Princess Masako

Princess Masako
Prisoner of the Chrysanthemum Throne

BEN HILLS

JEREMY P. TARCHER/PENGUIN

Penguin Group (USA) Inc.
New York

JEREMY P. TARCHER/PENGUIN
Published by the Penguin Group
Penguin Group (USA) Inc., 375 Hudson Street, New York, New York 10014,
USA • Penguin Group (Canada), 90 Eglinton Avenue East, Suite 700, Toronto, Ontario
M4P 2Y3, Canada (a division of Pearson Penguin Canada Inc.) • Penguin Books Ltd,
80 Strand, London WC2R 0RL, England • Penguin Ireland, 25 St Stephen's Green,
Dublin 2, Ireland (a division of Penguin Books Ltd) • Penguin Group (Australia),
250 Camberwell Road, Camberwell, Victoria 3124, Australia (a division of Pearson
Australia Group Pty Ltd) • Penguin Books India Pvt Ltd, 11 Community Centre,
Panchsheel Park, New Delhi–110 017, India • Penguin Group (NZ), 67 Apollo Drive,
Mairangi Bay, Auckland 1311, New Zealand (a division of Pearson
New Zealand Ltd) • Penguin Books (South Africa) (Pty) Ltd, 24 Sturdee Avenue,
Rosebank, Johannesburg 2196, South Africa

Penguin Books Ltd, Registered Offices:
80 Strand, London WC2R 0RL, England

First published by Random House Australia
First Jeremy P. Tarcher/Penguin hardcover edition 2006

Most Tarcher/Penguin books are available at special quantity discounts for bulk purchase
for sales promotions, premiums, fund-raising, and educational needs. Special books or book
excerpts also can be created to fit specific needs. For details, write Penguin Group (USA) Inc.
Special Markets, 375 Hudson Street, New York, NY 10014.

Library of Congress Cataloging-in-Publication Data

Hills, Ben.
Princess Masako : prisoner of the chrysanthemum throne / Ben Hills.
p.   cm.
ISBN-13: 978-1-58542-568-6
ISBN-10: 1-58542-568-0
1. Masako, Crown Princess of Japan, 1963–   2. Hiro no Miya Naruhito, Prince, grandson
of Hirohito, Emperor of Japan, 1960– —Family.   3. Princesses—Japan—Biography.
I. Title.
DS891.42.M37H55   2006   2006037105
952.04'9092—dc22
[B]

7-07 3460 1350

Printed in the United States of America

3   5   7   9   10   8   6   4   2

While the author has made every effort to provide accurate telephone numbers and Internet
addresses at the time of publication, neither the publisher nor the author assumes any
responsibility for errors, or for changes that occur after publication. Further, the publisher
does not have any control over and does not assume any responsibility for author or third-
party websites or their content.

Contents

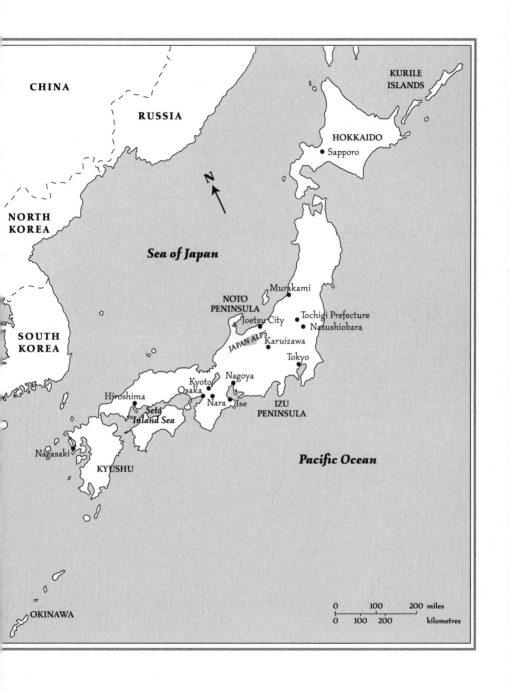

CHINA

RUSSIA

KURILE
ISLANDS

HOKKAIDO
● Sapporo

N

NORTH
KOREA

Sea of Japan

Murakami
●
NOTO
PENINSULA
Joetsu City
●   Tochigi Prefecture
● Nasushiobara
JAPAN ALPS
Karuizawa
●

SOUTH
KOREA

Tokyo
●

Nagoya
●
Kyoto
Osaka ●
Hiroshima ●   ●
Nara ● Ise   IZU
PENINSULA

Setō
Inland Sea

Pacific Ocean

Nagasaki ●

KYUSHU

OKINAWA

0   100   200 miles
0   100   200   kilometres

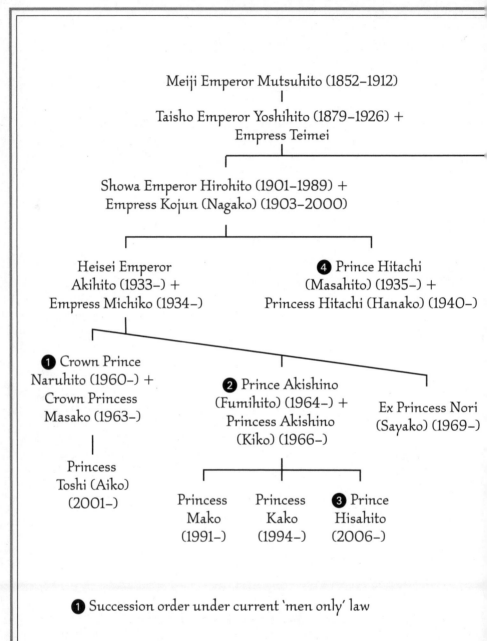

Meiji Emperor Mutsuhito (1852–1912)

Taisho Emperor Yoshihito (1879–1926) +
Empress Teimei

Showa Emperor Hirohito (1901–1989) +
Empress Kojun (Nagako) (1903–2000)

Heisei Emperor
Akihito (1933–) +
Empress Michiko (1934–)

4 Prince Hitachi
(Masahito) (1935–) +
Princess Hitachi (Hanako) (1940–)

1 Crown Prince
Naruhito (1960–) +
Crown Princess
Masako (1963–)

2 Prince Akishino
(Fumihito) (1964–) +
Princess Akishino
(Kiko) (1966–)

Ex Princess Nori
(Sayako) (1969–)

Princess
Toshi (Aiko)
(2001–)

Princess
Mako
(1991–)

Princess
Kako
(1994–)

3 Prince
Hisahito
(2006–)

1 Succession order under current 'men only' law

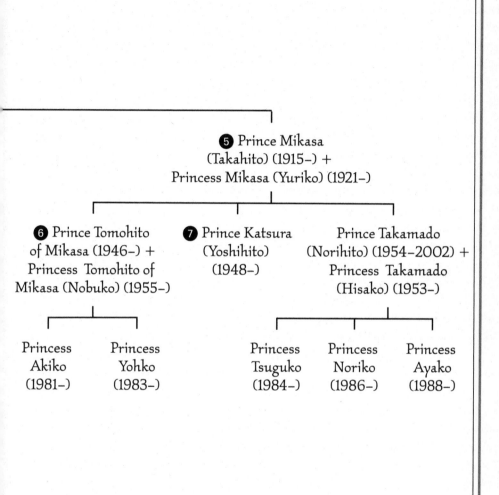

⑤ Prince Mikasa
(Takahito) (1915–) +
Princess Mikasa (Yuriko) (1921–)

⑥ Prince Tomohito
of Mikasa (1946–) +
Princess Tomohito of
Mikasa (Nobuko) (1955–)

⑦ Prince Katsura
(Yoshihito)
(1948–)

Prince Takamado
(Norihito) (1954–2002) +
Princess Takamado
(Hisako) (1953–)

Princess
Akiko
(1981–)

Princess
Yohko
(1983–)

Princess
Tsuguko
(1984–)

Princess
Noriko
(1986–)

Princess
Ayako
(1988–)

**Genealogy of the
Japanese Imperial Family**

Preface

NO SUBJECT IS MORE VEILED IN MYTH AND MYSTERY than the family of the Japanese emperor. The court of the world's last, and longest-reigning, imperial dynasty is a hot-bed of rumour and conjecture, conspiracy and intrigue, glimpsed by the outside world through the translucent *shoji* screens of the palace as a fleeting shadow-play. 'Across the moat' is another country and another time, haunted by its history, where vestal virgins perform ancient rites by night in secret shrines and outsiders are rarely allowed to penetrate.

It was into this medieval virtual reality that a smart, vivacious, Harvard-educated woman named Masako Owada confidently strode one rainy summer day, convinced by her supporters that she could breathe new life into the antique institution. Her marriage to the heir to the Chrysanthemum Throne, the self-effacing Crown Prince Naruhito, would be the key to modernising the monarchy and creating a new and more relevant role for its royals, they hoped. But 13 years later, that dream lies in ruins. Masako has become a prisoner of the institution she tried to reform, her health broken by the demands placed upon her – suicide has been mentioned, divorce is openly discussed, the prince may even renounce his claim to the throne. The ageing emperor is ailing with cancer and it was feared that the very survival of the 2600-year-old monarchy was at risk because Masako has not borne a son and heir.

Trying to sort fact from fiction, spin from substance, is a challenge any time, anywhere, but it is particularly difficult when dealing with the secretive bureaucrats of the *Kunaicho*, the Men in Black, who control the imperial household. Access to the royal couple is out of the question; requests for interviews with family and friends are ignored or refused on their orders. There were times during the 15-month, 50,000-kilometre trek that I took researching and writing this book when I was convinced I would have had more access to eye-witness accounts had I been writing a biography of that other emperor, Napoleon.

However, eventually I did manage to track down and interview about 60 people scattered around the world, some of whom have never spoken publicly before. Most are in Japan, but others are in the United Kingdom, the United States and Australia, which has a special place in the affections of the royal couple. Many are the ubiquitous 'royal watchers', an amorphous band of journalists and academics who make a living filter-feeding tiny diatoms of information from their contacts in the imperial bureaucracy and the Owada family circle. Others are old friends, colleagues and teachers of Masako's and former school and university pals of the crown prince and his father, the Emperor Akihito, who still manage to stay in touch.

Wherever possible I have identified my sources, but a

few people close to the couple insisted on anonymity – breaking the code of silence can have dire consequences, particularly for a Japanese bureaucrat – and I respect their wishes. I am thankful to Chie Matsumoto, who helped with research and translation in Japan, and Emma Firestone, who guided me around Harvard and arranged meetings with academics and graduates who knew Masako there.

As far as written sources are concerned, these are acknowledged in the References section at the back of the book. I am very grateful to the Foreign Correspondents' Club of Japan for allowing me use of their facilities, and particularly the helpful staff of the library for making available their extensive newspaper and magazine clippings files. Among the many journalists who helped with useful contacts, background and commentary I would like to particularly thank my friend the author Jun Hamana, David McNeill of the *Irish Times*, Richard Lloyd Parry of *The Times*, London, and Julian Ryall, who writes for newspapers including the *Scotsman*. The book would not have been possible without the hard work, criticism and encouragement of my wife, the photographer Mayu Kanamori, who gave so generously of her time in sifting the odd speck of gold from the mullock-heap of Japanese books, magazines and newspaper articles about the star-crossed couple. I thank my agent, Margaret Gee, for suggesting the idea to me in the first place, my publisher, Jeanne Ryckmans, for her support and encouragement, and my eagle-eyed editors, Sara Foster, Gail Umehara and Roberta Ivers.

This book does not attempt to advance any particular agenda, nor does it pretend to be the last word on this unfolding tragedy. As it went to press, after a nail-bitingly precarious pregnancy, there was rejoicing in the streets of

Tokyo as Naruhito's younger brother, Prince Akishino, and his wife, Princess Kiko, were blessed with a baby boy – the first to be born into the royal family in more than 40 years. This rescued the monarchy from extinction, at least for now, and saved the government from having to kow-tow to the wishes of an overwhelming majority of its citizens and change the law to allow a female to become emperor. It does try to shed a little light on some of the important social issues with which Japan is grappling in this dawning decade of the twenty-first century – the role of women, attitudes towards mental health and IVF parenting, the relevancy of the monarchy, the power of the bureaucracy. But at its heart it is about a romance gone wrong, a young couple crushed by forces over which they have no control, a marriage which neither will survive undamaged, but from which neither seems capable of escaping.

A final note on style. Anglicised versions of Japanese names are given with the family name last, as most Japanese now do on their business cards. Toshi Sato is Mr Sato. All dollars are Australian, converted at the rate of AUD 1 = USD 0.75 = JPY 80. Measurements have been converted to their metric equivalents, and dates are given according to the Western calendar rather than the Japanese imperial calendar.

Ben Hills
September 2006

1

The Men in Black

THE MEN IN BLACK COME FOR HER AT 6.30 ON A DREARY Tokyo morning, hardly an auspicious start to what is supposed to be the happiest day of a woman's life. Nor have the weather gods smiled – the *tsuyu* season, the 'plum rains' which coincide with the ripening of the fruit, has arrived the earliest anyone can remember this summer. The two palace chamberlains, in their long, fusty black dress coats, unfurl black umbrellas as they climb out of the black limousine. The chauffeur in his brass-buttoned jacket sits rigidly gripping the steering wheel with his white-gloved hands. The police motorcycle escort dismounts and stands stiffly to attention. Watching the scene on TV, it looks to me more like a State funeral than the royal wedding we have been waiting for.

The Owada family, on whom the cortege has come to call, live in a bunker-like rain-stained ferro-concrete mansion in what is normally a quiet little backstreet in the well-heeled suburb of Meguro, lined with maple trees and hedges of azaleas. But on this June morning in 1993 it is the bustling epicentre of the Japanese media world. Crammed into a small parking area opposite the house, clad in hooded anoraks for their all-night vigil and bristling with lenses and microphones, is a battalion of some 400 reporters, photographers and news cameramen from all the major national newspapers, radio stations and TV networks. Some have been manning the stake-out 24 hours a day for five long months, paying the car-park owner $400 a week for the privilege, and with little to show for it other than a daring paparazzi shot of the Owadas' pet Yorkshire terrier cocking his leg against a tree on his daily walk.

Why the frenzy? At the age of 33, Japan's mild-mannered Naruhito Hironomiya, heir apparent to the world's most ancient continuous monarchy, is getting married. He's the oldest unwed crown prince in the country's history, and his parents had begun to despair that he would ever find a bride and ensure the dynasty continued. But at last, after more than seven years of rejections, he has persuaded the woman he loves to tie the knot. Masako Owada, a strong-minded career woman, graduate of Harvard, speaker of six languages and all-round high achiever, has reluctantly succumbed to the pressure, though not with any obvious enthusiasm. 'If I can be of support to you, I would like to humbly accept,' was the strange, stilted way in which she finally accepted his proposal. For his part, the prince, when the engagement was announced, declared: 'I will do everything in my power to protect you.' That ominous nuance was not remarked on until much later.

Since the official confirmation of Japan's worst-kept secret in January 1993, the whole country – well, the part of it that watches daytime TV and reads celebrity magazines – has been waiting for this day. With little else to cheer, the stock market slashed to window-jumping lows and growing numbers of the unemployed sleeping in subway underpasses, the impending wedding promises a welcome piece of pageantry, a boost to the country's bruised sense of national pride. The more excitable tabloids are comparing it with the scintillating spectacle a decade before in that other rainy, snobby, tea-drinking offshore island when Britain's Prince Charles married *his* commoner Cinderella, Diana Spencer. The more bullish economists are predicting the nationwide celebrations and the sale of tacky souvenirs will pour $44 billion into the stagnant economy.

On this, her day of days, the ever-obsequious Japanese media are far too polite to point out the obvious schism between their manufactured romance and her reality, between the fairytale of Charles and Diana (which had, coincidentally, just ended in tears) and what Princess Masako can really expect as an empress-in-waiting. Never let unpalatable truths get in the way of a good story, especially when it may risk the wrath of a powerful institution like the monarchy. Not so restrained were some foreign commentators. *Vanity Fair* headlined its acerbic story 'Masako's Sacrifice'. *Newsweek* magazine's international cover story, 'The Reluctant Princess', was deemed so disrespectful that its local distributors insisted it be bowdlerised in its Japanese edition to a bland 'The Birth of a Princess', for fear of offending people in high places.

To follow Masako through her wedding day will give a foretaste of what the rest of her life will be like after the last toasts in *sake* have been drunk, the last guests have left clutching their wedding gifts, the bunting has been pulled down and the books full of the signatures of well-wishers packed away.

To the Western observer – and to many Japanese of her generation – this brave, or foolhardy, woman is about to give up not just her career but her family, her friends, her future and – some would say – even the twentieth century. When she crosses the palace moat she will enter a secretive world of oppressive protocol and arcane religious ritual, a medieval imperial court where she will be required to bow at an angle of precisely 60 degrees whenever she meets the in-laws, and to address her husband (in public, at any rate) as 'Mr East Palace'. Her only role in life will be to play the part of a demure and deferential consort mincing along three paces behind her husband; her only task to produce a son and heir to the Chrysanthemum Throne. Her every move will be monitored, her every public word scripted by the Men in Black, officials of the *Kunaicho*, the Imperial Household Agency, the officious bureaucracy which controls the lives of Japan's royals. What she will go through over the long years ahead will make Princess Diana's ordeal look like a picnic.

But that is all in the future. Back in Meguro, the bunker door is opened. The head of the besieged household emerges, a distinguished-looking gentleman of the old school with grey, receding hair, owlish eye-glasses and a perpetually pained expression as though he has just stepped in something nasty. Or perhaps it is just the media attention he finds so distasteful. His name is Hisashi Owada and he is one of Japan's most powerful mandarins, the head of *Gaimusho*, the foreign affairs ministry. He steps into the street, dressed in his own inevitably black morning coat, and bows to the two emissaries as raindrops speckle his spectacles.

4

It is not, of course, the father that the media and the palace officials have come to see this drizzling dawn, but his daughter, Masako. The crowd surges, the cameras go kerchunka-chunk, the small crowd of mainly middle-aged mums and dads wave little red and white rising sun flags which someone has handed out. And now here she comes, her thick black hair bobbed, a nervous smile flickering across her face, immaculately turned out in an aquamarine outfit with a matching hat and a strand of pearls around her neck – the first of four costumes which she will wear before this day is done. 'Masako-*sama*' cries the crowd, clapping, already giving her the royal honorific which will attach to her name.

Hers is the face which has launched a thousand magazine posters, flapping from the ceilings of Tokyo's subway carriages. Most Japanese men would say she is good-looking, though not in the cutesy-pie mould of the typical *tarento*, the simpering pubescent starlets of popular culture. Her nose and chin are rather too prominent, her skin a shade darker than the classical ivory, her teeth crooked. It is a face with character, which is no doubt one of the things that attracted the prince. At the age of 29 she has an athletic build now that she has shed the kilos she stacked on in her university days – Masako was a champion softball player at high school, and still loves tennis and skiing. She walks with a confident stride, and is 164 centimetres (5 feet 5 inches in the old currency) in her stockinged feet, an embarrassing centimetre or so taller than her husband-to-be.

Her mother, Yumiko, a severe-looking woman in a cream suit with her hair drawn back in a chignon, steps into the street to bid her farewell, followed by Masako's younger twin sisters, twenty-somethings Setsuko and

Reiko. Hovering in the background are her grandparents. The girls can no longer keep up appearances, and are openly weeping as the officials shelter their sister with their umbrellas and escort her to the limousine. She has already said goodbye to her darling Chocolat, the cute little terrier which has become something of a media celebrity in its own right over the past few months. Her mother's parting words sound to some more like a general dispatching his troops into battle than a mother wishing her daughter a happy married life. 'Please take care of yourself and do your utmost for your country,' she exhorts Masako. 'I feel a mixture of emotions,' her father lectures reporters in his donnish way. 'I hope that she will gallantly fulfil the duties which come with being a public figure.' Then, almost as an afterthought, he adds, 'And, as a parent who is giving his daughter away, I want her to be happy.' The family then faces Masako, and with a stiff formality – and no hugs or kisses – solemnly bow their farewells. The plum rains tumble from a pewter sky.

What needed no explanation to the tens of millions watching around the country was that marriage in Japan, even among the common folk, is a far more weighty undertaking, particularly for a woman, than in the West, where it is increasingly seen as a contract that can be ripped up at the first sign of trouble. From this day on Masako ceases to be part of the Owada family – her name is expunged from the official family register – and she becomes a member of the family of Japan's reigning emperor, the ailing Akihito, the 125th in the imperial lineage. As a member of the royal family, she will not have the right to vote and she will not even have a surname any more, let alone those other essentials of modern life: a passport, credit card, health insurance, or a car. There will be no public record of her very existence. It may be months, or even years if the precedent of her new mother-in-law is anything to go by, before she is allowed to see her relatives again. And unlike Charles and Diana, there will be no way out – separation and divorce are unthinkable for Japan's royals.

The previous Christmas she had written her family a desperately sad little card, decorated with holly, which showed quite clearly that Masako had more than an inkling of what she was letting herself in for:

Dear Father and Mother,
Sorry for making you worry so much about me this year, but with your support I was able to think it through and make the right step towards a new life. This Christmas and New Year may be the last we will be able to spend together. I really appreciate it that you raised me all these years in such a warm and happy family. Tough times are waiting for us, but I hope we get through.

She signed the card with the *kanji*, the two Chinese characters that make up her name and which mean something like 'feminine elegance'. It is a good name – one of the members of the pre-World War II extended royal family, Princess Tsune, was also called Masako – which has led many to speculate that right from the start the Owadas had high ambitions for their first-born child. But surely not in their wildest dreams could they have imagined that one day they would find themselves standing in the rain watching their daughter being driven away for such a date with destiny, union with a family that believes it is descended from the gods, wife of a man destined one day to take the role defined by the constitution of the world's second most important economy as 'the symbol of the State and the unity of the people'.

The car with its police outriders swishes slowly along the slick streets towards the imperial palace, the walled and moated site of the shoguns' castle, a hidden world of woodlands, palaces, parks and shrines. At the height of Japan's Roaring Eighties bubble, economists calculated that this oasis of greenery in the heart of the grey city, which occupies just 46 hectares, was worth more than Canada. Overhead, airships hover, surveying the gathering crowds for signs of dissent or disorder. Even in these innocent pre-9/11 days, even in orderly Tokyo, 30,000 police have been mobilised to ensure security. Not everybody loves a lover.

The threat is not from Islamist terrorists but from an odd assortment of militant groups which oppose not so much the nuptials as the entire 'Emperor system' as they call it. Communists – who in the early 1990s still represent a significant bloc of votes in the parliament, and publish one of the country's most popular newspapers – believe the monarchy should be abolished, and are boycotting the ceremony. Other marginalised groups are outraged that detectives have been hired to make sure that there is no 'bad blood' in the bride's family tree which would prevent her from marrying into the royal family – or, indeed, into any socially prominent family. There must be no taint of a connection with the indigenous Ainu people, ethnic Koreans (even those who have been in Japan for three or four generations) or *burakumin* – 'village people' – which is a politically correct name for an underclass of Japanese excluded from society. All three communities have already loudly protested against such discrimination.

The media have reported that two 'fire bombs', actually little more than jumped-up firecrackers, have been thrown in attacks on *Kunaicho* officials. In Japan, such symbolic threats – it has been years since anyone was actually hurt in an anti-monarchy protest – invoke a symbolic security response. So much safer than the real thing, especially since the only point is to get the message across.

All the soft-drink vending machines along the route the wedding cavalcade will take later in the day have been removed, supposedly lest any hot-head hurl a can of Pocari Sweat (a popular soft-drink, believe it or not) at the royal couple. I have seen police frogmen dragging the murky green waters of the palace moat, searching for goodness knows what lurking danger – *E. coli* seems to be the gravest threat. Cars have been ordered not to park with their boots towards the imperial palace, less dissidents fire rockets from them. Plain-clothes police have infiltrated a coffee lounge thought to be patronised by Communists. Known agitators have had a knock on the door from their neighbourhood bobby, warning them not to even think about trying to use the wedding as a backdrop for their agitprop.

Sailing blithely past is the princess-to-be, concentrating no doubt on the intricacies of the imperial rites and rituals ahead of her. Particularly the bowing. Just as the Inuit are said to have 18 words for snow, Hawaiians 47 for banana and Albanians 27 for moustache, the Japanese preoccupation is with bowing, for which there are half a dozen words. The precise style and angle are dictated by the social standing of the bower and the bowee, and heaven forbid Masako should commit the unpardonable gaffe of confusing her *saikeirei* (which the dictionary describes as 'a very low, worshipful type of bow that involves the nose nearly touching the hands') with her *pekopeko* ('to bow one's head repeatedly in a fawning or grovelling manner').

To prepare for the great event – and for the life in the imperial court that will follow – Masako has had a dress rehearsal, and has submitted to 62 hours of indoctrination from aged sages on subjects such as the history of the imperial family, its religious ceremonies, the special language used at court (some of it as incomprehensible as Latin to the average educated Japanese), calligraphy, even the construction of *waka,* an antique verse form of 31 syllables which the royals are required to compose for recitation on special occasions. Her doting husband-to-be is particularly adept at it, and dedicated his entry in the last New Year's poetry recital to his fiancée:

> *I gaze with delight*
> *As the flock of cranes takes flight*
> *Into the blue skies.*
> *The dream cherished in my heart*
> *Since my boyhood has come true.*

But even so, no matter how meticulously planned, things can go wrong even at a great occasion of state. No doubt they both remembered the embarrassing gaffe a decade before when Diana Spencer managed to muddle up Prince Charles's name as they exchanged vows at the altar of St Paul's Cathedral before an audience of 3500, including most of the crowned heads of Europe. But that is about as far as one should take the comparisons. The two ceremonies could not have been more different, both in spirit and in spectacle.

A TV audience of a billion people watched Diana alight from a crystal coach to walk down the aisle of one of

Europe's grandest cathedrals with bridesmaids supporting the seven-metre train of her ivory silk gown. Elgar's 'Pomp and Circumstance' thundered from the great organ, and the ceremony was conducted by the primate of the Anglican Church, the Archbishop of Canterbury, Dr Robert Runcie. Masako's marriage, on the other hand, will be conducted in secrecy and near-silence in a gable-eaved wooden shrine according to the rituals of Shinto, Japan's ancient animist religion. There will be no ring of white Welsh gold, in fact no ring at all. Instead of a bouquet of yellow roses the bough of an evergreen tree will be brandished. Bowls of *sake* will be drunk, a white-robed priest will officiate, and an official virgin will be present. And as for the outfits – the reason the Owadas had to be up so early was to allow two full hours for Masako to be cosmeticised and costumed up for the ceremony.

The reason for these strange customs (strange not only to foreigners, but to most younger Japanese who nowadays choose Western-style outfits, tiered wedding cakes and waltzes) lies in the dual role of Japan's royal family. On one hand, Hirohito having renounced his divinity after the disastrous war in which it was the national rallying cry, the emperor is now, constitutionally at least, a mere mortal. He is the symbol of the Japanese people, but bereft of even the token power of a British sovereign to 'advise, encourage and warn' ministers and assent to Parliament's laws. But what the postwar constitution, dictated by the victorious Americans, ignores entirely is the emperor's role as the principal shaman/priest of Shinto. This unique and ubiquitous belief system predates Buddhism and centres on the worship of the 'spirits' of the sun and the wind, landscape features such as mountains and rivers, *inari* the rice-deity whose shrines are guarded by white foxes, the ancestors of the living, and fallen heroes like the *kamikaze* suicide pilots enshrined at Yasukuni Shrine, Japan's great and controversial place of worship for the war dead.

The job for which Naruhito has been groomed since the day he was born involves an exhausting calendar of religious ceremonies which often take hours to perform and will involve him rising before dawn and purifying himself with sacred water before donning special robes. The anniversaries of the deaths of every one of his 125 ancestors must be strictly observed. Superstitious farmers fear that without the emperor donning his gumboots every spring and ceremonially planting the first stalks of rice, their harvest may fail. He is not the Pope of Shinto, nor even its titular head in the way Queen Elizabeth II is of the Church of England. Shinto has no ecclesiastical hierarchy, no sacred text, and no belief in God or a universal afterlife; in fact, it doesn't really qualify as a religion at all. Most Japanese of Masako's generation never worship, but happily embrace a trilogy of faiths. They see no contradiction in being taken to the local Shinto shrine to be recorded at birth, marrying in Christian ceremonies (thousands of them in Australian churches as part of a honeymoon package), and having their bones buried in Buddhist family tombs.

The emperor is not just Shinto's principal practitioner, he – in practice the Imperial Household Agency – is the custodian of Japan's most sacred shrines, places of worship guarded by vermilion *torii* arches and bearing bells which supplicants ring to summon the spirits. These include the imposing building of unpainted timber with its raised floors and roof tiled with cypress bark which stands in the palace grounds called the *kashikodokoro*, literally the 'awe-inspiring place'. This is where today's ceremony will take place. The shrine is dedicated to the emperors' legendary ancestor, the sun-goddess Amaterasu Omikami, who, according to legend, stirred the sea with a jewelled spear to create the Japanese nation. It contains replicas of the symbols which legitimise the imperial lineage: precious stones, an antique sword and a bronze mirror which is said to have been used back in the time of the gods to entice Amaterasu out of a cave where she was sulking to shed light on the world.

The deep religious significance of the occasion presents the *Kunaicho* with a dilemma they must have spent months sucking their teeth over. Agency officials want the world to see Japan as a modern country headed by a constitutional monarch, but they cannot abandon the traditions that they believe are central to the role of the emperor and to Japan's identity as a nation. They want the wedding to be a great, glittering event like that of Charles and Diana, attracting distinguished foreign guests, boosting the economy, celebrated by the public, watched by millions on TV and thus showing Japan (and themselves) in a favourable light.

On the other hand, they are not stupid. The agency's top brass knows there are aspects of the ceremony which non-believers may find curious or even comical – for instance, when she goes to pay her respects to the spirits at Shinto's Vatican, the Grand Shrine in the seaside town of Ise, the very modern Masako will have to submit to having her belly rubbed with rice bran by two virgin shrine attendants to ensure her fertility. '(If this gets out) we will be seen as a high-tech nation with barbaric customs,' fretted the magazine *Bungei Shunju*. On top of all this, the wedding is being financed by the taxpayer to the tune of $40 million and there are concerns it may be seen to contravene Japan's strict separation of Church and State, the ban on the use of public money to promote Shinto, thus provoking protest.

The *Kunaicho* has resolved the problem with a typically Japanese diplomatic sleight-of-hand. The wedding celebrations will be spread over a gruelling three days, incorporating more than a dozen different functions to which some 2700 people have been invited. In contrast with Charles and Diana's nuptials, they have decreed that no foreigner will be allowed anywhere near the actual wedding. Overseas dignitaries, royals and prime ministers will be invited to only one of the six scheduled grand banquets. The business with the bran will be done in strictest privacy.

And so as Masako prepares to take her vows, the 900 guests taking their places under their dripping umbrellas on the small stadium which has been constructed near the shrine are all Japanese. They are led by the diminutive, grinning Prime Minister, Kiichi Miyazawa, and most of his Cabinet, who little suspect that within weeks they will suffer the almost-unprecedented ignominy of being voted out of office. There are top bureaucrats from all the great ministries of State, judges, ambassadors, captains of commerce – a real *Who's Who* of Japan's rich and powerful. The Owada family is there, of course, along with most of Naruhito's relatives, including his playboy younger brother Akishino, and his sister Sayako. The only conspicuous absentees will be Emperor Akihito himself and his Empress Michiko – protocol decrees that they not attend their own son-and-heir's wedding.

Before she can accompany her bridegroom behind the *shoji* screens and the bamboo curtain into the dark recesses of the shrine, Masako – who, like her mother, actually went to a Catholic school – has to be bathed in holy water, and dressed in wedding robes which almost defy description. The theatrical costumes the bride and groom will wear were in fact designed in the late nineteenth century, though they are modelled on those worn in the Heian court 1000 years earlier, when the imperial household lived in sumptuous luxury in the old capital of Kyoto. It took eight handmaidens more than an hour just to swaddle her in the dress, a number called a *juni hitoe*, which consists of 12 cloak-like layers of different coloured silk fabric woven with gold thread, the outermost of which is emerald green and adorned with a pattern of white jasmine flowers. The whole outfit cost about $350,000, weighs 16 kilograms, and reduces the normally free-striding Masako to a stilted shuffle. Her raven-black hair has been soaked in camellia oil and moulded into a bun around a hair-piece, pinned in place with a golden comb. She is carrying a hefty white cedar fan and her normally mobile face is a mask. Crimson lips highlight a complexion so pale with pancake make-up she looks like a *kabuki* performer.

The TV cameras pick her up as she totters along the boardwalk to the shrine a few steps behind her husband. Four years older than his bride, Naruhito is a little shorter than Japanese men of his generation, but from what we can see of him neat and fit-looking – he is a great hiker, and has climbed most of Japan's highest mountains. He has a nice smile, though this is not on display for this most solemn and serious occasion. The most noticeable features of his smooth, round face are the pronounced epicanthic folds of his upper eyelids, which make it difficult to tell from a distance whether his eyes are open or closed. His younger brother, Prince Akishino, has joked with him that the reason it has taken him so long to find a bride is that he is not the girls' cup of tea. 'You're too short-legged and too

Mongolian-looking,' he once quipped, according to a bitchy piece by the journalist Edward Klein.

Naruhito is dressed almost as gorgeously as the bride. He is wearing a *hakama*, a broad divided skirt of heavy cream silk, with cream-coloured booties inside black lacquered clogs peeping out beneath. Over the top of this is a billowing gauzy garment dyed the colour of sunrise with saffron and jasmine seeds, called an *oninoho*. It is decorated with nesting storks, in case anyone still fails to grasp the whole point of the marriage. In his hand he carries a sort of giant white shoehorn called a *shaku*, which is the crown prince's sceptre of office, and strapped to his head is a black lacquered hat with a curious extension at the back, rather like a beaver's tail. They enter the shrine, and here we are obliged to Asahi TV for providing an animation of what they imagine is going on inside.

The six Japanese TV networks have been giving the whole affair saturation coverage since it first became public. What they have lacked in immediacy (all the major stories of the royal romance have been broken by foreign media, for reasons we will go into later) they have made up for in sheer quantity and uninhibited tackiness. Anchors have appeared on sets tricked up like wedding parlours. We have seen a full-scale studio mock-up of Masako's Harvard dormitory room. Fuji TV has flown in the American actress Brooke Shields, Naruhito's pin-up when he was at Oxford University a decade before, to give studio commentary. NTV has mounted a 14-hour wedding-day special, which began at 6 am. Some of the coverage has left me rubbing my eyes with disbelief. Was I hallucinating, or did I really see a trained monkey named Tsurusuke peering into a crystal ball and predicting that the happy couple would have three children, the first of them a girl?

And here is the computer simulation of the ceremony even the most trusted Japanese guests are not allowed to see. Actually, it is simple and solemn and rather charming – I can't imagine why the *Kunaicho* would not allow a single discreet TV camera to intrude on the scene. Only half a dozen people are present, including the chief palace ritual-ist, an elderly man named Fusatada Koide, who is dressed in a pure white robe; a chamberlain carrying the sacred samurai sword; a lady-in-waiting; and an older woman identified as one of the four 'vestal virgins' who attend the imperial shrines. Naruhito is presented with a bough of the sacred *sakaki* tree, an evergreen which is traditionally planted around shrines, which he ceremonially offers to the gods. He then recites a pledge of loyalty, and the couple sip *sake* three times from each of three tiny lacquered bowls, a good-luck toast known as *san san kudo*. Masako says nothing apart from her name, which she inserts at the end of the prince's pledge. And they are married – in the eyes of the sun-goddess at any rate. Unlike those of other Japanese, royal marriages are never registered with the civil authorities. The whole ceremony has taken just 18 minutes.

And then it is time to meet the in-laws for lunch. Offi-cially meet them, that is. Highly unusually, there has already been one informal dinner party when the Owada family was invited to the palace to dine with Akihito and his family. It was the first time that this had happened, and it was widely interpreted as a gesture by the emperor – or, more importantly, by his wife Michiko, who was also a commoner when she married her crown prince – to reassure the Owadas that their reluctant daughter would be offered support and protection from bullying by the palace bureaucracy. This time the meeting is far more formal.

The prince and his new princess have now changed into less colourful Western attire. Masako is wearing a cream brocade gown designed by Hanae Mori, Japan's first international superstar designer, teamed with a diamond-encrusted tiara and necklace. The prince is in a white bow-tie and black morning coat, with a sash across his chest, and a gaudy gold medal and a red and blue cockade, rather like a best-in-show award for champion poultry, pinned to his coat. The emperor and empress, equally formally dressed, are waiting for them in a huge reception hall in the palace. They are surrounded by servants and seated on red lacquered stools on a sort of *tatami* dais made of rice straw and rushes, with red lacquered tables in front of them on which are arranged tiny dishes of sweetmeats. Each menu item, like every aspect of the ceremony, has a cultural symbolism – for instance, bowls of sticky white rice and red beans will feature prominently throughout the three days of feasting, as this is 'celebratory food' reserved for special occasions.

Masako and Naruhito make their way across the polished wooden floor, bow to the required 60 degrees, then seat themselves at their own little tables, which are lower and located four or five metres away. Lunch sounds delicious – clear soup with a dumpling in it, mullet roe, a savoury custard with eel and mushroom, golden baby *ayu* (grilled freshwater sweetfish), followed by a cherry blossom sweet. But one cannot imagine that amid all this exquisite formality there was much time to enjoy the meal, let alone chat about the baseball or the weather, before they were ushered into a studio for the official portraits, and then dispatched to their new home.

The place Masako and Naruhito will call home for the moment is just down the road from her in-laws' palace.

Although the trip, across the moat and along the broad boulevard of Shinjuku-dori is only four kilometres or so, it takes the eight-car cavalcade half an hour. From their black open-topped (the rain has by now eased off) Rolls-Royce with a golden chrysanthemum in place of a licence plate, the royal couple waves to the enthusiastic crowd, which has now built up to about 200,000, pressing against the crush-barriers waving their paper flags. It is a public holiday in Tokyo, with more than one reason for celebration. Miyazawa's government has seized the opportunity to wipe clean the records of some 30,000 criminals, including an astonishing 5800 people, mostly members of the ruling Liberal Democratic Party, convicted of political graft and corruption.

Looking at the passing procession, it occurs to me that waving lessons have also been part of the princess training course Masako has been put through, as she now flutters her hand at just the right royal angle, smiles with the required balance of warmth and dignity, and walks the obligatory three paces behind her husband. Since criticism of her performance at her first and only press conference earlier in the year, she has done her best to meet public expectations – in spite of a constant campaign of sneer, smear and innuendo from influential sections of Japanese society who thought she was not worthy to be the next empress.

The criticism is coming from three main sources. The Imperial Household Agency regards Masako, who spent many years abroad, as not 'Japanese' enough to maintain their traditions, not sufficiently deferential and too willing to speak her mind. They have conducted a vicious campaign against her through leaks to selected journalists in off-the-record briefings in bars and coffee lounges, resulting in scurrilous stories about former boyfriends, and suggestions that her family had been implicated in a terrible pollution scandal. Next there are the *kuge* and *kazoku* families, Japan's former nobility, who maintain a haughty social standing even though they lost their titles of 'marquis' and 'count' and so on half a century ago when hereditary titles were abolished – except for the royal family. These dynasties were until quite recent times the sole breeding ground for royal brides and concubines, and were angry and resentful when first Akihito, then his two sons, took the unprecedented step of marrying commoners. They have been continually bobbing up on TV in their pearls and twinsets with disdainful remarks about Masako's manners and appearance. The last group of Masako's critics is the influential old girls' association of the elite Gakushuin school and university, where the young royals and scions of other prominent families are educated. They had gone so far as to provide a computer print-out of graduates they believed were suitable can-didates to marry the crown prince. Deeply huffed when Naruhito turned them all down, they too have been campaigning against Masako behind the scenes and in the media.

As an indication of the depths of their resentment, listen to Minoru Hamao, a pompous old fossil who for 20 years was the chamberlain of the East Palace, the crown prince's chief courtier, and one of his closest confidants. Hamao has written a number of books about the royal family, and became a favourite on talk-shows looking for the voice of Japan's ultra-conservative Establishment. At that first joint press conference announcing their engagement – not a live free-for-all as is usual in the West, but a scripted affair where tame journalists submit polite questions in advance

– Masako brought a breath of fresh air into proceedings when she talked quite freely about her plans and ambitions. Instead of listening to what she had to say, her critics put the stopwatch on her and tutted that Masako had spoken for 9 minutes and 37 seconds, 28 seconds longer than Naruhito. Protocol apparently decrees that she should have meekly deferred to her groom-to-be, allowing him to speak for twice as long as she did. This is what Hamao had to say about it:

> *I felt she was a bit too impudent. Above all, she talks too much. She even talks about things she has not been asked about. She does as the Americans do – she walks in front of a man because Westerners say 'ladies first'. All this may be acceptable in the United States, but I believe she should display more modesty in Japan.*

This would be the last time Masako would be allowed to speak in public for several years. The *Kunaicho* put the gag on. Though she was no doubt seething with indignation at Hamao's impertinence, she had no option – other than abandoning the marriage, bringing unbearable dishonour to her family – than to swallow her pride and learn to do things the imperial way. From now on, every moment she spends in public will be like this. There will be no room for spontaneity, no impromptu moments. She will not even be able to let that fixed smile slip for a second, for fear that the paparazzi would capture the moment, giving the editors an excuse for the headline they have all been waiting to write: 'The Unhappy Princess'.

She has, so far, managed to navigate the prickly obstacle course of protocol without another major incident. The imperial family's engagement presents have been delivered to that house in Meguro without incident. No steak-knives or electric frying-pans, as you would imagine. A court official in a morning coat has solemnly presented the family with: two enormous red sea-bream weighing five or six kilograms each and arranged so as to form the character for the lucky number eight; six 1.8 litre bottles of *daiginjoshu*, the Grange Hermitage of premium *sake*; and five bolts of the finest silk with which to make evening gowns, fabric hand-spun in traditional patterns such as the poetically named gold and white *keiki zuicho nishiki* or 'shining silk birds of good luck', and *gakukyo no toki* or 'moments of musical joy'.

The only other moment of embarrassment her critics have been able to pounce on has actually not been of Masako's doing at all. It is the custom for the parents of the bride to provide expensive dowries, and a constant stream of other gifts, to the emperor and other members of the imperial household. This practice proved so ruinous that a previous royal in-law, the Viscount Masanori Takagi, actually committed suicide because of the financial burden – yet another reason why most Japanese parents would be very reluctant to see their daughter marry a royal. However, nowadays if a family does not have the means to provide a suitable dowry – as Masako's father, powerful bureaucrat but nevertheless a modestly paid public servant did not – the imperial family gives them the money to buy the gifts.

Estimates of just how much this dowry cost range up to an eye-popping $4 million, and when you look at the goods that Masako had delivered to the palace in the days leading up to the wedding it is possible this was no exaggeration. A convoy of five pantechnicons pulled up, and a team of 40 removalists laboured most of the day unloading some 500 cardboard cartons, cases, chests and other pieces of furniture. Fine rugs, kimonos worth thousands of dollars, futons, specially carved ward-robes . . . the stream of possessions never seemed to stop. And the embarrassment? Curiously enough, all this extravagance is supposed to be done in a tasteful and non-ostentatious way; certainly nothing should suggest that the bride comes from a wealthier background than her royal groom. When it was discovered that three pawlonia-wood bedding chests had been covered in gold foil by a well-meaning craftsman, he had to issue red-faced apologies before scraping the gilt back to the bare timber.

So when the wedding cavalcade pulls up outside Masako's new home, she knows they are not exactly going to be starting from scratch. 'Home' is Naruhito's tem-porary official residence, pending renovations to the *Togu Gosho*, also called the East Palace, because it is, well, east of the imperial palace. It sits in the middle of a huge swathe of parkland, lakes, and stands of ginkgo and the silver-birch trees that form the crown prince's official seal. It's extraordinary to think that in the heart of one of the world's most densely populated cities is a wild area where, according to one visitor, the royal couple will make friends with a feral fox.

Tourists seeking a glimpse of the palace are constantly confounded because the tour buses pull up in front of a set of towering wrought-iron gates topped with gold-tipped spikes and flanked by antique guard-boxes, through which can be seen an avenue of immaculately clipped pine trees leading up to one of Tokyo's most imposing neo-baroque buildings, the Akasaka Palace. It is a magnificent *faux* chateau of granite and marble modelled on the Palace of

Versailles, once residence of that other Sun King, France's Louis XIV. And it was built, in 1909, as the residence for Naruhito's great-grandfather, Crown Prince Yoshihito, later to become the sad, mad Taisho Emperor. But it hasn't been used as such for decades because of the huge cost of its upkeep, and the fact that such imperial ostentation has gone out of style. In 1969 the palace was closed down for a five-year refurbishment, and it was re-opened as an official state guesthouse, occupied only on special occasions such as international economic pow-wows and summits of heads of state.

Nowadays crown princes live in substantial but much more modest digs. Naruhito and Masako's residence is hidden away behind the Akasaka Palace, invisible from the street. The extensive grounds are surrounded by a simple stone embankment and a bamboo fence, with the only sign of security some video cameras mounted on poles, and the occasional guard-post where police patrol up and down. At the time of the wedding, they shared the compound with other members of the royal family. Naruhito's parents were in residence at the East Palace with their daughter, Princess Sayako; brother Akishino and his family were a short walk away; another relative, Naruhito's great-aunt Chichibu, also lived on the Akasaka estate until her death in 1995.

From the accounts of visitors, the palace is a sprawling two-storey Japanese-style building covering some 670 square metres, with sections that serve both as public entertaining areas, beautifully furnished in the Western style, as well as the couple's private quarters. It is surrounded by ponds full of *koi*, colourful giant carp which can cost thousands of dollars each, tennis courts, jogging tracks (Naruhito is a keen outdoorsman), sculpted gardens of flowers and shrubs, and even a vegetable patch where the royal couple can grow their own eggplants and tomatoes. To look after them, they will have a staff of 50 chamberlains and ladies-in-waiting, chefs, chauffeurs, official secretaries, even doctors. These are the *Kunaicho* officials who from this day on will decide what they do, who they see, where they go, and what they say. Welcome to your new life as a princess, Masako.

Some have compared Masako's existence with that of a bird in a gilded cage. A less clichéd metaphor might be a luxurious safari park, in which the royal couple is the pampered last breeding pair of an endangered species. You can glean an idea of the sort of life she will lead behind the Chrysanthemum Curtain from comments Masako would make five years after the wedding. Remember, this is a woman who was a high-flying diplomat at Japan's foreign ministry, attended three of the world's great universities, was an international traveller and author of an economics thesis on Japanese trade. When she was asked what she had enjoyed doing the previous year, this was her reply:

> . . . *last summer I discovered a weakened male stag beetle sitting outside one of the palace windows. Because it was in somewhat of a sad state, I took him under my care and began to look after him. Later on we were successful in breeding him with a female which laid eggs, and now we are rearing the larvae . . . so now I am wondering whether I have taken on a rather arduous three-year task.*

But that is getting ahead of the story. On the evening of her wedding Masako discovers just how strictly her keepers will keep her caged. The bride and groom, at least one of them most likely a virgin, will not even be allowed unscripted intimacy on their first night together. No champagne by candlelight in the jacuzzi. Their first supper together has to be a ceremony called a *kuzen no gi* at which, with attendants hovering, they dine on grilled snapper, soup and rice. Masako is required, like a dutiful old-fashioned wife, to pour her husband a cup of *sake* so that he can drink to her health.

The days that follow are a dizzying whirl of banquets and receptions. Everyone who is anyone in Tokyo is there: the politicians, captains of industry such as Toyota's Tatsuro Toyoda and the late Akio Morita, the founder of Sony; authors including Hiroyuki Agawa; entertainers like the *kabuki* actor and 'living national treasure' Utaemon Nakamura VI. The only celebrity absentees are the gigantic sumo wrestlers who normally attend such royal celebrations, lumbering around like animated Easter Island monuments. They have been struck from the guest-list because at the last royal wedding, that of Prince Akishino, a champion wrestler named Chiyonofuji committed the unpardonable *faux pas* of actually eating the grilled sea-bream that was set in front of him. At upper-crust weddings, the fish is a gift to the guest, who should take it home in the little *bento* box provided, along with all the other spoils – towels, packets of tea, sheets, little silver bonbonières and so on. In Japan the guests bring money, the bride and groom provide the presents.

Masako can forget about any idea of a get-away-from-it-all honeymoon, too. While Charles and Diana flew off to join the royal yacht *Britannia* for a cruise around the Mediterranean, Japan's newlyweds had to make do with ceremonial appearances at shrines in Nara, the eighth century imperial capital with its magnificent Buddhist temples and herds of free-ranging sacred deer; and at Ise, a town on the picturesque Shima peninsula which juts out into the Pacific three hours by bullet train and local express south-west of Tokyo. They are not there, however, to see the sights but to pay their respects to the gods, Naruhito's ancestors.

Ise is the most sacred Shinto site in Japan, lofty wooden shrines dedicated to the sun goddess, with thatched roofs and great gold-tipped beams, set in the timeless twilight of a forest of vast and ancient *cryptomeria* pines. Walking around the grounds is a solemn and rather spooky experience. It is always an acute disappointment to the thousands of pilgrims who flock here that these shrines, which have been destroyed and rebuilt every 20 years since the seventh century, are closed to the public and can only be glimpsed through four stockades of fencing. However, Naruhito and Masako, swapping her smart designer suits for ceremonial robes, will be ushered in by priests and shrine maidens dressed in white, for ceremonies including the aforementioned ritual with the bran. No matter how diligent the coaching, one cannot help wondering what a modern career woman like Masako really thinks of all the mystical mumbo-jumbo.

Amid the whirling weeks of parties, presentations and ceremonial occasions, there is one moment in particular which I feel is worth recording. Warwick McKibbin is head of the economics division of the Research School of Pacific and Asian Studies at the Australian National University in Canberra. An impossibly young-looking economics professor, who also has a gig as a professorial fellow at the prestigious Lowy Institute in Sydney, he regularly commutes to Tokyo and Washington where he works out of the Brookings Institution, a famous think-tank. When he was a young doctoral student at Harvard University 20 years ago, McKibbin was assigned to tutor Masako for her economics degree, and got to know her well – a friendship which continues to this day.

The Australian professor was one of a dozen or so foreign friends who attended one of the celebratory banquets, and he cherishes having been invited back to the palace for a very low-key, very private celebration with Masako and Naruhito afterwards. They chatted for a while, quite informally, and the crown prince poured him a beer and began enthusing about the garden he was culti-vating. 'Come and have a look,' he said, throwing open a door and inviting him out into the night, where light misty rain was still falling.

Suddenly, says McKibbin, half a dozen men in white coats materialised out of the drizzle. 'I don't know who they were,' he says, 'but the message was pretty obvious. The crown prince said that we had better go back inside, and that was it. I never got to see the garden.' It was the moment he first really grasped the rigid and restrictive rules that his friend would have to live by for the rest of her life.

And even then, after an exhausting 18-hour day, it's not yet over. The royal rituals actually follow them into the bridal chamber. Just as Naruhito and his bride are thinking about their first night of bliss together, there is a knock on the bedroom door. Who's there? Why, it's a wizened 87-year-old official named Kizuo Suzuki, a former East Palace chamberlain, and his wife. They are carrying a lacquered tray decorated with (here comes that heavy-handed hint again) storks, on which are four silver dishes, each containing 29 tiny rice-cakes the size of marbles called *mochi*, one for every year of Masako's life. Every night for four nights, the aged retainers explain, the couple must pray for a baby, then eat one rice-cake each. On the fourth morning, the tray, the silver dishes, and the remaining *mochi* will be taken to an auspicious spot in the palace gardens and buried. Pregnancy should follow shortly thereafter.

Or not.

2

Daddy's Girl

FROM THE SUMMIT OF THE HILL YOU CAN SEE WHY FOR centuries Murakami Castle was an impregnable stronghold for the Tokugawa shoguns, the dynasty of 'barbarian-subduing generalissimos' who once ruled Japan. Behind you, stretching down into the dark forest, are narrow ravines, guarded by *chevaux-de-frises*, upturned rocks to obstruct horsemen and leave them vulnerable to the bowmen above. Ahead is the broad stormy sweep of the Sea of Japan. The flank is guarded by a lazy, gravelly bend of the Miomote River. Although now there remain only broken foundations, blocks of lichen-encrusted stone, a small shrine and a massive tombstone inscribed with ancient *kanji* characters, this ancient fortress must once have been a formidable deterrent to both invading barbarians from across the sea and rebellious local tribes.

Even in a modern, urbanised, post-industrial society such as Japan's, most families still trace their roots back to the countryside, to remote, rustic retreats like Murakami.

There is a reverence for rural life found in few other countries, a reminder that just two generations ago the majority of Japanese earned their living from the land. Even today parents tell their children to eat up all their rice 'so the poor farmers will not starve to death'. Every summer at the time of the Buddhist festival of *Obon*, *shinkansen* bullet-trains shoot out of the great cities of Tokyo, Nagoya and Osaka jam-packed with millions of people returning to the home-towns of their grandparents to pay respect to their ancestors. There, bonfires blaze into the night to attract home the spirits of the dead, and jovial crowds dressed in colourful *yukata* sip *sake*, munch octopus balls and dance by lantern-light in circles in the street to the rhythmic beat of *taiko* drums.

Even though it is three generations since the Owada family moved from Murakami to the bright lights of Takada (now called Joetsu City), amid the snow-caped mountains of Niigata Prefecture, the private detectives hired to investigate Masako's background would have been obliged to come here – 400 kilometres or so across the country from Tokyo, at the dead-end of a highway lined with gaudy *pachinko* palaces, pinball parlours where workers and housewives gamble for prizes of giant fluffy toys. The investigators from Tokyo came to make inquiries into whether Masako's pedigree was sufficiently pristine for marriage into the imperial family. Perhaps they even spoke with Tetsuro Honma, a historian who is curator of a museum dedicated to the Owadas at the local council chambers, though he would be much too discreet to say so.

Murakami is a pleasant little backwater of 32,000 people on the way to nowhere, which prides itself on its '*sake, sake* and *nasake*' – word-play combining its principal produce, rice-wine and salmon, with an untranslatable quality that means a mixture of compassion and kindness. It has an ageing population, little secondary industry apart from a big rice-cracker factory, and is not mentioned in any international tourist guide. So when Masako's engagement to the crown prince was announced there was great civic jubilation. The town staged a fireworks display, flew flags, paraded festive palanquins which one of the Owada ancestors commissioned through the streets, and made plans for a tourist boom. Alas, that does not seem to have eventuated, and after a few months of excitement Murakami reverted to its old sleepy ways. The bones of the Owada ancestors were quietly dug up and relocated. Their princess never came.

There is a festival going on the day I arrive, a *matsuri* which involves a kind of lion-dance, a reminder that China is only a few hundred kilometres across the sea (see the map on page vii). Honma is waiting for me, a pedantic little man with an armful of historical documents who never uses two words when 20 will do. He ushers me into the Owada museum, which is full of family memorabilia, a huge red bowl of the local lacquerware embossed with golden dragons, wedding photographs, the family tree. The most interesting exhibit is a gadget containing an ink-block used in calligraphy.

When Masako married her name had to be obliterated, literally, with black brush-strokes from the family's *koseki*, the official record which is kept in the custody of the local authority. Japanese law requires all households to report births, deaths, marriages, divorces and criminal convictions to their local authority to be recorded on this registry.

Just why the Owadas had not transferred their registry to the Tokyo ward where they have lived for many years is not clear. So when their daughter married they had to travel all the way to Murakami to blot out Masako's name with that ink-block and brush. From now on, she is no longer an Owada but a member of her husband's family until death, when her semi-incinerated bones will be interred in a tomb with those of *his* ancestors. That is how final marriage often is in Japan – no running back to Mum if things don't work out.

In the sixteenth century, explains Honma, three great battles were fought hereabouts, which culminated in Tokugawa Ieyasu – the greatest of the shoguns, who unified Japan and founded the castle-town in a swamp that would become Tokyo – capturing the seemingly impregnable castle. In 1720 the Tokugawas installed the Naito family as the local war-lords, and in 1787 the first Owada, Shinroku, came to Murakami to serve them. He and his son Heigoro, Masako's great-great-great-grandfather, were the last of the samurai, the hereditary warrior class celebrated in a thousand Japanese soap operas.

However, it would be a mistake to imagine the Owada ancestors as the haughty sword-wielding warriors of movie epics such as *The 47 Ronin*, living by the oaths of loyalty laid down in the *bushido* code of chivalry and indulging in practices such as *tsuji-giri*, meaning 'to try out a new sword on a passer-by'. No, urges the unsentimental Mr Honma: 'Think of the castle as corporate head-quarters, and the samurai as *sararimen*.' Public servants might be a better comparison. Heigoro, in fact (although you would never know it from the adulatory commentary in the Japanese media at the time), was a third-grade samurai, the lowest class of the 700 or so employed by the Naito lords. He was a kind of feudal Mr Plod, and a display of knotted ropes on the wall of the museum shows that his particular speciality was trussing up wrongdoers in various ingenious ways. He was paid only with a daily ration of rice sufficient to fill a wooden measure the size of a shoe-box. As the veteran Japan journalist Murray Sayle put it in an elegant article for the *New Yorker*:

> *The Owadas were the poor, prickly-proud retainers of a hard-luck lord, the kind who often went without supper but still picked their teeth in public to make a good show.*

In 1853 Commodore Matthew Calbraith Perry sailed an armada of nine warships, the 'black fleet of evil intent', as the Japanese named it, into Tokyo Bay, ending Japan's nearly three centuries of international isolation and triggering the Meiji Restoration, the installation of the emperor at the centre of power, the overthrow of the shogunate, and the end of the samurai. It took 15 years for the first ripples of the impending revolution to reach remote Murakami, and the local warlord, branded 'an enemy of the emperor', departed for Tokyo immediately to help defend the shogunate. He left in charge his adopted 17-year-old son Joshi Nibutani, who promptly committed suicide. The town, left without a lord, was split into two camps: those who supported the shogun and those who sided with the emperor. But eventually common sense prevailed and Murakami surrendered without a fight. On the emperor's orders, the castle was dismantled block by block. The samurai melted away into the night, the Owadas to Takada to look for work.

By a stroke of good fortune, although now destitute, the family retained the key to its future – a share in the salmon-fishing cooperative which controlled Murakami's most important industry. Every summer, millions of salmon migrate up the Miomote River to spawn, a silver torrent of fish packed so densely you can almost stroll from bank to bank without getting your feet wet. Wander into an ancient wooden store like Kakkawa, and you will discover what happens after they are netted. Rack upon rack of fish, some of them weighing a mighty nine kilograms, dangle from the roof of the shop where they will cure for a year before being shipped off to the gourmets of Tokyo. To care for the children of the impoverished former samurai, the cooperative established an education fund which operated right up until the 1960s. Both Masako's father and grandfather received their early education thanks to this charity. They are known as *sake no ko*, 'salmon children'.

In fact, education became the touchstone of this ambitious family, and through it within three generations the Owadas would regain their social status. Takeo Owada, Masako's paternal grandfather, worked his way up to become principal of a prefectural high school in what is now Joetsu City, and then for many years was head of the city's board of education. He lived well into his nineties – Masako would have known him – and he believed education was the greatest asset a parent could give his children. 'There are three important things in life – study, study, and study,' the old man lectured his offspring, and his offsprings' offspring.

All seven of this remarkable man's children who survived infancy (including, unusually for those days, the two girls) graduated from university or teaching college. It must have been a tremendous struggle, in those dirt-poor, defeated 1940s and 1950s for him to find the money. Quite extraordinarily, the five boys all graduated from the

University of Tokyo, the most prestigious of the country's 89 national universities, which is the training ground for the mandarins who run what used to be known as Japan Inc. Akira, the oldest, became a lecturer in Chinese literature at Senshu University; Takashi a lawyer; Osamu head of the Japan National Tourist Organisation; and the youngest of the boys, Makoto, became an inspector at the Transport Ministry's Ports and Harbours Bureau. And the girls married well. Yasuko wed the late Tadashi Katada, managing director of what is now Krosaki-Harima, a giant of the international fire-brick world. Toshiko married Kazuhide Kashiwabara, then managing director of the Industrial Bank of Japan (IBJ). These were the relatives Masako grew up with, her uncles and aunts, high achievers all of them, a theme which would run through her life from her earliest days.

And then there was Hisashi Owada, the third-born, the aloof, unsmiling figure whom we met earlier as he farewelled his daughter, bowing stiffly in the rain. Masako's father was born in September 1932, and little has been revealed of his early life in the boondocks of frigid, mountainous Niigata Prefecture, the only part of Japan where the traditional thatched wooden houses are built three storeys high to surmount the snow that can drift five metres deep. Even today scores of people die in avalanches and roof collapses during the bitter winters. As one of a family of nine growing up during the war on a school-teacher's pay, Hisashi and his siblings must have known hardship and deprivation, as did all Japanese of their generation.

Education was Hisashi Owada's get-out-of-Niigata-free card. The 'salmon child' was a diligent student and won a place at the University of Tokyo, Japan's equivalent of

Harvard, Oxbridge, or the École Nationale D'Administration, the finishing school for France's ruling class. He was
studying Liberal Arts and Sciences when, at the age of 21,
he passed the fiercely competitive civil service entrance
examinations and joined the Diplomatic and Consular
Service, as Japan's fledgling foreign ministry was then
known. Smart, ambitious, and – all-important in a
Japanese organisation – a team player, at least in his
younger years, Owada was chosen as one of the ministry's
fast-track career officers. He was sent to study at
Cambridge, where he graduated in law, and later
completed a PhD course – his passion was legal scholarship, and he was known to his colleagues from his didactic
manner as 'the professor'. He embarked on a stellar career
in which, like any loyal *sarariman* of his generation, the
interests of the corporation (or, in his case, the ministry)
had to be placed ahead of the wellbeing of the family.

Today, people who know Owada speak highly of his
drive and intellect, but describe him as a prickly hard-to-
know personality, with little warmth or tolerance of others.
'He was very *ambitious*,' says a former colleague at the
ministry, speaking on condition of anonymity, pursing his
lips and tilting his head as he spits out the word. This is far
from praise in an organisational culture where consensus
and cooperation are the keynotes. Sir Adam Roberts, an
Oxford University don and one of the world's leading
scholars of international relations, taught Masako and
remains her friend and an occasional visitor to the palace.
He met Masako's father on a number of occasions when
Hisashi was a guest lecturer at Oxford, and subsequently at
international conferences and seminars. 'I thought he
lacked emotional range,' he says, 'and he did not take
kindly to criticism.' Gregory Clark, an Australian journalist

and longtime commentator on Japan, saw quite a bit of Owada in the 1970s when Owada was running the quaintly named Oceania Division of the Foreign Ministry, which includes Australia. 'In those days he was very competent and went out of his way to cultivate journalists,' he recalls. 'But we had a falling-out over something, and that was it.'

Striving ever upwards on the career ladder, Owada accepted postings first to Moscow, then to the United Nations in New York, then to Washington, then back to Moscow, then Paris, New York again, and finally The Hague. In between postings he was to take semesters as a visiting professor in international treaty law, his speciality, at Harvard and at Oxford. Back in Tokyo, working out of the ministry's famously dingy grey granite-faced office block in the public service precinct of Kasumigaseki, he worked his way up through the ranks until in 1991 he achieved the pinnacle of his ambition, head of the ministry.

Although Japan's mandarins are modestly entitled *jimujikan*, literally 'administrative vice-ministers', no Japanese is in any doubt who holds the real power in Tokyo. The politicians who in Western democracies direct policy come and go in Japan and are not held in high regard by the public, who see them as venal and corrupt. Since the end of World War II Japan has had more prime ministers than notoriously unstable Italy, and nearly as many governments – until the charismatic Junichiro Koizumi took over in 2001, Japan had had 46 administrations in 56 years, and frequent Cabinet reshuffles meant that most ministers barely had time to find their way to the toilets before their term was over. As well, hundreds of members of the dominant Liberal Democratic Party (LDP), including one notoriously corrupt former prime minister,

Kakuei Tanaka, have been jailed for taking bribes. Little wonder bureaucrats like Hisashi Owada claim the credit for the economic success of Japan's post-war recovery, though not, curiously enough, for the calamitous decade and a half of recession which followed the bursting of the economic bubble in 1990, which seems to have been all the fault of those rotten politicians. They have come to regard themselves as the real ruling class.

Owada married in 1962 when he was 30, during one of his stints working at the ministry back in Tokyo. He and his future wife were introduced by a mutual friend, Takeo Fukuda, an elder statesman of the LDP, rather than at an *omiai*, a date often arranged by a professional matchmaker. This is still, incidentally, the way a surprising number of Japanese, around one in seven, meet their partners. Not that there is anything wrong with the practice, particularly when one considers that Japan has a divorce rate less than half that of the United States. In fact, with the boom in on-line dating agencies, the use of matrimonial intermediaries is enjoying a revival even in the West.

Yumiko Egashira would have been regarded as an eminently suitable match by Owada's parents, impecunious but eager to regain the family's lost social standing as they were. Five years younger than Hisashi, she was pretty, but more importantly she came from the 'right' background. A well-brought-up, well-educated young woman with a degree in French literature from the highly regarded Keio University, she was working at the time for an airline company. Her father was a wealthy banker, managing director of the Industrial Bank of Japan, then a financial powerhouse of Japanese industry and ranked among the world's top ten banks; now swallowed up by the Mizuho financial group after bankrupting itself with reckless loans.

Both her grandfathers had been admirals in the Imperial Japanese Navy, with one, Yasutaro Egashira, having commanded a battleship in the war between Japan and Russia at the beginning of the twentieth century. Another thing they had in common was that Yasutaro was also descended from samurai, though in his case they were far away – servants of the lords of Saga, the shoguns' domain on the Ariake Sea, not far from Nagasaki on the tropical southern island of Kyushu. There was one skeleton in the Egashira family closet, but it would be more than 20 years before this came to light.

The year after their marriage, Masako was born, on 9 December 1963 in a public hospital in the Tokyo suburb of Toranomon. With typical obsession with trivia – it is only the important issues that they often miss – the Japanese media reported later that the future princess was 51 centimetres long, and weighed 3870 grams at birth. Home in those days for the Owadas was a humble '2LDK' – a small apartment owned by the Foreign Ministry consisting of two bedrooms, a living room, dining room and kitchen. One of the earliest photos shows Masako in a traditional photographer's studio, clutching a toy panda. The family is kneeling on cushions on a *tatami* mat in front of a painted oriental screen, the men in dark suits, the women in dresses and pearls, apart from one of the grand-mothers who is clad in a kimono, with a broad silk *obi* cinched around her waist. They are all trying hard to smile, except granny, although it would certainly, even in the 1960s, have been cause for greater celebration if their first-born had been a boy.

Along with many other Asian societies, Japan still places a premium on males. They alone can carry on the main branch of the family tree, the *honke*, which is important to socially ambitious families like the Owadas, who take great pride in their ancestry. More practically, in spite of token official efforts at gender equality, men earn a lot more money and monopolise the top jobs in business and the bureaucracy to a far greater extent than in the West. Get into any elevator in Tokyo and watch how the women – even if they happen to be quite senior executives – slide into place beside the doors and push the buttons while the men call out the numbers from the back. No doubt Masako's mother murmured to her husband that they were young, there would always be another chance for a boy. But as luck would have it, the only other time Yumiko Owada would fall pregnant was two years later – and the twins, as they turned out to be, were both also girls.

Eric Johnston is a long-time correspondent in Japan, currently based in Osaka, who is deputy editor of the *Japan Times*, the country's leading English-language daily newspaper. He has been reporting on the royal couple for more than a decade and he believes that the key to Masako's personality is her complex relationship with her father:

Some people who worked with [Hisashi] say that he is a real son-of-a-bitch, a brilliant mind, but extremely cold and aloof. Masako is the son her father never had, but desperately wanted. Everything she did, including the marriage, was to please him. She has a huge father complex.

There would not be much time for a typically Japanese upbringing, before the demands of Hisashi Owada's career collided with the needs of his family. No prize for guessing which won. At the age of 18 months, Masako was transported from the leafy streets of suburban Tokyo to the bleak concrete blockhouse of a diplomatic compound not far from the Kremlin in Leonid Brezhnev's Soviet Union. Her mother was also later to sacrifice her own career to be with her peripatetic husband – she had to turn down a job as professor of calligraphy. Hisashi's ambition, then as always, came first.

At least Foreign Affairs, being one of the more enlightened arms of the Japanese bureaucracy, did not insist that mother and daughter remain at home for the duration. This is what still happens to many loyal *sararimen* – their company exiles them to a poky apartment in a far-flung outpost like Hokkaido's snowy capital of Sapporo, while their families stay in Tokyo. This is great for the economy of places like Susukino, the rip-roaring red-light district, where karaoke parlours, restaurants, and bars where one can pay to molest women dressed as schoolgirls, are stacked ten storeys high. But it does little for families, and often leads to children estranged from their fathers and overly dependent on their mothers.

The Moscow posting set the scene for what many believe to be the second important influence on Masako's personality: constant mobility leading to a lack of sense of belonging, a feeling of foreignness. By the time she married, she would have spent very nearly half her life abroad, developing the rare ability – or curse, for a Japanese – of being able to see Japan from an outsider's viewpoint. Her kindergarten, primary and secondary schooling were in Moscow, New York, Tokyo and Boston, the language of the playground switching from Russian to Japanese to English. Her university studies were at Harvard, Tokyo and Oxford universities, three institutions on opposite sides of the world, with very different academic demands and social norms. We will look later at the culture shock of a well-brought-up young Japanese woman confronted with the sex-and-drugs-and-rock-and-roll scene that swirls around Harvard Square. Every time she settled down somewhere for a few years and formed a new circle of friends, it was time to move on. Small wonder that friends, even today, talk of there being 'two Masakos' – one, the bright, sparkling internationalist, the other a modest, introverted Japanese wife and mother.

Yukie Kudo, like Masako, is one of the best and brightest of her generation, a graduate of the University of Tokyo's law school (the faculty which the elite of the elite attend), and a master of economics from the prestigious London School of Economics – a place, she sniffs, where you have to earn your degree, unlike in the United States where 'almost everyone passes'. She first met Masako on the Tokyo campus, where they used to hang out in coffee shops, and she agrees with this Jekyll and Hyde view of Masako's character, which she puts down to the destabilising effect of constant travel:

> *People say that Masako has a strong personality, but to me she is like 'moving water'. She lacks a true identity because she was brought up in many parts of the world. She is very adaptable, and her character does not seem to have developed; it changes from day to day. One day [at university] she is wearing casual jeans and a sweater with a hole in it; the day after, she is wearing an impeccable Hanae Mori suit. She suffers from inconsistency and instability.*

To compensate for an absentee father – Japanese bureaucrats work hours which awe their counterparts in other countries, often putting in 30 or 40 hours of overtime a week when the occasion demands – the young Masako seems to have had a stimulating stay in Moscow. She attended the Jetskisato No. 1127 daycare centre, little knowing that learning Russian would come in handy many years later when, as crown princess, she would find herself chatting to former Soviet President Mikhael Gorbachev, who was seated next to her at a state banquet. A photo shows her at the age of three trying out a pair of child-sized skis, a sport she still enjoys. She has talked of trips to the embassy dacha, a rustic country house on the outskirts of Moscow, where in the summer she picked flowers, and in the autumn apples.

But it would, of course, be a mistake to idealise the family's time in Kutusovski Prospekt – or daily life of any sort in the paranoid depths of the Cold War Soviet Union. Russia and Japan were still – indeed, are still – technically at war, no peace treaty having been signed after the end of World War II owing to a territorial dispute. Masako's mother was so concerned about the quality of medical treatment available there, that when time came for the twins to be born in the summer of 1966 she flew off to a clinic in Switzerland. Reiko and Setsuko enjoy dual Swiss/Japanese citizenship, speak French, and like to be called by their Gallic first names, Madeleine and Marie.

Imagine, then, at the age of five this little girl saying *poka*, goodbye, to all her Russian friends, and getting on a plane to go, not 'home' to Japan – which Masako hardly knew anyway – but off to the United States, to the Big Apple. Hisashi had been assigned to Japan's mission to the United Nations, one of the ministry's most important postings, and his family would have to accompany him – not that I imagine they shed many tears at leaving a hardship post like Moscow. At least they would now have rather better weather, creature comforts like supermarkets with goods on the shelves, and superior accommodation in the upscale Riverdale district. Overlooking the Hudson River, Riverdale is dotted with church spires and the mansions of wealthy bankers and politicians – the likes of Teddy Roosevelt once lived here. It has extensive swathes of parklands, even though it is next door to the gritty Bronx, and is only a few kilometres from the UN head-quarters tower on the East River. It is here, on Henry Hudson Parkway, that the Japanese government has the apartments in which it houses its diplomatic corps – Masako's new home for the next three years.

Another year, another country, another language, another life. It was 1969, the year man walked on the moon, rollicked in the mud at Woodstock, and marched down the Washington Mall to protest against the war in Vietnam. Not that this would have registered much with the curious little girl who got off the plane at New York's John F. Kennedy Airport to be driven to her new home.

Not yet five years of age, Masako was put into New York City public kindergarten No. 81 where, hardly surprisingly, teachers remember her as a rather quiet child, at least to start with. For the first four months she just sat there listening to this new language before she ventured her first words in English: 'May I go to the bathroom?' Pictures show her, a chubby little girl, doing the things kids like to do: picnicking in the park, riding a pony, costumed up for Halloween (she's the skeleton), posing in front of a snowy mountain with her sisters. Nowhere in most of these American photographs, the 'authorised' shots released by the Imperial Household Agency, is Hisashi to be seen. As in some families in the West, child-rearing is still seen as 'women's work' in Japan – the father's place is at the office. Some *sararimen* refer to their homes as 'the aircraft carrier' – the place where they crash-land late at night, refuel, and take off from at dawn.

In 1971 it was time to move on once again, this time to the home country Masako had never known. Clambering ever higher in the bureaucracy, Owada was to return to the ministry to be groomed for one of its most sensitive and influential postings, private secretary/advisor to his friend Takeo Fukuda, who had been appointed foreign minister, and was later to become prime minister of Japan. Later that year he would be further honoured to be chosen to accompany the Emperor Hirohito on his first postwar trip outside Japan to Europe, though he would be no doubt deeply offended by the reception he received from some. With memories of the war still raw, crowds turned their backs, politicians boycotted ceremonies, the Dutch burned the Japanese flag and the British satirical magazine *Private Eye* ran a front-page headline: 'Piss Off Bandy-Knees!'

On their return the family moved to the pleasant suburb of Meguro, where Hisashi – moving up in the world – commissioned an architect to design the three-storey brutalist mansion where the Owadas would live with Yumiko's parents, the Egashiras. The family fortunes appear to have improved – the land alone on which the house was built is calculated to be worth $3.4 million, a substantial amount even by the standards of the super-heated Tokyo property market, even with interest rates running at little over one per cent. The Owadas could now also afford a maid. Belatedly, Masako began her 'real' schooling, Japanese schooling, the only kind that really counts in this conservative society.

Masako was labouring under a double handicap – at

the age of seven, other kids of her generation had already begun their education; and, having lived abroad, she would be stigmatised as a *kikokushijo* or 'returnee child'. This phenomenon is now well recognised – the Education Ministry actually keeps statistics, and reckons that about 12,000 children enter the Japanese education system every year having spent at least a year abroad. But back in the 1970s, it was just beginning to become a concern. Japanese were not allowed to travel freely overseas until 1964, and by the early 1970s the advance guard of Japan Inc. began returning home after years abroad. These people, many of them senior bureaucrats and businessmen, discovered to their dismay that their children had missed out on important elements of their schooling – studying Chinese *kanji* characters, for instance, or Japan's unique spin on history – which would make it difficult if not impossible for them to complete their education success-fully. Moreover, exposure to lively and challenging classrooms abroad made many unwilling to accept the rigid disciplines of the Japanese education system, where rote learning and absolute obedience are demanded. In short, their 'Japaneseness' had been compromised. The media began to fret about a 'drop-out generation' who, having been contaminated by Western notions of individu-alism, would never be able to fit back in to conformist Japan.

Masako's parents had tried hard to preserve a quiet island of Japanese culture while the family was abroad. They spoke Japanese at home, favoured Japanese cooking, and Yumiko read the children Japanese fairy stories. But there is evidence that the girl still found it very difficult to adjust when she returned. Yumiko was determined that her three daughters would go to a strict private Roman Catholic girls-only school, the same school she and her mother had graduated from. Futaba Gakuen is in Denenchofu, now a trendy outer suburb of Tokyo, and is one of a network of 'little charitable schools' founded in the seventeenth century by the Blessed Nicholas Barré, a Jesuit from Amiens in France. The nuns, who still play an important part in the school's pedagogy, came to Japan in 1872 as missionaries, with the aim of teaching English, French, and Western manners and skills to Japanese women. Although not regarded as an academic powerhouse – Masako is the first diplomat the school has produced, and very few of its graduates make it to the University of Tokyo – the school selects only girls from good families, and it emphasises *shitsuke*, a word which combines the precepts of good upbringing, behaviour and discipline. The school day begins with prayers, and ends with the students performing menial tasks. The motto emblazoned on the badge-pocket of Masako's navy blue uniform was *Simple Dans Ma Virtue – Forte Dans Mon Devoir* (Simple In My Virtue, Strong In My Duty).

But Masako, for the first and last time in her life, failed the entrance exam. Even primary schools have them in highly competitive Japan, where your life can be predetermined as much by the school you manage to get into as by your natural talent. In fact some kindergartens even assess toddlers by their ability at tasks such as unwrapping sweeties and correctly folding and disposing of the wrappers. So instead of the $7500-a-year Futaba she was first enrolled at the council-run Haramachi primary school near her home in Meguro, and then – after just a few weeks there – vaulted up to the second grade of another council school called Tomihisa, a subway ride away in Shinjuku. It was not until the following year that she was finally able to make the grade at Futaba, the fifth school she had attended in five years, and her third language of instruction.

In spite of these formidable handicaps, it didn't take Masako long to catch up. She did well at her studies, learned to play piano and tennis in her spare time, joined a handicraft club, and when she was in grade six decided she wanted to be a veterinary surgeon. After school, she tended rabbits, chickens and fish, a hamster and a chameleon. For a school project once she dissected and stuffed a *kojukei* bird, a Chinese bamboo partridge. She bred mice in a barrel, which caused a minor neighbourhood scandal when she took them home for the school holidays, and they escaped into her parents' toffy neighbourhood. Her classmates nicknamed her 'Owa', and she seems to have been a popular kid, a bit of a tomboy, not some spoiled upper-class brat. She played pranks, though what passes for naughty behaviour in Japan probably wouldn't raise an eyebrow elsewhere: nibbling at her tuckbox before the lunch break, climbing onto a roof to pelt fellow students with snowballs, tape-recording the sound of a siren and playing it in class, causing a stampede of students out of the building.

I drove around the school one summer's day with an old school-friend of Masako's, Kumi Hara, to try and get a feel for the place. It was during the summer holidays, so it was deserted – normally there are 700 or 800 students at their desks in the rather grim-looking cream concrete towers, decorated with statues of the Virgin Mary, or playing on the barren asphalt sportsground, shielded by pines and guarded by a high chain-link fence. Kumi Hara is an engaging woman a couple of months younger than Masako, who was in the same class when

Masako graduated to Futaba's junior high school. They used to hang out together after school. She is a talented Bossa Nova singer – there's a market for everything in cosmopolitan Tokyo – working nights at the delightfully named Jazz Live Spot Full House, a low-ceilinged dive decorated with posters of jazz greats and Hanshin Tigers baseball stars, in the outer suburb of Koiwa.

'They were quite strict,' she concedes, talking about the nuns, who watched like hawks to make sure the dress code was observed: socks folded three times to precisely 15 centimetres above the ankle, dress to the knees, hair bobbed if it reaches the collar, red scarf knotted just so, hat at the correct angle. When boys were allowed to visit the school for the annual festival, the girls had to prudishly wear black tights under their skirts. Lunch was home-made *bento*, typically rice-balls wrapped in seaweed. After-school chores, as at most Japanese schools, involved the students in cleaning up the rubbish and sweeping and polishing the classroom floors. If discipline and modesty were lacking at home – which they weren't – Masako had it drummed into her by the nuns.

Masako, says Kumi Hara, became one of the top students of her class, although she was quite outspoken, and not afraid to challenge her teachers when she thought them wrong. 'She was a very good student, very focused, always on top of her subject,' she says. 'During the ten-minute break between classes other students used to swot up, but Masako didn't need to.' English was her forte, naturally, after her time in America – she regularly got 'excellent' grades – although she was no slouch in other subjects, and had begun to study her fourth and fifth languages, French and German. Her younger sisters used to tease her that she spent too much time studying and not enough on 'girly' pursuits, as though even at that age she had decided on one of the male-dominated professions, rather than life as a housewife. They called her *onii-chama* ('big brother'), she complained in a kind of diary she used to exchange with school-friends.

Vacations were spent at the family *besso*, a holiday-house in the chic resort-town of Karuizawa. Once an exclusive mountain summer retreat for the upper class and expatriates, now that the *shinkansen* bullet-train has brought it to within an hour's ride of Tokyo the quaint little timber-fronted main street has become infested with tourists and overrun with fast-food joints and souvenir shops selling bottles of the local blueberry jam and maple syrup. But tucked away on the outskirts, among expensive golf courses and woods of pine and maple, are some handsome old European-style mansions where people like the Owadas, and even Japan's royal family, like to escape the stifling Tokyo mid-summer heat and spend a few lazy days or weeks of summer. It was to Karuizawa that many years later Masako would retreat to try to heal her wounds with the balm of those happy childhood summers. But that is getting ahead of the story again.

Kumi and Masako were both keen baseball fans, and tried to persuade the school to start a team. The nuns refused, saying it would cost too much to buy the equipment and find a ground. Kumi Hara, however, suspects it was because they did not regard Japan's national sport as sufficiently ladylike. Instead, the girls revived the defunct school softball team, and soon Masako had a number of *kobun*, a coterie of followers, and the team began to win. With a strong pair of shoulders, Masako fielded at third base, and batted in what is called the clean-up position, coming in at number four when the bases can be loaded, and often saving the innings, and the game, with a mighty home-run wallop, sending the ball soaring over the fence, and her team-mates galloping home to victory. By the third year, the Denenchofu Futaba softball team was swigging orange juice from the district championship trophy urn.

Her love of baseball also led her into a liaison which would alarm Western parents, but which in Japan – certainly in those days – was probably regarded as a bit of harmless teenage hero-worship. The Yomiuri Giants are the rich and pampered superstars of the Japanese national baseball league, commanding the sort of fanatical support which is elsewhere probably only achieved by Manchester United, Britain's soccer champions. Masako got a crush on an outfielder and '*pinchi hitta*' named Haruaki Harada, a strong, handsome man who was a mainstay of the team for nine years and who was, incidentally, married. She carried his photo around, and she wore the same No. 8 on her softball jersey. The two girls, from the age of 13 or 14, used to go to the Giants' practice ground on the flood-plain of the Tama River in the suburb of Setagaya to cheer him on. Afterwards, they would hang out with the base-baller in coffee shops, share clandestine Italian meals with him, and even, later, go drinking in night-spots such as the old Green Room in sleazy Roppongi.

'If only I'd kept those letters,' he muses. 'They would be worth heaps.' Harada is sitting in the Dolci Mari Risa, a trendy cake shop in Denenchofu not far from the school, toying with a glass of iced tea. He is still – approaching 60 – a good-looking man with a tanned face, solid frame and stiff salt-and-pepper hair, wearing a pink striped short-sleeved shirt and slacks, with the thick bangle of a gold watch on his wrist. He is reminiscing about 1979 when the

Giants went away to training camp down south on Kyushu island, and the love-lorn 16-year-old Masako sent him chocolate and a love letter on St Valentine's Day. 'There would not be just a card, but two or three pages of letters. She would tell me how much she admired my baseball, how much she liked me, in fact . . . well, just things.' He is almost blushing. He had photos taken with the girls, but was not game to pin them up on the wall until after Masako married, for fear his wife would misunderstand. 'There were always a lot of girls hanging around the base-ballers, and, quite frankly, some parents worry about this. I don't think the girls tell them [the parents]. Many of my friends have gone on to marry them, marry their fans.'

They kept up the friendship for ten years, meeting occasionally, sometimes going to see Kumi Hara sing Bossa Nova. Harada, who now works as a talent scout for the Giants, was very impressed with the young Masako – and not altogether surprised when he heard she was to marry the crown prince, though 'quite frankly, I would not like my daughter to marry into the royal family'. He says of Masako: 'She came from an upper-class family, but she was not stuck-up. She was pretty, she was physically fit, she was studious. She always had the air that she might do something that would surprise you.' He did not, needless to say, get an invitation to the wedding – baseballers are not in the same league as sumo wrestlers when it comes to imperial patronage.

It is also highly unlikely that Masako told her parents about her crush on the handsome baseballer. They were strict and proper and certainly would have had ambitions for their eldest daughter beyond a sports star, no matter how celebrated. Kumi Hara accompanied the Owadas to classical concerts, and visited the family occasionally at their home in Meguro. She remembers it as a very formal household, with no place for teenage high-jinks. Masako's parents, she says:

> . . . *brought her up to value status, not happiness.*
> *They were social climbers. It was a strict upbring-*
> *ing, and there was always a tense atmosphere in the*
> *house; it was like walking on eggshells. The house*
> *was full of books, but there was no TV. Her parents*
> *were very strict and expected a lot of [Masako]*
> *because she had the potential.*

Like Eric Johnston, Kumi Hara says Hisashi was the dominant figure in Masako's life: 'Masako was her father's girl. She was brought up to be the boy of the family, and she really wanted to follow in her father's footsteps.'

Literally. As 1979 rolled around it was time for Hisashi Owada to uproot his family again to take another step up the ladder of ambition.

3

Mummy's Boy

THERE IS SOMETHING ALMOST SURREALISTIC ABOUT THE scene in the photo that Colin Harper pushes across the table. In a bush backyard, against a backdrop of tea-tree bushes, two teenage boys with violins tucked under their chins and a Vivaldi score on a stand in front of them play sweet music in the evening air. Around them, mosquitos buzz while a corps of clicking cameramen jostle for position. So this is what a Japanese prince gets up to on his holidays.

It is a chilly late August afternoon in the winter of 1974, and Naruhito, Prince Hironomiya (it means 'shrine of broad vision'), to give him his full title, is making his first overseas trip at the age of 14. Masako, nearly four years younger than the prince, is already a seasoned world traveller, now back at school in Tokyo after spending most of her childhood in Moscow and New York. But Naruhito has had a far more sheltered and secluded upbringing, as do all the Japanese royals.

Since World War II the historically xenophobic Japanese monarchy has tried to modernise and internationalise its image. Naruhito's grandfather Hirohito was the first emperor in 2600 years to set foot outside Japan, and a cousin, the late Prince Takamado, was one of the first to be educated abroad. He was known, incidentally, as the 'Canadian prince' (because that was where he lived while attending Queen's University) until his untimely death from a heart attack in 2002 on the squash court of the Canadian Embassy in Tokyo. And now it was time for Naruhito, destined to be the 126th emperor of Japan, to have a taste of life abroad, forging what would turn out to be an enduring bond with that other large English-speaking ex-British colony and former wartime enemy, Australia.

The idea for an Australian home-stay seems to have come from Naruhito's father, then the Crown Prince Akihito, who had visited the year before and had apparently also heard good things about the place from a royal relative, Prince Katsura, who had studied at the Australian National University in Canberra. The trip was endorsed by the Imperial Household Agency, which approached Sir John Crawford, then the university's vice-chancellor. They sought his help in arranging a visit for the young prince, explaining rather quaintly:

We have decided on Australia, which is a sound, young and healthy country, because it is comparatively close to Japan [and] this is his first overseas trip – also because the language spoken there is English, the language he is studying. [Because] we want him to experience different walks of life on his own, we think that Australia – which is in many ways the opposite of Japan – is appropriate.

That picture was taken at Point Lonsdale, a sleepy seaside holiday resort on one of the crab-claws of land that pinch the entrance to Port Phillip Bay. A place more 'the opposite' of the hectic high-rise Tokyo that Naruhito would have glimpsed through the windows of his official car would be hard to imagine. Across the treacherous straits where pilots wait to guide tankers to the ports of Melbourne lies Portsea, Australia's wealthiest postcode, where the city's old-money Establishment has its multi-million-dollar summer hideaways. But Point Lonsdale is an altogether more laidback kind of place – men in shorts, hats and long white socks trundle bowls down the green, pensioners sip pumpkin soup in the cafes, kids skim pebbles into the grey-green waters of Bass Strait from the rocky beach. And here, in Kirk Road, a quiet street lined with gum trees a few minutes' walk from the ocean, was where Colin Harper had his modest holiday house, a rambling place of timber and fibro, linoleum-covered floors and a couple of sleep-outs.

Harper is now retired, a courteous silver-haired gentleman sitting in the lounge of his home before a flickering faux log fire, surrounded by the mementos of his famous home-stay guest: New Year's cards, photos, letters, a silver urn embossed with the imperial crest, a silver-framed portrait of Naruhito looking very military in his brass-buttoned school uniform. Back in the 1970s Harper was a big wheel in Melbourne business – he was to become a director of the ANZ Bank for more than 20 years, chairman of pharmaceutical company CSL, and vice-president of the Australian Institute of Company Directors. He also happened to be a member of the council of the exclusive Melbourne Grammar School, whose century-old bluestone buildings are the training ground for Melbourne's Anglican aristocracy, and the *alma mater* of three prime ministers.

Out of the blue one day he received a call from the head-master – Sir John Crawford had rung to tell him that the *Kunaicho* was looking for a respectable host family for the prince. Could he help? The criteria were: they had to have a son around the same age as Naruhito, and a spare room. Gobsmacked at the idea of a royal house-guest, Harper asked for 24 hours to think it over.

The criteria were not the problem. The Harpers' younger boy, Alex, was 14 and his brother Adam 16. And they had plenty of room in Shipley Lodge, their comfort-able two-storey home in South Yarra, built in 1850 by a family which migrated from Yorkshire bringing with them the materials for the house – the Welsh slate, the timber, the cast zinc verandah. But what Harper needed to talk over with his wife, Barbara, was the attitude of her parents. Her stepfather, Lieutenant Commander Clive Robinson, had been harbourmaster at Singapore when the Japanese invaded, and her mother, Jenette, a doctor. Both had been captured and brutally treated in the notorious Changi concentration camp, an experience from which Clive never recovered psychologically. Even though the war had been over for almost 30 years, and Japan – as Harper was well aware from his work as a banker – had now become Australia's most important trading partner, many Australians still harboured hatred towards their former foe. Harper has kept an ugly letter scrawled in wavery blue ink, one of several pieces of hate mail he received when the prince's holiday was publicised in the newspapers:

... you are a lot of crawlers ... you have got that ugly-looking Jap prince and taken him to Pt Lonsdale after all the atrocities they committed – and they will

do the same again. Tell your sons what the Japs did in the war.

So they talked it over with Jenette, who said: 'I'd rather you didn't, but as I live in Sydney and you live in Melbourne I really don't need to know.' And so the decision was made. On 18 August 1974, as most Japanese were preparing to stumble back to work after the Obon midsummer holidays, a polite young man, neatly dressed in slacks and a blazer, was delivered into the arms of his Australian host family on a cold Melbourne winter morning. Although they had been told Naruhito would 'eat anything' (the imperial family alternates between Western and Japanese cuisine) the first thing they did was take him to the slap-up Sunday buffet at the old Southern Cross Hotel where they watched him pile his plate up with that traditional Japanese *sarariman*'s staple, *karei raisu* – curry and rice. Relief. Melbourne's first Japanese restaurant had only just opened, and the raw seafood fare had been unkindly described by a reviewer as 'squids' turds and rubber bands'. The second thing they did was take him to the zoo to see his first kangaroo.

'He was a very friendly, very cheerful boy,' recalls Alex Harper, now a Melbourne opthalmologist, 'but we knew he must have had a pretty strange kind of life.' Indeed. Although it was officially a 'private' visit, Naruhito brought quite an entourage. He was accompanied from Japan by his chamberlain, a valet who laid out the boy's clothes every morning, and a bodyguard from the palace police. A second secretary arrived from the Japanese Embassy in Canberra, and an Australian government contingent headed by one W. G. N. Orr, the grandly titled Deputy Director of the Office of Government Ceremonial and Hospitality, two police and a media liaison officer. Security caravans were parked on nearby blocks in South Yarra and at Point Lonsdale. Although it was supposed to be a private holiday, no one was under any misapprehension that if the slightest thing went wrong it would cause international embarrassment, and could even damage the fragile relationship between the two countries.

And, of course, the media were everywhere. All the Japanese TV networks and major newspapers sent their correspondents to stake out the prince – as well, of course, as the naturally curious Australian news organisations. Even though Gough Whitlam's nominally republican Labor Government was in power, Australia loved – and still loves – a royal of any sort, let alone one who is heir to something as exotic as the Chrysanthemum Throne.

On the whole, the publicity given to the carefully staged events was positive. Pictures of that impromptu back-yard concert – Naruhito and the other Harper boy, Adam, playing the violin – were flashed around the world. *The Age* had a page one photo of him playing tennis, accompanied by a fawning article claiming that 'With his immaculate ground-strokes, he sent the ball whizzing across the net in a yellow blur'. TV showed the three boys tinkering with their bicycles, and going for rides around Point Lonsdale. They went out in a police-launch, on a brilliant day when the sea was like glass, and Naruhito delighted in watching the penguins and seals frolicking. He took a side-trip to climb Ayers Rock, as Uluru was then known – the prince had been a keen mountain-climber since the age of five. He played the violin (Chopin this time) for distinguished guests at Government House in Canberra after a State dinner thrown by then Governor-General, Sir John Kerr.

Naruhito appears to have been remarkably unaffected by the attention. 'He had no side, he was very natural, very easy to get on with,' recalls Colin Harper. 'My boys got on with him very happily, very well. He was a nice educated boy with plenty of spirit, plenty of go, and very inquiring.'

There were just a couple of occasions when Naruhito managed to slip the leash, to snatch a bit of unscripted fun. Once, on the way back from a barbecue, they drove up Mt Macedon, a scenic spot north of Melbourne. When they arrived at the lookout on top of the mountain, they found the view obliterated by thick fog. 'Ah,' quipped Naruhito, 'Kissinger's lookout.' The story loses something of its flavour without the context of the times – the US Secretary of State, Henry Kissinger, was unpopular in Japan and relations between the two countries were strained over the war in Vietnam, and US recognition of China. But it does show that, even at the age of 14, Naruhito was taking a keen interest in international affairs – an interest that would have appalled his minders if they had heard the remark. Any hint of a political opinion is strictly *verboten* to Japan's royals.

Another time, Harper found himself curled up in a bean-bag with the future emperor, consulting a dictionary to try and work out what was on his mind. Naruhito had done two years of intensive English, but struggled with the spoken language – foreign languages are taught like Latin in Japan, to be written and read, not as a means of verbal communication. Eventually they got it: the boy wanted to try his hand at golf. There is a scenic 18-hole course carved out of bushland a short walk from the Harpers' holiday-house, and Harper agreed to take the prince out for a hit the following morning. But when they mentioned their plans to his equerry there was a sharp intake of breath.

How easy it is to step on a mine in the no-man's land of Japanese imperial protocol. Golf wasn't in the schedule, and that was bad enough. Much worse, Hirohito, who was still on the throne, had had the nine-hole course in the palace grounds ripped up after bombing Pearl Harbor in 1941 and banned the game as being 'too American'. If the emperor found out that his grandson had been playing golf there would be all hell to pay.

They solved the problem, giving the media the slip by telling them that the prince intended to go fishing at Indented Head, sending the camera crews haring off miles in the wrong direction. Then Harper and the boys sneaked over the back fence of the golf course and had a few swings at a ball. In the middle of all this, the ranger came roaring up the fairway on a motorbike to ask what they thought they were up to. He, too, had to be sworn to secrecy. 'To this day, the story hasn't been told,' chuckles Harper. 'The Japanese media would have had a field-day.'

As for any lingering anti-Japanese sentiment, that was dispelled on their final night when a farewell dinner was arranged at the historic old Ozone Hotel in nearby Queens-cliff. Eighteen of them sat down to dinner, and at one stage during proceedings there was a minor panic when a minder noticed that Naruhito was missing. The heir to the Japanese throne had slipped into the public bar, and was learning to play pool. 'There was no problem at all,' says Harper. 'The locals quite took to him. They said "Oh, you're that Japanese prince, aren't you," and showed him how to play.'

The Harpers – along with a number of other Australians whom the prince got to know over the years – remained friends. But they were not to see each other again for almost 20 years, when Colin Harper was visiting Tokyo on

ANZ bank business, and a meeting was arranged through then Australian Ambassador to Japan, Rawdon Dalrymple. Naruhito was by now in his thirties, and had been officially designated crown prince, and installed with his retinue in the East Palace. Harper was shocked at what had happened to that boy he remembered as having so much 'spirit and go':

> He had been put through some form of submission . . . he was under a lot of pressure [to find a bride]. He was quite clearly bored to sobs. I asked him why he didn't go out more, and he said the problem of arranging [with the Kunaicho] any sort of trip outside the palace was unbelievable. 'So we never go out,' he said. 'I have been playing tennis, and I really am beginning to hate the sight of tennis balls.' He was really very unhappy.

In spite of these restrictions, Naruhito in fact had a far more 'normal' life than any of his ancestors. If anyone needed to do a bit of checking up on the family tree of the prospective spouse it was surely Masako's parents. The crown prince's grandfather, Hirohito, was the sovereign/deity in whose name Japan invaded Asia and the Pacific causing more than 20 million deaths. Many supported the distinguished jurist Lord Wright of Durley, chairman of the United Nations War Crimes Commission, who believed he should have been top of the list to be hanged for war crimes. His great-grandfather Yoshihito was the tragic Taisho Emperor, the son of a concubine. He suffered from meningitis and suspected lead poisoning and was rarely seen in public after 1913 when he was supposed to open parliament. Instead of reading his speech, he rolled the manuscript up and stared at the assembled MPs through it as though it was a telescope. His great-great-grandfather was Mutsuhito, the debauched, xenophobic Meiji Emperor, who was the father of modern Japan and also of 15 children by five different women, none of them his wife. Quite a remarkable dynasty. (See the genealogy on pages viii and ix.)

Naruhito's father Akihito, by contrast, is Japan's first modern constitutional monarch, the first not to be worshipped as a living God (Hirohito renounced his divinity in 1946 at the insistence of the occupying American forces), and the first to attempt to reconcile Japan with its former Asian enemies. Still, in his seventies, a small, smiling, dapper man with a thatch of iron-grey hair, he has done much to restore respect for the monarchy and atone for his father's war guilt. Kenneth Ruoff is a world authority on the current emperor, and Associate Professor of History and Director of the Centre for Japanese Studies at Portland State University in the Pacific North-West of the United States. He says that Akihito, the Heisei Emperor, and his commoner wife Michiko have 'brought down the imperial house from "above the clouds"'. In his award-winning biography *The People's Emperor* he writes:

> *Since ascending the throne in 1989, Emperor Akihito has put his stamp on the monarchy and Japan, not only with his informal style, but with his sustained efforts to bring closure to the post-war era by issuing apologies to neighbouring countries for Japan's wartime actions. [His] marriage in 1959 was widely interpreted by Japan's burgeoning middle class as symbolising liberty (because it was a 'love*

*match' rather than an arranged marriage) and
equality (because Michiko was of commoner stock,
instead of belonging to the ex-aristocracy).*

The dour and enigmatic Hirohito had just about given up
on any hope of a son and heir. He and his aristocratic wife
Nagako had four girls in a row, and his courtiers were
urging the emperor to take a mistress, the mysteries of the
Y chromosome and the exclusive role of the father in deter-
mining the gender of the child having not been discovered
in the 1930s. There is an old Japanese saying '*sannen tatai
konaki wa sare*', which can be interpreted as 'If (your wife)
has no boy after three years, leave her'. Up until Hirohito's
father's day, this would have raised no eyebrows. About
half the Japanese emperors would be classified as illegitimate by today's standards, being the children of concubines
procured from the noble families of the day. But Hirohito
rejected this solution as out of sync with the role Japan
sought to play in the modern world, and on 23 December
1933, the year Japan invaded China, their persistence paid
off and Akihito was born. Flags fluttered, sirens sounded
and bonfires were lit throughout the land.

The child's upbringing was devoid of family love, as was
the custom. Removed from his parents when he was a week
old, Akihito was suckled by a wet-nurse, raised in the
imperial nursery, and at the age of three taken to his own
palace to be brought up by tutors, chamberlains and nurse-
maids. The only time he saw his mother, father and siblings
was during a formal once-a-week visit and for celebrations
such as New Year. 'Although I had many mothers, I never
knew motherly love,' wrote China's last emperor, P'u Yi,
who was raised in similar isolation by eunuchs, behind the
walls of the Forbidden City. A Japanese royal princess once

confessed to the author Toshiaki Kawahara: 'I did not shed a tear when my mother died, but I was sad and could not stop crying when my maid resigned.'

Akihito's entire childhood was spent in wartime. At first, the Japanese military machine seemed invincible, advancing as far as Darwin, Sri Lanka and even the American mainland, which was attacked with bomb-bearing hydrogen balloons. But by 1944 General Curtis LeMay's B29s had incinerated Tokyo with a greater loss of life than the atom-bombing of Hiroshima and Nagasaki put together. Akihito and his younger brother Prince Hitachi were evacuated to the resort retreat of Nikko. He was 12 when his father went on the radio to announce, with typical circumlocution, that 'the war situation has developed not necessarily to Japan's advantage', and surrendered.

Young Akihito's one stroke of good luck was that in 1946, General Douglas MacArthur, commander-in-chief of occupied Japan after the war, persuaded his father to engage a foreign tutor for the boy. The woman chosen 'to help (Akihito) study English and obtain a sense of the international world' was an American Quaker, a children's book author named Elizabeth Gray Vining. A brisk, no-nonsense widow, she called the prince Jimmy because she found his Japanese name too difficult to pronounce. She later wrote that he was a 'poor little boy' because he had to live apart from his family, and described him as 'a small boy, round-faced and solemn (but) loveable-looking'. She is credited with having a profound influence on the development of Akihito's character, as well as bringing a little human warmth into his life. Certainly the son turned out to have little in common with the plumed militarist on a white horse who came to symbolise his father's reign.

Hirohito, according to Akira Hashimoto, a lifelong friend of Akihito's, justified entrusting the upbringing of his son and heir to others by saying 'I am the man who could not stop the war – such a man cannot give a good education to his son'. But, in truth, he was a remote and inscrutable figure, nicknamed 'Mr Ah, So' by the Americans because of his non-committal response to any query, whom one cannot imagine playing an active role in child-raising. And, in any case, he was merely following the tradition dictated by the imperial court for centuries, a system of which he himself had been a victim.

Like most of his ancestors, Hirohito was brought up by a succession of military officers, *Kunaicho* retainers and Confucian scholars who drummed into him the virtues of a frugal life of stern dynastic duty. Most influential of these was Maresuke Nogi, an infantry general who had fought in the Russia–Japan war of 1904–05. The day Hirohito's grandfather, the Meiji Emperor Mutsuhito, died in the summer of 1912, Nogi called the young prince into his office, gave him a lecture about his imperial obligations, and told him he would have a new tutor when his schooling resumed. The day of the funeral, Nogi and his wife Shizuko retired to their quarters where they bathed together before she dressed in widow's black, and he in white undergarments. Nogi composed a poem, in which he declared that he was committing *junshi* – the samurai practice of a loyal retainer following his lord into death, which had been abolished centuries before. They bowed solemnly to portraits of the emperor and of their own ancestors. Then Nogi plunged a dagger into his wife's neck, and disembowelled himself with a sword.

It is hardly surprising that with an upbringing like this, Hirohito had little to draw on when it came to a parenting role for his own children. This is what Akihito's wife, the Empress Michiko, wrote about her husband's lonely childhood many years later:

> *When I hear from him about how much he wanted a family, and had to live his life without his family, I begin to cry. When he told me that 'I must not die before I have my own family', never in my life have I heard such heart-breaking words, not even in a novel. Therefore I decided that I would try my hardest to make a warm home for this prince [Akihito] who had to endure living 25 years of his life in this way.*

Somehow Naruhito's father survived this loveless childhood and determined that it would never happen to his own family. His first major break with tradition was in choosing his own wife, and in choosing her for love, rather than having her chosen for him as a suitable social alliance. Up until then, all heirs to the throne met their wives-to-be through *omiai*, dates arranged by matchmakers and approved by the *Kunaicho* – usually the daughters of Japan's 500 or so noble families, or distant relatives from distaff branches of the royal family like Nagako, his mother. The *Kunaicho* did present Akihito with a number of 'bride candidates', but none of them met with his approval until one day in 1957, playing tennis while holidaying at that mountain resort of Karuizawa, he found himself in a mixed doubles game with Michiko Shoda.

The woman who would become Naruhito's mother was pretty, vivacious, a graduate of the Seishin (Sacred Heart) University, and the daughter of an eminently respectable family – her father was an industrialist, Hidesaburo Shoda, the president of the Nisshin Flour Milling Company. She was also no shrinking violet – in that first tennis match she and her partner wiped the court with the crown prince, while her mother cringed with embarrassment in the bleachers. She was the right age (23, nearly three years younger than Akihito), and she was a few centimetres shorter, another essential requirement. But, like her future daughter-in-law, she did not meet the other criteria of the *Kunaicho*, and she never gained the approval of her mother-in-law, the haughty Empress Nagako. Like Masako, she would be subjected to merciless bullying in the years to come, leading eventually to a health crisis.

Akihito, however, would not be denied, and two years after they met the bureaucrats relented and they were married in a traditional ceremony much like that of Naruhito and Masako. 'Until then, I did what the chamberlains told me to do,' he said. 'But I thought that at least marriage I should decide for myself.' The public agreed – polls showed that 87 per cent of people were in favour of the novel idea of a 'love match' for their next emperor. And it also triggered a mini economic boom as people rushed out to buy their first television sets to watch the great event.

The second radical break with the imperial past was their determination that their own children would have a better upbringing than the loneliness and deprivation suffered by Akihito. Their first child was born on 23 February 1960, in a rather dilapidated building hastily converted into a maternity hospital in the grounds of the palace. 'I was born in a barn inside the moat,' the prince was later to joke. A panel of imperial scholars chose the name Naruhito for him, meaning something like 'vast virtue'. When – if – he ascends to the throne he will exchange this for a unique 'reign name' and a new calendar will begin.

Michiko prepared herself for the task of child-raising by studying what was, by the medieval standards of the Japanese imperial court, a radical guide to 'modern parenting' by the American guru Dr Benjamin Spock. Dr Spock counselled that 'cuddling babies and bestowing affection on children' would make them 'happier and more secure' – not spoilt. Michiko soaked up the advice. She breast-fed the baby herself – in fact, she breast-fed him for 11 months – rather than use a wet-nurse. She had a special kitchen built at the palace so she could cook for the family, another innovation. She played with the boy in a nursery, which she had fitted with a specially padded floor-covering to protect him from falls.

Michiko kept a loose-leaf book in which she wrote instructions for the servants on how to look after her precious boy. So intrigued were the Japanese at the idea of a royal for the first time actually grappling with the same child-raising issues that they had to cope with, Michiko was persuaded to turn it into a book, *Naru-chan Kenpo* or *The Naruhito Constitution*. It became a best-seller, with its insights into such things as how to play with the child ('only one toy at a time'), how to extract small stones from his mouth, to 'rub his skin hard' when he wakes up in the morning, and 'give him a proper hug at least once a day'. When the child has his afternoon nap, the top button of his shirt must be unbuttoned. When she had to go on a trip, Michiko would leave tape-recordings of herself singing songs or reciting nursery rhymes which the servants would play to the child. Japan's royals make a great show of living modestly, and the empress let it be known that she patched Naruhito's clothes herself, and mended his broken toys.

In short, the picture emerges of a doting, some would

say overly prescriptive and protective mother. This is not uncommon in Japan, where fathers typically play very little part in the upbringing of their children, leading to a phenomenon psychologists nickname *mazakon* – an abbreviation of the Japlish phrase *mazaa konpurekkusu* or 'mother complex'. Children, particularly boys, who develop these intense relationships with their mothers tend to be overly dependent and to have difficulty forming relationships with other women. In extreme cases, a survey in the 1980s found that some Japanese mothers treated their boys to sexual favours as a reward for studying hard. There is no evidence that things went this far with Michiko and Naruhito, but people who know the prince well say that she is still the dominant person in his life.

'He's definitely not gay or impotent,' says Isamu Kamata, answering the unspoken question that would come up much later when Naruhito and Masako failed, year after year, to produce the child expected of them. 'He is a true gentleman, kind, broad-minded, very thoughtful, very healthy, he likes music. I give him 99 points [out of 100]. I am very proud that we have such a man as crown prince. But he does have a *mazakon*. He respects and listens to his mother more than usual. She is quite dominant.'

Kamata, a sprightly man in his seventies, is chairman and chief executive of Jabil Circuit, a Japanese computer circuit-board maker, as well as an accomplished amateur musician. We met over a tuna bagel at the Foreign Correspondents' Club of Japan, whose top-floor restaurant looks down on the leafy grounds of the imperial palace. Kamata has been a friend of Emperor Akihito since they were together at Gakushuin, the exclusive school which the royals attend. He has known Naruhito since he was a baby, and frequently goes to the palace to make up a musical ensemble: Michiko on the harp or piano, Akihito on the cello, Naruhito on the viola, and Kamata and a friend making up the rest of the strings. Forget *Chopsticks* – a typical evening's entertainment might include the second movement of Schumann's *Piano Quintet in E Flat*, Mozart's string quintets in C Major and G Minor, and his difficult and dramatic *Piano Quartet in G Minor*, an especial favourite of the empress. Sometimes the royals come to his place for these classical jam sessions, though Kamata is not too keen on that. They bring a retinue of up to 30 officials, police and other hangers-on, and Kamata is expected to feed the lot of them cakes, tea and sushi.

Naruhito, you may have noticed, has switched from the violin of that Point Lonsdale performance to the viola, a larger, more mellow instrument which plays a more subservient role in the orchestra and which stars in very few concertos. The viola is the butt of many musicians' jokes; in fact there are whole websites devoted to mocking people who play it. ('Two musicians are driving along when they see a conductor and a violist crossing the road ahead of them. "Which one shall we go for first?" asks one. "The conductor," says the other. "Business before pleasure." ') Typically, says Kamata, the modest prince switched instruments because he thought the violin 'too much of a leader, too prominent'. Of his technique, he says: 'I would say that he is accomplished, rather than gifted. Of course he does not have a professional technique, but he plays with feeling; his interpretation is very sensitive.'

The Elizabeth Gray Vining role in Naruhito's early life was filled by a man we have already met – the stern old lackey who was so disapproving of Masako's performance at her inaugural press conference. However, Minoru

72

Hamao, one of Japan's few Roman Catholics, would have had little in common with the liberal-minded Philadelphia Quaker who was Akihito's mentor. He was a member of the palace old-guard who revered the glory days before the war when the emperor was not only a living god, but the country's wealthiest mortal.

Then the *Kunaicho* was called 'the Ministry Above the Clouds', and controlled an empire of industry and real estate which would be worth billions today. These days it has been downgraded to the status of an agency, is a tenth of the size, and dependent on a grant from the taxpayers. Then positions were hereditary, which helps explain the agency's iron-clad resistance to reform. Hamao's grandfather was Hirohito's chamberlain, his mother a chambermaid to one of the royal princesses. He himself attended the elite Gakushuin school, and in his numerous books he laments the fact that the imperial bureaucrats are no longer chosen from the ranks of the old nobility, but seconded from common or garden ministries such as finance, police or foreign affairs.

What we know about Naruhito's childhood comes mainly through the rose-tinted filter of his minders, particularly from Hamao's books. The kind of journalistic intrusiveness that saw Britain's 14-year-old Prince Charles splashed over the front pages for escaping his Scottish boarding school to sip cherry brandy in a pub does not exist in Japan. Hamao has known Naruhito since he was one year old, when he was appointed his personal chamberlain/tutor, one of around 100 staff then working in the East Palace. The boy, you infer from his writings, grew up in a goldfish bowl – a household which included no fewer than eight chamberlains, three doctors, and three chefs (one to cook Japanese dishes, one Western, and one specialising in bread and desserts), with servants whose sole job was brushing clothes, polishing shoes, caring for the silverware and so on. It is not known whether, like Prince Charles, he actually had a valet to put the toothpaste on his toothbrush, but that would not surprise. Whenever he went on an outing – to the zoo, for instance, or the aquarium – it was a media circus.

However, his devoted mother did not take Dr Spock's dictums too literally and seems to have been anxious not to overly pamper the child. When he was four, Michiko wrote: 'One thing I have felt strongly during these past four years is that my son has not had any opportunity to see people from the outside world working really hard. I do not want him to grow up with the mistaken notion that food will always appear on the table as if by magic every meal-time.' Akihito also lectured his son to 'avoid a lifestyle which is above the clouds and divorced from the citizens'. So when Naruhito misbehaved – rattling his chopsticks on his rice-bowl, for instance, or failing to complete his homework – Hamao was given permission to stand him in the corridor, shut him in a dark cupboard, or, as an ultimate deterrent, spank him on the bottom.

While Masako was belting the softball out of the ballpark and chopping up birds, Naruhito's favourite pastime – as a child and now – was mountaineering. Like Masako, he holidayed in the resort town of Karuizawa, and scaled his first mountain (actually, Mt Hanare is more a hill with pretensions) at the age of five, mocking his studious father who lugged along a three-volume botanical tome in his backpack to identify plants they came across. At last count he had conquered more than 140 peaks in Japan, Nepal, Alaska, Great Britain – and Australia, where as a schoolboy, you will remember, he scaled Uluru. Though, as usual, one should not take Japanese official history too literally. Don't imagine the gentle prince fearlessly rappelling down icy crevasses on a rope – that would be far too risky for the *Kunaicho* to allow. 'He is more a trekker than an alpinist,' says Jun Hamana, a fellow member of the Japan Alpine Association who has conquered serious peaks in the Himalayas, 'boots and camera.'

Naruhito, it goes without saying, was being groomed for his destiny from the moment he was born, though in a very different way from European royals, and from his own predecessors who regarded military service as an essential part of their royal training. Prince Charles and his sons were sent to complete their education in uniform – indeed, controversy raged when William and Harry graduated from the Royal Military Academy Sandhurst and let it be known they wanted to serve in the Iraq war. Denmark's Crown Prince Frederik trained as a frogman, Norway's Crown Prince Haakon also served in the navy, and Thailand's Crown Prince Vajiralongkorn studied at Australia's Royal Military College, Duntroon, and served as a career officer in Thailand's army, as well as training to be a Buddhist monk. Naruhito's grandfather Hirohito practised martial arts, and his instructors even constructed a machine-gun firing-range for him in the palace grounds.

But such warlike pursuits would be anathema in postwar Japan, with its pacifist constitution, where so many millions had died in the name of their commander-in-chief, the emperor. Akihito was spared the rigours of such military indoctrination, and ensured that his son's education was also largely academic. As well as the three Rs, Naruhito was well-tutored in the classics of Japanese history and culture, particularly the *Nihonshoki* and the *Kojiki*, the earliest written works in Japanese, which date from the eighth century AD and consist of a confusing mixture of history, myth and spiritualism. He also studied the *Manyoshu*, the '10,000 leaves', a 1200-year-old collection of verse. His only contact with the martial arts was confined to taking part in the annual high-school *kendo* fencing tournament and attending sumo wrestling matches. Such is the education of a modern emperor-to-be.

Naruhito is, in all likelihood, the first Japanese crown prince to have had a genuinely happy childhood. As well as the mountain-climbing and the music, he skied, he skated, he rode a little pony from Okinawa, he became quite a handy tennis player and occasionally he cycled over to his chamberlain Hamao's house in the palace grounds to play with his five children. Like Masako, predictably, he barracked for the champion Yomiuri Giants in the Central Baseball League – though his hero was the big-hitting No. 3, Shigeo Nagashima, later to become the team's manager. In later years, he came to enjoy crooning sentimental pop songs such as 'Let's Meet in Yurakucho' in karaoke bars, and became an accomplished drinker. 'He drinks like a python,' says his brother Akishino, himself no mean boozer. Even his mother said Naruhito was 'my drinking teacher'.

While Masako was digesting new languages and cultures in the Soviet Union and the United States, Naruhito, poking around the palace grounds one day, discovered the remains of an ancient roadway, which kindled a lifelong interest in the history of transportation. Both his university theses were to be based on its obscure and seldom-visited byways. Japan's royals all choose esoteric and inoffensive hobbies like this – not because they are necessarily peculiar, but for fear of causing the slightest hint of controversy.

After the war, the Emperor Hirohito disappeared into a

specially built laboratory in the palace grounds where he devoted the rest of his life to the study of jellyfish. The current Emperor Akihito is also an ichthyologist and has published 26 scientific papers on goby fish, tiny spiny-finned minnows. He even had one, *platygobiopsis akihito*, named in his honour after Douglas Hoese, the former chief scientist of the Australian Museum in Sydney, who corresponded with the emperor for many years, identified it as a new species. Even Naruhito's larrikin younger brother Akishino has a doctorate in agricultural science. He enjoys dissecting catfish (his wife bakes him cookies shaped like them) and he spent five years cross-breeding a Chinese Buff Cochin chicken with an American Bronze turkey, producing a meaty new breed of fowl he christened the Buff Bronze. Naruhito's hobby, however, has a rather more poignant point, escapism from his ruled and restricted life, as he pointed out once at a press conference:

I have had a keen interest in roads since childhood. On roads you can go to the unknown world. Since I have been leading a life where I have few chances to go out freely, roads are a precious bridge to the unknown world, so to speak.

When he was four years old, led by his chamberlain Minoru Hamao, the road led him to the gates of the Gakushuin kindergarten, a ten-minute walk from the East Palace. Even today you could hardly call the children who attend Gakushuin Tokyo's hoi polloi, the common folk Naruhito's parents were keen for him to mix with. They are embarking on one of the most expensive and exclusive educations in the country, with kindergarten fees starting at around $20,000 a year. Gakushuin offers a seamless conveyor belt from kindergarten to university for the scions of Japan's old aristocracy and postwar *nouveaux riches*, guaranteeing its graduates a social network which will set them up for life, and access to the plum jobs in business and the bureaucracy. So sought-after is a place at Gakushuin that some years ago when I was living in Tokyo a local businessman whose child failed to make the grade was caught offering a $95,000 bribe to try and buy his way in – to a kindergarten, for goodness' sake.

Before the war, the Peers' School, as it was known, was in fact part of *Kunaicho*'s empire, the finishing school for members of the nobility, and a fertile recruiting ground for future royal brides. But nowadays it is a little more egalitarian, and this is where Akihito and Michiko decided to send Naruhito, his younger brother Akishino and little sister Sayako for their schooling. 'Please educate them as normal students . . . do not give them a special education . . . they should follow the rules and be punished if called for,' was the admonition of their father, the emperor. Perhaps overdoing the modesty thing, the boy was made to walk to school and wear a hand-me-down uniform.

Gakushuin is also where a gangling young man from Melbourne became the second Australian in the crown prince's life.

Andrew Arkley is waiting in his apartment just around the corner from Tokyo's raunchy gay nightlife district of Shinjuku Nichome. His flat is crammed with souvenirs of his schooldays with Naruhito, or Den-Den (a play on his title *denka*, or 'highness') as they used to call him. In the kitchen drawer are the lacquered chopsticks the classmates were presented with on a school outing. On a table is an elaborate gold-bound yearbook in which the class wrote their farewell messages. Hanging in the wardrobe is the school uniform, a replica of that worn by students at the Bremen Naval Academy in Bismarck's Prussia, a navy blue jacket with black braid, brass buttons up the front and studs shaped like cherry blossoms on the collar. Arkley can still struggle into it – he keeps himself lean swimming, and doesn't weigh a whole lot more than in 1975 when he and Hiro (another nickname of the prince's) met at Gakushuin's senior high school.

That was the year the service organisation Rotary inaugurated a scheme to build cultural ties between the two former enemies by sponsoring two Australian students to attend high school in Japan for a year. Arkley, then a lanky 16-year-old attending a State high school in the bayside Melbourne suburb of Beaumaris, was chosen along with David Emery, whose father was a Rotarian from Epping, in Sydney. Both boys did a crash-course in Japanese and early that year, with snow and ice still gripping Tokyo, arrived to settle in with their host families. They had the usual cultural shocks: 'I kept forgetting to take my shoes off,' says Arkley, 'and I knew the baths were going to be hot – but not that hot!' But the Australians settled in well – so well, in fact, that more than 30 years later, after returning to Australia a couple of times, Arkley has decided to make Japan his home.

At Gakushuin senior high, Arkley found himself in the year ahead of the crown prince, but they got to know each other well because of their membership of the school geography club. 'He had just been to Australia, and he seemed to like the place and the people,' says Arkley. 'He was also pretty keen to improve his English, so we would spend hours together talking.' At Gakushuin, says Arkley, 'the policy was that he should be treated the same as everyone else . . . so that meant everyone was treated well.' 'Well' means that, unlike at other schools such as Masako's, the students did not have to scrub the floor after classes, there was no corporal punishment, and geography club outings were a treat.

Once the crown prince and his fellow club members went on an expedition (by bus, accompanied by a posse of security guards, with a second empty bus following in case of a breakdown) to the wild and mountainous Noto Peninsula, across the country on the Sea of Japan. At every guest house where they stayed, the entire staff – the general manager, the chef, the chambermaids – would come out into the street and bow deeply to the bus as it pulled out. 'Everyone was treated like royalty,' recollects Arkley. 'It was really very funny – even Hiro was laughing.'

Arkley says that wherever the prince went he was tailed by security guards, and 'even at university there was no way he could just disappear'. Not that he appears to have tried very hard, unlike his father who once – famously – 'escaped' to the bright lights of the Ginza one night, causing the entire Tokyo Police Department to be turned out to search for the fugitive prince. '[Naruhito] was very responsible,' says Arkley. 'He has always been a good boy. From the time I have known him, he would never say a bad thing about anybody. The idea of him doing anything to upset anybody . . . it's beyond his capacity. His main aim in life is to get the skills and knowledge to become a good emperor one day.'

Taking turns with all the other 134 students of Naruhito's year – no favouritism could be shown – Arkley and Emery were invited back to the palace to hang out with the prince. He found the East Palace 'quite modest – a rather cold sort of place and I was surprised that they had this harsh neon lighting'. He had meals with Naruhito's parents – again, humble fare like *tonkatsu* (crumbed pork cutlets) – and found the current emperor 'very nice, not at all intimidating, though he seemed to have official duties all the time. I never saw him without a tie, even at ten or eleven at night'.

Later, when Arkley returned to Tokyo to complete a university degree, he got to know Naruhito even better, dining with him and his friends in Chinese restaurants, even going back to the palace late at night to get drunk with him. Drinking is more than a social lubricant to many Japanese males, it is the only opportunity they get to speak their minds without fear of consequence. Squeeze into any bustling bar under the Yurakucho railway arches and watch the uninhibited way *sararimen* and their bosses slip out of their corsets of social convention for a night of boozy bonding. Naruhito was no exception:

We all knew the pressure he was under [this was when Naruhito was being pressed to choose a bride] so we would just go over and get drunk with him. Beer, whisky, wine, sake . . . whatever was going. He was a good drinker, and I only remember one night when he had too much and had to excuse himself. He just said very quietly and politely 'I might have to go upstairs' and disappeared.

As far as his studies were concerned, Naruhito appears to have been more the diligent plodder than the bright intellect his future wife would turn out to be. In 1978, while she was topping the class in English at Futaba high school, the prince was enrolling at Gakushuin University, across town in the suburb of Meijiro. It is a huge campus, about three kilometres around, into which are crammed 40-odd buildings, a hodge-podge of architectural styles from early twentieth-century mock Gothic to an ancient timber lodge that might once have been the vice-chancellors' residence, to a peculiar concrete pyramid. In summer, the place is humming, with cicadas screeching in the ginkgo trees, and girls in 'sailor suit' uniforms squealing from the sidelines as boys clash hockey and lacrosse sticks on the red, gritty sports ovals.

At university, Naruhito, the high-school goody-goody, seems to have done his best to be 'just one of the guys'. When it came time for him to be initiated as a freshman, the other students politely approached the prince and asked whether he would mind terribly if they threw him into a goldfish pond – the traditional rite of passage. 'Be my guest,' said Naruhito, or words to that effect, and the emperor-to-be submitted to a dunking. He ate with the other students in the university cafeteria – *soba* and *udon* noodles at $1 a bowl – he joined the *ikebana* flower-arranging club, and he studied more assiduously than most, earning him the nickname '*ji-san*', a phrase which has the feel of 'old codger'. His chosen field of study, the history of transportation, was hardly likely to set the world on fire. The title of his thesis has been quoted in full by the Japanese media, leaving people to draw their own conclusions about a man who could spend four years labouring over '*A Tentative Review of Maritime Transportation in the Seto Inland Sea in the Medieval Period*'. A welcome change, nevertheless, from the piscatorial preoccupations of his father and grandfather.

His tutors, at any rate, were impressed. His supervisor, Professor Motohisa Yasuda, an eminent Japanese historian, had this to say about Naruhito on his graduation: 'He was very diligent and quiet, not the type to be loud.

I was very impressed with his beautiful use of language – he did not use student slang or trendy colloquialisms. He has definitely been brought up properly since he was very young.' In his university yearbook entry, Naruhito's personality is described as: 'Quiet, studious, cheerful, good sense of humour, fair, honest, generous, considerate and easy-going'. Under the heading 'Ambition', the prince wrote 'To teach English history at university'.

And, indeed, if this diligent and altogether nice, if rather namby-pamby, young man had been allowed to quietly drift off into some academic backwater a lot of people would have been spared a lot of grief. But it was not, of course, to be. There could be only one future for Naruhito from the moment he was born: to one day occupy the Chrysanthemum Throne, and to produce an heir to ensure the continuance of the dynasty. And already the distant drumbeat of duty was beginning to sound more loudly. When would the prince, now pushing 23, find a wife?

The Last Emperor

I t was a steamy hot day in the central African jungle. Raddled, bare-breasted women stood in front of their mud huts pounding millet in hollowed-out tree stumps as our bus bumped and rattled its way into town from the airport. Children threw stones at scavenging dogs. Men lay in the shade of mango trees drinking home-brewed beer and swatting flies from their faces. In one of the world's most desperately poor and benighted countries I was on my way to an extravaganza the likes of which the world had never seen before or since – the coronation of a new emperor.

The twentieth century has not been kind to monarchs of any description. Kings and queens, czars, shahs, emirs, sultans (and sultanas, their female equivalents), maharajas, princes and padishahs, grand dukes and duchesses have toppled like ninepins. When Japan's Emperor Hirohito was born in 1912 there were almost 100 monarchies. Ninety per cent of the world's population – including India and China, the most populous states – was ruled by royals, whose 'divine right' was

conferred by heredity. They ranged from the mellow constitutional monarchs of Britain, to the off-with-his-head absolute
dictators of the Ottoman Empire. Republics were oddities you
could count on the fingers of one hand: France, the United
States and Switzerland.

By the time the fireworks went off to celebrate the millennium, less than ten per cent of mankind had a royal head of
state. In the intervening century, war, revolution and the very
occasional democratic vote had swept away two-thirds of the
monarchies. Today there are only 30 royal families left in
the world, all but a handful of them with powers tempered by
constitutions, elected parliaments and independent courts. Only
three countries (Spain, Cambodia, and the kingdoms of Uganda)
later changed their minds and restored their monarchs. One, the
remarkable King Simeon II of Bulgaria, returned home in 2001
after half a century in exile, formed a new political party, and got
elected prime minister. It would be nice to say that this trans-
formation has been uniformly of benefit to mankind, but one
has only to look at China, the Soviet Union and the loathsome
Marxist dictatorships of North Korea and Laos to see that abol-
ishing a monarchy does not necessarily lead to either democracy,
respect for human rights, or a better life for the citizens.

Nor, for that matter, does establishing one, as the citizens of
the Central African Republic were about to find out.

At the start of the twentieth century, there were five rulers
who were called emperors. Only one of these dynasties survives,
that of Japan – although its empire has long vanished. In fact,
there is some dispute about whether *tenno*, as Japanese call
their monarch, should really be translated as emperor – the
Chinese characters mean something like 'heavenly ruler above
the clouds'. Two emperors, Charles I, the last of the Habsburgs,
and Wilhelm II of Germany were overthrown at the end of World
War I, their empires dismantled, and the new republics of

Germany, Austria and Hungary re-drawn on the map of Europe. In 1948, Britain's last emperor, George V, surrendered India and the cryptic inscription 'Ind Imp' (*Indiae Imperator*) was removed from the back of the British coinage. The most famous of the century's emperors, thanks to Bernardo Bertolucci's visually stunning movie, was P'u Yi, China's last emperor, who was over-thrown as a five-year-old child in 1912 then restored as the puppet monarch of Japanese-ruled Manchuria until World War II ended in 1945. But he was not actually the last emperor. In the desolate, famine-ravaged kingdom of Ethiopia on Africa's Horn, the Emperor Haile Selassie I, King of Kings, Lord of Lords, Conquering Lion of the Tribe of Judah, Elect of God etc. etc., ruled for almost half a century until he was deposed in a Marxist coup in 1974, and died – some say by suffocation – a few months later.

And then there was Jean-Bédel Bokassa, the man whose coronation I had been dispatched to cover that December day in 1977. The Central African Republic is as close as you can get to Joseph Conrad's *Heart of Darkness*, a land-locked kingdom the size of Texas in the geographical centre of Africa, where rebel bands lurk in the lawless jungle, disease kills most people before they turn 40, and the population lives in grinding poverty on less than $400 a year. Bokassa, once a colonel in the French Army, had seized power in a coup in 1966, and since then his country had spiralled into bankruptcy as he and his cronies looted its coffers and brutalised its people.

The cynical French former colonialists kept him in power for a decade for the sake of his country's uranium exports, greased with gifts of diamonds and big-game hunting trips which Bokassa gave the French president Valéry Giscard D'Estaing. His rule was to stamp him as one of the modern world's most infamous dictators, right up there with Uganda's murderous Idi Amin and Kim Il-sung, who starved to death, imprisoned or executed millions of his fellow North Koreans. Bokassa's rule was absolute, his temper ferocious, and many believed him deranged – when an Associated Press correspondent tried to interview him, he smashed the correspondent's glasses into his face and had him thrown into a prison from which he was lucky to escape alive.

But absolute power was not enough. The vain and preening Bokassa craved the 'divine right' of his hero, Napoleon Bonaparte, and so he appropriated some $30 million, a large chunk of his country's meagre revenues, to have himself crowned emperor. The front row of the Catholic cathedral in the capital of Bangui was filled with fashionably dressed whores whom Bokassa flew in from Paris to help him celebrate. Dressed in a gold-encrusted uniform with a white-plumed cockade in his tricorn hat, the bearded Bokassa seized the crown from the archbishop and placed it on his own head, as Napoleon had done. A plane-load of rose-petals was flown in from France to scatter on the ground at his feet, where hundreds of European and African diplomats, celebrities and officials of aid organisations guzzled Champagne, caviar and *fois gras* at a debauched open-air banquet. It was the most obscene display of extravagance amid poverty, even by the standards of Africa in the 1970s.

No one lamented three years later when French paratroopers finally overthrew their puppet, and Bokassa – along with an unknown number of his 17 wives and 55 children – was flown into cushy exile at a chateau near Paris. He did return to Central Africa, now reverted to a republic, in 1986, and was put on trial for treason, embezzlement, and the murder of 100 schoolchildren whom he had personally butchered in 1979 because they protested at having to buy the expensive uniforms he decreed they should wear. He was convicted twice of all charges, apart from one of cannibalism (human body-parts had been found in freezers in his palace) and sentenced to death. To the great disappointment of his victims, that sentence was never carried out and Central Africa's first, and hopefully last, emperor died in 1996 of a heart attack.

The world's 30 remaining monarchies are: Andorra, Bahrain, Belgium, Bhutan, Brunei, Cambodia, Denmark and territories, Japan, Jordan, Kuwait, Lesotho, Liechtenstein, Luxembourg, Malaysia, Monaco, Morocco, Nepal, The Netherlands and territories, Norway, Oman, Qatar, Saudi Arabia, Spain, Swaziland, Sweden, Thailand, Tonga, United Arab Emirates, the United Kingdom and most countries of the Commonwealth, Vatican City.

The following countries abolished their monarchies in the twentieth century:

1910:	Korea, Portugal
1912:	China
1917:	Russia
1918:	Austria, Germany, German royal states, Finland, Lithuania, Poland
1924:	Turkey, Mongolia
1931:	Spain (restored 1975)
1944:	Iceland
1945:	Manchuria, Vietnam, Yugoslavia
1946:	Hungary, Bulgaria, Italy, Albania
1947:	Romania
1947–1950:	India and Indian princely states
1953:	Egypt
1956:	Pakistan
1957:	Tunisia
1958:	Iraq
1960:	Cambodia (restored 1993)
1961:	South Africa

1962:   North Yemen
1966:   Burundi
1967:   Ugandan states of Buganda, Toro, Bunyoro
           and Ankole (restored 1993), South Yemen
1968:   Maldives
1969:   Libya
1973:   Afghanistan, Greece, Ethiopia
1974:   Malta
1975:   Laos, Sikkim
1979:   Iran, Central African Empire
1987:   Fiji
1992:   Mauritius

4

Magna Cum Laude

OR MASAKO OWADA, THE AUTUMN OF 1979 WAS TIME
to pack her bags yet again. As Naruhito was settling
down at Gakushuin University his future wife was
farewelling her friends once more, and leaving behind the
culture in which she had just begun to feel comfortable.
Touchingly, 40 of her giggling teenage classmates came to
the airport coach terminal to sing her a goodbye song,
to the surprise of her father's colleagues from the ministry
who thought they must be there to welcome a rock star.
Even though she was a bit of a swot, Masako had become
popular at school, and made some friends which she
would keep, at least until her marriage. She recited a
farewell poem in German which she had written for the
occasion, and climbed aboard the coach. It would be seven
years before she would return to Japan.

Even though she had attended primary school for three
years in New York, nothing better illustrates the culture
shock the young Masako would have to cope with than

her new school. The contrast between the strict, prudish nuns of Futaba and freewheeling Belmont High School in semi-rural Massachusetts could not be starker. Set beside a large lake in grounds full of silver-birch trees, Belmont's emblem is not a symbolic green sprig, but a pirate with a dagger clenched between his teeth wearing a tricorn hat emblazoned with a skull and crossbones.

The school has grassy sports grounds, where Masako would continue to play softball, an ice-skating rink, and a huge parking lot for the staff and teenage students, many of whom drive themselves to school. Instead of religious icons, the walls are covered with great splashy pictures of comic-book characters. It is co-educational, and as for tucking one's socks over three times to just 15 centimetres above the ankle, the uniform is gangsta rapper chic – forage caps on backwards, baggy pants, football jumpers and sneakers. And make-up – banned on pain of expulsion at Futaba – is *de rigeur*. Ethnic homogeneity is replaced with diversity – one in five of the students at Belmont is Hispanic or African-American. The notice-board, rather than having notes about upcoming softball fixtures and music clubs, has the phone number of the Samaritans' suicide helpline, and newspaper cuttings with cautionary headlines such as '20 Shots of Scotch Prove Fatal to Student' and 'Six-pack Cost Him $4722'.

Julie Yeh, a Taiwanese student who befriended Masako, says that, compared with their new American classmates, they were both initially rather socially naïve. Masako was shocked at the drug use and the dating. When they went to the school prom, Masako blushed at the couples kissing in the dark, and since they didn't know how to dance, the two girls spent the night watching movies in the school auditorium. 'We were pretty nerdy,' she said, 'but she seemed to enjoy herself. She was always happy.' Another former classmate, Faye Binder Wisen, was quoted later as saying: 'She wasn't a dweeb, but she wasn't really in the mix of things.'

But after completing a refresher course in English, Masako seems to have found a niche in the raunchy culture of her new school. Other students remember her as the 'quiet and studious' type and some say she earned a new nickname of 'Brain'. Betsy Pew Karban, now an art teacher whom I tracked down in Elyria, Ohio, did not know her well but says she was in the maths team and the French club, where she excelled. She continued writing German poetry, winning a Goethe Society award. One year she took part in a senior high-school production of *M*A*S*H*. The assistant principal at the time, William Sullivan, was quoted as saying Masako 'was a very quiet kid who just passed through the school without causing any great ripples. If she walked in the door today I wouldn't know her'. The only public report of her time at Belmont High, apart from her academic record, is a write-up in the local paper which dubbed her 'Slugger' Masako, after a softball success.

This time there would be no poky government apartment for the Owadas. Hisashi had been appointed to a prestigious position as visiting professor of international law at the Law School and the Centre for International Affairs of what is arguably the New World's most famous university, Harvard. However, the plan was that he would remain on the Foreign Ministry payroll with the title of Minister at the Embassy in Washington, and would resume his career with another plum posting the following year. The visiting professorship came with a handsome two-storey house on a hill at 56 Juniper Road, an area favoured by many Harvard professors with families. There are good schools and a country club nearby, and the district is only 20 minutes' drive from the Harvard Square. Juniper Road was to be Masako's address for the next two years, and Harvard her home for the following four.

Oliver Oldman must be one of the oldest still-practising academics in the United States, and he knows the Owadas well. A sprightly man with a ready smile, he can spare only 45 minutes because he is on his way to a welcome dinner for the Harvard Law School's new intake of students. At 85 he has been on the faculty for 50 years and a professor since 1961. When we spoke, he was still teaching one class a week his esoteric speciality of Japanese local government tax law. His office is indescribable, like a moraine of paper left behind by a fast-retreating glacier. There is not a surface which is not covered by half a metre of books, papers and reports. On a side table is a photograph of a smiling Crown Prince Naruhito and Princess Masako, posing in front of an enormous glass screen sand-blasted by the Oldmans' artist daughter with a pattern of palms and cranes – their wedding present to the couple.

At the time of Hisashi Owada's secondment to Harvard, Oldman was the head of East Asian Legal Studies, and got to know him well, both professionally and personally. The two families dined together, and Oldman invited the Owadas to his 'cabin' – actually a charming two-storey wooden house – on the banks of Lake Sunape in New Hampshire, where they swam and sailed. Masako loved these vacations, and even Hisashi unbuttoned a little, displaying some connoisseurship of food and wine. 'She was an intelligent, open, sympathetic person,' says Oldman. 'She got along very well with people, with her fellow students and so on.' Although Owada could hardly be described as a charismatic lecturer – his courses attracted 15 or so of the 6000 students at Harvard – Oldman successfully lobbied for his one-year appointment to be extended to two.

The two years flew by, and here is Masako, in a white gown and mortarboard (they celebrate these milestones properly in the United States) receiving her matriculation diploma, and an award from the National Honour Society, a kind of honour roll of high-achieving high-school gradu-ates. 'Friendships forever,' she writes in her class yearbook, along with the initials of her favourite pals. The only cloud on the horizon is that it is now the autumn of 1981, and Hisashi Owada has, once again, heard the call of duty. The Foreign Affairs Ministry has decided he has been having far too good a time at their expense for the past two years, and has posted him back to Moscow. 'We used to joke that this was his punishment,' says Oldman. 'He had been hoping for Paris, but he got Moscow.' Would Masako, still a few months shy of her eighteenth birthday, have to uproot herself all over again, for the fifth time in her life?

It must have been quite a family crisis. Masako wanted to go on to university – her father, typically, was urging her at her high-school graduation to study a subject which would 'benefit humanity'. However, Russia was not the place to do it, even if her language skills had been up to it. She could, perhaps, have returned to Tokyo to stay with one of her aunts and uncles and try for admission to a university there, but having been out of the Japanese education loop for so long, no matter how bright she was, she would have had no chance of getting admitted to any of the top universities, let alone the gilded halls of the University of Tokyo. The answer was sitting right under their noses, although there was one major problem, and it was not academic. Masako's grades were good enough to get her into Harvard with flying colours, but who would look after her, with her parents across the Atlantic in Moscow, and the rest of the family on the other side of the Pacific in Tokyo?

'Ollie' Oldman and his wife Barbara stepped into the breach. 'Hisashi asked Barbara and I if we would stand *in loco parentis* for Masako after they left, and of course we were delighted to say yes.' So for the next four years, the Oldmans acted as Masako's guardians, the people a lonely teenager could turn to in time of trouble, seek advice from, or confide her personal problems in. She stayed with them from time to time, though her official residence was one of the Harvard college dormitories. She helped them hang baubles on the tree that first snowy Christmas. She left her skis with them over summer – Masako became quite an accomplished downhill skier, tackling the slopes at Sunape, and the black runs of the more demanding Cannon Mountain in New Hampshire. She helped serve the food at the reception when the Oldmans' son Andrew married. She sent them a postcard from the beautiful French university town of Besançon in the Jura Mountains where she went one summer – typically, not to holiday but to study French, while staying with a host family. Another summer 'holiday' was spent improving her German with the Goethe-Institut in Germany.

It says quite a bit about Masako's maturity and sense of responsibility that her parents were prepared to leave a 17-year-old girl alone in a place like Harvard, even with a couple like the Oldmans to keep an eye on her. Harvard University is not, as many think, in starchy Boston, Massachusetts, the historic port-city whose 'tea-party' launched the American Revolution; nowadays more often in the headlines as the home of the resurrected Red Sox baseball team, gay marriages and paedophile priests. It is a 20-minute ride away on a decrepit subway in the pleasant suburb of Cambridge, a town of handsome clapboard houses with shingled roofs, parks where grey squirrels scamper around with acorns in their mouths – and universities. This is Education Central, the greatest concentration of scholarship in the world – in an urban area half the size of Sydney are no fewer than 165 tertiary institutions, an academic city with more than 100,000 students and staff. The two most important are both built close to the banks of the sluggish Charles River: Harvard, and the great engineering university, the Massachusetts Institute of Technology.

'We call this the statue of the three lies,' says my guide, pausing under an elm tree on a lush lawn in front of a bronze statue of a seated man in a cloak and knee-breeches with a book, presumably the Bible, in his lap. The buckled shoe on his left foot is worn shiny by generations of students who rub it for luck. 'JOHN HARVARD. FOUNDER. 1638' reads the inscription in the granite plinth. In fact, Harvard University was founded two years earlier, in 1636. It was founded by the Pilgrim Fathers. And the third lie: the statue is not a likeness of Harvard, generous benefactor though he was – the sculptor had never even seen a painting of him.

Nevertheless, the oldest university in the United States remains its most prestigious and its richest. It tops almost every international poll for academic and research excellence, including the benchmark rankings by Shanghai's Jiao Tong University. Through relentless fund-raising, its war-chest has grown larger than the entire annual economic output of 121 of the world's poorest countries. The Harvard Management Company, which is responsible for the university's endowment, has $35 billion to invest.

It is, as you would expect, bruisingly competitive to get into – only 13 per cent of the 15,000 students who apply each year, one in eight, is accepted. But Harvard does have its share of 'the cream' – the rich and thick. It has many 'legacy' students, those given preferential treatment because their parents are Harvard alumni, and often generous benefactors. And it has a large contingent of young people whose principal talent is the ability to throw, catch, hit, kick or bounce a ball, winning them sporting scholarships.

Still, Harvard remains a beacon for the best and the brightest young minds across the United States and around the world; or, at least, those who can afford the current fees of around $55,000 a year. Countless captains of commerce and industry, Nobel Prize-winners and politicians – including no fewer than six US presidents – are Harvard alumni. Which explains why, when any of the Ivy League colleges would have been happy to accept her, Masako, with her father's blessing, chose Harvard as the stepping-stone to a career in the diplomatic service. Their only difference of opinion was that he would rather she followed in his footsteps and studied law, while she saw economics as the key to understanding the relationships between nations.

For once, Masako asserted her independence. She won a scholarship and enrolled in Harvard's Economics Department in the autumn of 1981, as the trees around the campus blazed with Fall fire. The Oldmans helped her carry her luggage and a few sticks of furniture up to the room on the top floor of Thayer Hall, a Georgian-style brick building which is right in the heart of the Harvard campus. All freshmen, 'the frosh', as Harvard calls them, are required to spend their first year, often their first time

away from home, in 'The Yard', where their college super-
visors can keep a closer eye on them. They eat, 600 at a
sitting, in Memorial Hall, a grandiose colonnaded cathedral of a building, all marble floors and stained-glass
windows, built to honour the dead of the Civil War.

Through the university gates beckon the bright lights of
The Square, the hub of Harvard social life. It's a lively
scene with bookshops and restaurants and bars, buskers
performing around the subway entrance, and dead-eyed
homeless kids begging. A girl with black and purple hair,
piercings and vandalised black net stockings shakes a
cardboard drink-cup at me with a sign: 'Adopt Me –
Or Change'. You get an idea why parents might be the
teeniest bit uneasy about off-campus life when you read
the *Unofficial Guide*'s review of the Hong Kong, a popular
Chinese noshery for many years:

*Ah, the inevitable Saturday night surrender after an
eve of inebrious liquors, after Redline has closed and
the final clubs have locked their doors you are glad
to find yourself in one of the Kong's brazenly-red
downstairs booths where many freshmen have
bonded over a plate of the Kong's unbeatable
crabless 'crab Rangoon'. Three years later they are
getting sloshed on their first 'Scorpion bowl'.*

*For as long as anyone can remember the Kong
has served as a late-night booze and nosh pit for its
hardy Yard and River following. At 2 am on a
Saturday night General Gau's chicken will seem to
be the best thing you ever tasted. Hopefully the next
morning you won't remember eating it. Fuel your
all-nighter with a take-out available until 2 am on
weekdays.*

Now Masako likes her Chinese cuisine, but this was most definitely not her scene. I located one of her college friends, Sunhee Juhon-Hodges, now an administrative law judge in Denver, Colorado. Juhon-Hodges, who was majoring in literature, was at the same house Masako chose after completing her first year on 'The Yard'. Lowell House is one of the 12 undergraduate boarding-houses, which each sleep 400 or 500 students in individual rooms or shared suites, comfortable neo-Georgian buildings built in the 1920s and 1930s, surrounded by park-like gardens dotted with elms and oaks. She and Masako chose Lowell, says Juhon-Hodges, for the same reason – it had a reputation as being a 'bookish' house rather than one famous for its rowdy parties or sports prowess. It is proud of its traditions, from its knitting circle to its Greek-philosophy reading club, its Winter Waltz to its Spring Ball, 'the Lowell Bacchanalia'. On Sunday afternoons, student '*klapper-meisters*' ring out peals on the 17 'Russian bells', acquired from a Moscow monastery, which hang in the bell-tower.

Masako seems to have enjoyed life at Lowell, and was particularly fond of the 'high teas', a tradition since the 1930s. Every Thursday afternoon the house-master, the distinguished mathematician William Bossert and his wife Mary Lee, held open house in the mansion, with its 35 rooms and a dozen fireplaces, which they called home. Students, alumni and distinguished outsiders as diverse as the Mexican labour union hero César Chávez, the actor Robert Redford, and Grateful Dead percussionist Mickey Hart used to mingle for the occasion. They would hob-nob over sandwiches, tea, and decadent cream cakes, the only time Juhon-Hodges saw Masako indulge herself. Bossert, now retired, says he remembers her as a bright, articulate woman '. . . who would have had no problem becoming a professor at a major US university'.

He says she seemed comfortable at Lowell, her home for three years, perhaps because the college has a 'rather starchy and anachronistic reputation'. You can get something of the flavour from looking at the pedigree of its founder, the former Harvard president Abbott Lawrence Lowell. A popular jingle of the day went like this:

I dwell 'neath the shades of Harvard
In the State of the sacred cod
Where the Lowells speak only to Cabots
And the Cabots speak only to God.

Masako, says Juhon-Hodges, got on well with the other upper-class young women – particularly 'Gigi' and 'Lisa', her two room-mates at Lowell House – privileged to attend this blue-ribbon university. She adopted the Harvard preppy look of the day: bobbed hair, Oxford cotton shirt or argyle sweater, with a silk scarf knotted around the neck, cords and Topsiders, canvas-topped yachting shoes. She did go out socially, and she liked to ski and to travel overseas during vacations. She went whale-watching off Rhode Island, and enjoyed visiting Quincy Market, a cluster of restored historic buildings near the Boston waterfront crowded with souvenir shops and restaurants specialising in Boston's signature 'scrod', a fillet of baked cod, and 'steamers', steamed long-neck clams. But 'she wasn't a socialite', say her classmates. Work always came first. Friday or Saturday Masako would find time for her small circle of friends; Sunday would find her burning the midnight oil, as she did most nights of the week.

Warwick McKibbin, the Australian economics professor we met earlier, was doing postgraduate studies at Harvard when he met Masako. 'Jeff Sachs [their professor] was away in Bolivia beginning [his work] to save the world. He wasn't around very much, so I sort of picked up the mantle of helping her with the thesis.' Three of them became a regular fixture around the computers in the studies and libraries of the economics department's Littauer Building: McKibbin, Masako, and a woman named Naoko Ishii, a career-track official at the Ministry of Finance who is now one of Japan's most senior female bureaucrats. McKibbin says that Masako impressed him as 'amazingly bright . . . quite assertive, quite different to what I had experienced previously as a "normal" Japanese. She was already very Westernised'.

As for Masako's social life, 'I don't think any of us really had any time for anything except work. She would call me up at odd hours of the morning, one or two am, when she was stuck on a problem. Fortunately I was usually awake – we [McKibbin and his wife Jenny] had just had a baby, and I often got to do the night-shift. When she completed her degree, she gave me a packet of beautiful silk handkerchiefs to thank me – it was really quite thoughtful, because I always suffered from hay-fever at Harvard.'

Masako became quite close friends with the then Japanese consul in Boston, and volunteered as a kind of self-appointed diplomat and cultural ambassador. The early 1980s was a time of mounting trade tension between Japan and the United States, and Masako seemed to take almost personally criticism of Japan's diplomatic and economic policies, which was beginning to dominate the American media. She became chairman of the Harvard Japan Society, and helped organise Japanese art exhibitions, sushi parties, *go* (a complex Asian board game) competitions and film nights. Surprisingly for the straight-laced Masako, one of her favourites was Tora-san, a cult scoundrel nicknamed 'the bum from Shibamata', played by Kiyoshi Atsumi, who starred in the longest-running movie series in the world, 48 movies in 27 years. She also organised dinners at Boston's only Japanese restaurant, Tatsukichi, which is now, sadly, closed down.

Someone else who knew Masako well at Harvard is Ezra Vogel, the Grand Old Man of Japanese letters in the United States, author of the most influential, and controversial, book on Japan in a generation, the 1979 tract *Japan As Number One – Lessons for America*. Still teaching at Harvard well into his seventies, Professor Vogel's office is the gloomy ground floor of a three-storey clapboard house a ten-minute walk from the campus. I ring the bell, and a twinkling elf appears at the door, balding, a little stooped, his leathery face creased in smile-lines, and wearing casual slacks and a striped green polo-shirt. He ushers me into his office, which has an antique Japanese painting on the wall, and on the mantelpiece what I first take to be a class picture with 30 or so people crammed into the shot – it's actually his rather large family. Thirty minutes, he says, and 30 minutes it is. These Harvard professors have BlackBerries dangling from their belts and mete out their time like Manhattan lawyers.

Vogel was director of US–Japan relations at Harvard's Center for International Affairs in the 1980s, and he first got to know not Masako but her father, Hisashi, back in 1977 when Owada was secretary to Takeo Fukuda. 'He was a very achievement-oriented person,' he says. 'He believed in hard work and excellence and worked very hard to achieve it. I am sure some of that rubbed off on his daughter.' They bumped into each other again, in Moscow, in Tokyo, in Paris – and then in 1979, when Owada was posted to Harvard. Vogel, who speaks Japanese, was invited to dinner at the Owadas' house, and met the young Masako, who had just enrolled at Belmont High:

> *She was very courteous and well-behaved, very mature; she came from a well-bred Japanese family. She helped her mother serve the guests, and was properly respectful, the way you expect of a good family. She was a pleasant, well-behaved and very bright young woman.*

Later, the professor saw more of Masako when she attended lectures and functions he organised for the Center for International Affairs, and he confirms that she had taken on the role of unofficial Japanese ambassador. 'She showed a lively interest in current affairs, and she was interested in [doing] things that promoted good relations, because already we were beginning to have trade tensions between Japan and the US,' he says. 'She had a kind of sense of responsibility for Japan, to try and see that Americans properly understood, and were not prejudiced against Japan, and had good information and were trying to think about ways to resolve difficulties. She was a responsible, thoughtful young woman.'

Juhon-Hodges agrees: 'The responsibilities she took on were really amazing. You would ask her on a Monday what she had been doing at the weekend, and she would have entertained, say, the Finnish Ambassador to the US or whatever. The idea of an 18-year-old doing that kind of thing . . . it gave you an idea of where she was heading.' Perhaps because of her own ethnic Korean background, she portrays the young Masako as having an almost Confucian sense of loyalty to her parents and to Japan:

Her duty to her family and to her country were pre-eminent. She could be playful, but she certainly wasn't at parties with a lampshade on her head dancing on the tables or anything like that. She was always very proper and very decorous. She wasn't a killjoy [but] she was obviously somewhat removed. I think she enjoyed the social aspect of Harvard, but study always came first. She was obviously a person of incredible intelligence, and she had an excellent grasp of the language. She worked incredibly hard, and she concentrated on an area [economics] that was very challenging.

Nor does it appear that there was much time for boys, naturally a subject of great speculation when Masako's engagement to the crown prince was announced many years later. Not that Juhon-Hodges knew, anyway – although Masako was discreet and 'there was never any deep disclosure of personal information'. Her social life consisted mainly of going out with a group to restaurants, art galleries and concerts, particularly of Western classical music. She did have one particular friend named Carlos, a Puerto Rican student, and once visited the Caribbean island at his invitation. 'But I don't think they ever went out just by themselves. I think there was always a group of them, her room-mates and so on,' says Juhon-Hodges.

The only breath of scandal came after the engagement, when American tabloid reporters began digging around – as they do – to try and find any 'dirt' in her past. A man named David Kao, a Chinese American then working as a

Boston management consultant, came forward to claim that he had had a relationship with Masako while she was at Harvard and was 'devastated' that she was marrying Naruhito. A *Chicago Sun Times* gossip columnist, Bill Zwecker, reported that Kao was threatening to 'go public with juicy details'. Kao claimed he had 'photos of Owada topless on a secluded beach . . . and has told friends he would like to sell them to the supermarket sleazoids'. However, Kao refused 'repeated requests' by the paper to produce any evidence, and its sources at Harvard 'confirm seeing Kao and Owada at several parties . . . but it appears unlikely there was any romance'.

Japanese reporters were dispatched to follow up the scoop, but came up with nothing – as did my attempts to locate the elusive Mr Kao. One can only conclude that either he allowed his imagination to get the better of him, or (as one of my more conspiracy-minded colleagues in Tokyo believes) the *Kunaicho* got to him first, and made him an offer for the pictures that he could not refuse. Either way, the scandal was nipped in the bud and Masako's reputation remained unblemished, at least in public.

Barbara Oldman was not aware of Kao, or any other boyfriend for that matter. We met for milkshake-sized cardboard canisters of bad coffee under orange sun-umbrellas at Au Bon Pain, an outdoor cafe on The Square where old men hustle chess for $2 a game. Mrs Oldman, like Juhon-Hodges, said that Masako had 'quite a few friends', but usually went out in groups of three or four. 'But I don't think she was naïve, I think she was quite savvy about men.' She goes on to relate a story of how, at a house party 'there was an extraordinarily good-looking Japanese man trying to cotton on to her'. He turned out to be a graduate student at Harvard, but Masako 'although she wasn't rude, made it clear she was not at all interested'. The man later married, and within six months the marriage broke down because 'it turned out he had a lot of lady-friends and didn't want to give them up'. Barbara Oldman nods knowingly.

When Masako's engagement was announced, a student named Tehshik P. Yoon wrote in the venerable university newspaper the *Harvard Crimson*: 'By tradition, the fiancée of the crown prince must be an aristocrat, no more than 25 years old, and must never have had a previous romantic relationship. Owada fails in the first two of these stipulations; her status on the last is unclear.'

It really does seem, unlikely as it sounds to a Westerner, as though Masako's studies always came first. To find out what she spent four years of her life doing, you have to seek admission to the Pusey Library, a rather modernistic place of strip-lighting, pale oak-veneer tables and benches, and a general air of efficiency. I had been rather hoping that old theses would be stored at the historic Harry Elkins Widener Library, the fourth largest in the world. It is a gigantic colonnaded neo-classical battleship of a building, shipwrecked in the middle of the campus, the bequest of a grieving mother whose son helped her into a lifeboat before he ran back to his cabin to save a rare copy of Francis Bacon's *Essays*, and went down with the *Titanic*. But, no, it is to the Pusey that you come if you want to research alumni, classes and theses past. Masako's, in its pastel binder, is brought out, a slender volume of 99 pages with the engaging title: *External Adjustment to Import Price Shocks: Oil in Japanese Trade*. It is dated 20 March 1985, and carries the notation that it was submitted (successfully) to Harvard's Department of Economics, for the degree of Bachelor of Arts, with Honours.

There are a couple of things worth pointing out about the thesis, before dealing with its substance. One is that the research was done in Tokyo as well as Cambridge, Massachusetts. She acknowledges receiving grants from the Japan Institute of International Affairs (a government-funded research institute), and from Harvard's Center for International Affairs to facilitate this – as well as the $8 an hour pittance she received for doing research-work during her vacations. Masako does not appear to have had a particularly generous allowance. Secondly, and more importantly, she gives credit for help from some very high-powered people indeed: Kazuo Nakazawa, director of financial affairs at Japan's Federation of Economic Organisations; Terohiko Mano, manager of the economic research division of the Bank of Tokyo; and Eisuke Sakakibara, then an advisor at the Japan Centre for International Finance, later to become the Finance Ministry's 'Mr Yen', a darling of the foreign media.

I asked her thesis advisor, the economics professor Jeffrey Sachs, whether he thought Masako, through her father, had advantages not available to others: access to the very highest levels of the Japanese bureaucracy for information and 'guidance' other students would give their eye-teeth for. This was his diplomatic non-answer: 'One of the things about Harvard is (it is) designed for very bright undergraduates who go out and seek high-powered advice . . . One of the tricks of the Harvard landscape if you are a very bright and ambitious student is to seek out people to help you.'

The thesis itself takes a contrarian view of the rapidly widening trade gap between Japan and the United States (and other Western countries). By the early 1980s Japan was running a $48 billion surplus with the US, and huge diplomatic pressure was building up on Japan to open its closed, cartelised markets – particularly in areas such as agriculture, computer chips, financial services, and the professions – to redress this imbalance. Masako's thesis is – guess what? – that the massive trade surplus should not be blamed on Japanese non-tariff barriers, but that it was the consequence of the two 'oil shocks' of the 1970s. As sky-rocketing oil prices slowed Japan's energy-importing economy and depressed its currency, it was 'only natural' that Japanese manufacturers would look for growth abroad, and that exports would boom. There are lots of impressive-looking econometric equations to back all this up. QED. Masako's sponsors got good value for their money.

It is not my job to point out the flaws in this argument, although it will be interesting to see whether another current account crisis occurs as a result of the 2005 'oil shock', as Masako's thesis predicts. Professor Sachs is the only one she had to convince.

Jeffrey Sachs has been described by the *New York Times* as the most important economist in the world. He was appointed a full professor at Harvard when he was 29, and is in fact only ten years older than Masako herself. He is an advisor or former advisor to an alphabet soup of international institutions: WHO (the World Health Organ-ization), IMF (the International Monetary Fund), OECD (the Organisation for Economic Cooperation and Devel-opment) and the World Bank. His current passion is a global crusade to eliminate third-world poverty through aid and trade; to this end he has toured Africa with the film-star Angelina Jolie, and Bono from the rock group U2.

I caught up with Sachs briefly in 2005 when he was in Australia for the Lowy Institute, promoting his latest book, *The End of Poverty*. He remembers Masako well as a 'very bright, very hard-working, very ambitious woman' who 'was on her way, I am sure, to a big career with the Foreign Ministry'.

'I was impressed with her poise, and her interest and her engagement and her determination to go on with graduate studies,' says Sachs. 'She made an impression on me well before she was a princess that she was a rising star.' As for her thesis: 'She produced a basic framework for analysing how an economy such as Japan's would adjust to oil price rises ... I thought it was a very admirable and clear job for an undergraduate, a very fine senior thesis.'

Much has been made by Japanese hagiographers of the fact that Masako graduated, in the summer of 1985, *magna cum laude*. This is taken by those unfamiliar with the US university system to mean that she is some sort of reincarnation of Albert Einstein. In fact, the majority of Harvard students graduate with some sort of honours; in the 1980s there was something of a scandal over this 'grade inflation', when the figure reached some 80 per cent of all students. The highest-possible grade for a final-year thesis is *summa cum laude* ('with the highest praise'), and in the 1980s around 15–20 per cent of students received this grade. Next came *magna cum laude* ('with great praise'), which accounted for another 25–30 per cent of students. Finally, there was the humiliation of a simple *cum laude* ('with praise'). So the best we can say is that Masako graduated in the top half of her year, probably in the top third. This is not in any way to belittle her achievement: an economics degree of any sort from Harvard University will get you a job anywhere in the world. It is, however, to say that from this moment on,

Masako would be unfairly burdened down by the weight of great expectations.

Armed with her new degree, with a fluent command of English and French and passable German, Russian and Spanish, Masako could have done as so many of her countrymen have done – taken a highly paid job in the United States or Europe, married a foreigner, and returned to the suffocating social conformity of Japan as infrequently as the demands of family allowed. 'Bananas' their critics wryly call them – yellow on the outside, white inside. But Masako, even though she had spent half her life abroad, had been deeply imbued with Japanese values by her parents – the 'other Masako' her friends remember. Recruiters from the major US banks, accountancy firms and financial institutions set up their stalls on campus that autumn to scout out promising graduates. But Masako refused their blandishments, even though the money on offer was great. Her mother, Yumiko, told friends that her young daughter had been offered more than her husband's base salary as a senior diplomat. 'We could all have a life of leisure,' she joked.

Instead, Masako chose to return 'home'. 'If I stay in America I will be like *nenashi gusa* (grass without roots),' she sighed as she packed her bags once again to leave for the country with which she had such a deep bond, but of which she knew so little.

Masako had already made up her mind that she would become a diplomat like her father. In fact, it seems to have been her ambition since she gave up her childhood dream of becoming a veterinary surgeon. Listing her interests in her junior high-school yearbook, the precocious teenager wrote: 'World issues (poverty, starvation, AIDS, the environment, politics and economics).' 'Sport' was added almost as an afterthought. Yukie Kudo, another bright young economist who was to become Masako's friend at the University of Tokyo, thinks her career choice was inevitable given the degree to which she idolised her father.

Even so, it was not a step to take lightly. The entrance examinations for the elite ranks of Japan's public service are savagely competitive; the hours are staggering; the pay is not great, though the perks and privileges can be juicy; and employment, even now, tends to be a lifetime commitment in Japan.

As well, women are treated particularly poorly in the Japanese workplace, worse than in any Asian country, bar Korea and Indonesia. There is still an overwhelmingly Victorian attitude that the man's place is in the workforce, the woman's at home minding the children. Although things have improved a little in recent years, surveys continue to show that Japan still has a long way to go to catch up with the rest of the world. Masako would have been well aware that on the World Economic Forum's ranking of 58 countries for gender equality, the Nordic countries, as you would expect, topped the list, and Islamic countries came last. Japan was ranked No. 38 in 2005, behind such bastions of feminism as Colombia, Uruguay and Bulgaria, and only just ahead of benighted Bangladesh. Australia, incidentally, came tenth.

Only in 2007 is the law to be repealed which prohibits women from working underground in mines or tunnels, supposedly for fear of offending the mountain goddesses. Really. Train companies have had to introduce special women-only carriages in peak hours, to protect women from the ubiquitous *chikan* who prowl the underground molesting them. One particularly repulsive specimen named Samu Yamamoto has even had the gall (and found a publisher) to put out an 'encyclopaedia of groping' in which he advises his fellow perverts how to avoid detection in winter by warming their hands and spraying them with an anti-static. In perhaps the most egregious recent reminder of the sexism embedded in Japanese society, Tokyo's governor, the populist right-winger Shintaro Ishihara, publicly referred to women as '*babaa*' – an expression which translates as 'old hag'. He went on to outrage even Japan's feeble feminist movement by asserting that 'for a woman to continue living after losing her ability to give birth is a waste and a crime'.

While I was in Japan researching this book, 131 Tokyo women did galvanise themselves to sue the governor for damages over his remarks in a civil case, Japan having no statutory penalties for such libels. What was surprising to the Western observer was not so much that a social Neanderthal like Ishihara, a character who delights in making such outrageous remarks, should say it, but that a court should let him get away with it. Tokyo's District Court Judge Yoshiteru Kawamura threw out the case, saying that 'it was difficult to say that his words caused serious emotional distress' to the plaintiffs.

In Japan, fewer women work, they earn only two-thirds of the pay of men, and they make up only 15 per cent of the ranks of the professions, management and administration, half the proportions of countries like the United States. Only a token handful of women sit on the boards of Japan's great public corporations, not one has ever headed a government department (at one stage even Japan's roving ambassador for women's affairs was a man) or become a superior court judge. Only one or two have ever been regional prefectural governors or even mayors of any of Japan's thousands of municipal councils. In the main, women are regarded as a pool of cheap, disposable unskilled labour, grist for the mill of Japan Inc, the '*Oh-eru*' or 'office ladies', making tea and pushing lift-buttons until the day they marry, when they will be expected to resign.

Masako would, almost certainly, have to give up any idea of marriage if she chose to climb the bureaucratic ladder. It is tough enough for a woman to balance a successful career with a successful family in the West. In Japan, where childcare is scarce and maternity leave is at the whim of the employer, where husbands perform on average 11 minutes a day of household chores and social disapproval of working mothers is common, it is all but impossible. As well, in the foreign service, Masako could expect to be posted overseas – few Japanese employers would be flexible enough to allow a husband to transfer with her to another city, let alone a foreign country. At the University of Tokyo Masako's friends would joke with her over coffee: 'If you are going to be a diplomat, you should marry an artist, because that's the only kind of person who can take his work with him wherever you are posted.'

Before Masako committed herself to what she must have realised was going to be the toughest fight of her life – to carve out a career in such a male dominated world – she sought advice from someone who had already been there. Four years earlier Mie Murazumi, also the daughter of a diplomat, had graduated in physics from Oxford University and become only the sixth woman ever to join the Foreign Affairs Ministry as a career-track officer, rather than a tea-lady. She was to have a distinguished career at the ministry, including a posting at the Japanese Embassy in Paris. In 1984 she was in Washington DC where her father, Yusashi, was Japanese *chargé d'affaires*. Yusashi knew Masako's father, and a meeting was arranged for their daughters. Masako arrived at tea-time, and asked Murazumi to give her some straight advice on a career at the Foreign Ministry. This is what she told her:

I said it's good [but] it's hard work, it's a lot of hard work. She asked whether there was any discrimination against women, and I said, 'Definitely not. This is a good place if you want to be just treated equally, because they are too busy to discriminate. Almost everyone has overseas experience, so maybe they have shed some of their Japaneseness. There is definitely no discrimination.'

Murazumi told me she was certain Masako had the ability to pass the diplomatic entrance examination, and have a great career in the ministry. But she wanted to make sure she knew about 'the good as well as the bad' side of life as a diplomat. The hours, for instance – in that grey bunker which houses the ministry's Tokyo headquarters, the lights burn well after midnight in times of crisis. But in spite of these cautionary tales, Masako left the meeting determined to give it a go. Sadly, and perhaps predictably, both women would fail to fulfil their potential. Mie Murazumi resigned from the ministry in 1993, the year Masako married, and for the same reason – a man. She is now living in the Pacific North-West of the United States, where I spoke to her, working as coordinator of the Asian Law Program at Washington State University.

So that northern autumn, Masako said goodbye to her friends at Harvard – goodbye, though not farewell, because she stayed in touch with at least a dozen of them, staff like Professor Vogel and fellow students like Warwick

Her first ambition was to become
a vet . . . Masako's mother, Yumiko,
introduces her to a goldfish.

An outing to a playground at
Karuizawa . . . Masako with her twin
sisters, Setsuko and Reiko.

On top of Mount Hakuba . . . A rare moment together – the Owada family on a rock-climbing expedition, 1976.

The birth of a prince . . . Akihito and Michiko admire their new son, Naruhito, 1960.

The dutiful heir . . . Young Prince Naruhito with the symbols of his office – sword and sacred evergreen bough.

The music-lover . . . Naruhito and Adam Harper perform for the media during the crown prince's first overseas trip, to Australia.

COLIN HARPER

First taste of freedom . . . Naruhito and the sons of his Australian host family, Adam and Alex Harper, tinker with their bicycles.

ANDREW ARKLEY

Boys' night out . . . Naruhito (*front, centre*) and some of his high-school pals, including Australian Andrew Arkley (*back row, second from right*), preparing for a bath on a school excursion.

We are the champions . . . 'Slugger' Masako with her
champion junior high-school softball team.

High-school buddies . . . Masako with some of her classmates from Belmont High at
Harvard Square, 1980.

Teenage heart-throb . . .
Masako enjoying a drink
at a Roppongi night-club
with her baseball idol
Haruaki Harada.

All dolled up for a big night out . . .
Masako (*right*) and her high-school
friend Kumi Hara.

Masako's *alma mater* . . . The memorial
church at Harvard University.

BEN HILLS

IMPERIAL HOUSEHOLD AGENCY

Magna cum laude . . . A plumper Masako (*second from right*) graduates from Harvard
University, 1985.

Farewell to a career . . . Masako says goodbye to her co-workers at the Foreign Affairs Ministry in 1993.

Princess-training . . . Masako is instructed in some of the arcane royal arts by a palace retainer before her marriage.

A last happy moment together . . . Masako bids farewell to her terrier, Chocolat, while parents, Hisashi and Yumiko, and sisters, Setsuko and Reiko, look on.

McKibbin. A decade later they were to be reunited as guests at Japan's 'wedding of the century'.

She moved back in with her parents in Meguro – renting one's own apartment is an impossible dream for most young singles in Tokyo. But before she could even think of sitting for the Foreign Ministry entrance examination, she knew there were some gaps in her education that needed to be attended to. She enrolled in the Law Faculty at the elite University of Tokyo, where her father had been a student a generation before, taking units of constitutional and international law. Masako was there only from April to October of 1986, but that was sufficient to get her over the line, though not a postgraduate degree, which always remained beyond her grasp. Her 'intake year' photograph shows the formidable competition she beat to follow her father into the ministry – of 800 people nationwide who sat for the exam, only 28 passed. And of those 28, only three were women. The mass-circulation *Asahi* newspaper published her picture with a write-up hailing Masako as 'a young and beautiful new diplomat'. Again the burden of heavy expectations fell on Masako's shoulders.

Talking now to former Foreign Ministry officials of the day, it is apparent that there was some resentment of Masako's appointment, though, since her father was by then second in charge, it would have been suicidal to say anything aloud. Masako herself was quoted by a friend as joking that 'I heard that some ministry officials who had a tough time training under my father are eagerly awaiting putting me through the mill'. Nepotism, of course, is nothing new in the Japanese system of government – many seats in parliament are 'hereditary', occupied by second- and third-generation members of the one family. But, from all the evidence, Masako achieved her place in the ministry on her own not-inconsiderable merits. Her father would not have attempted to influence her selection, at least not overtly, although his private advice and counsel over the dinner table would have been invaluable.

Masako started work at the ministry the following April, and immediately gained a reputation as a hard and diligent worker. *'Tafunesu ma-chan'* was her new nickname, something like 'Tough Cookie'. She ate at her desk on the seventh floor of the ministry's warren of a building like most junior officials – often humble *sarari-man*'s fare from the canteen like *karei-raisu*, one of Naruhito's favourites. Arriving home one night at 9 pm, her mother was quoted as saying with surprise: 'You're early.'

She was assigned, first, to the oddly named Second International Organizations Division which deals with Japan's relations with international agencies such as the OECD, a club of 30 rich countries committed to free trade and development. Her assignments included dealing with the OECD's environmental affairs committee, in those pre-Kyoto Treaty days when Japan was seen as an international pollution ogre. By all accounts she acquitted herself well – her command of spoken languages, so rare in Japan, was a huge advantage – and was popular with most of her work-mates. On occasion she would leave work for a night out with her parents and sisters, then return with ice-cream for colleagues doing overtime back at the sweaty office where the air-conditioning was turned off at 6 pm even on sweltering summer nights. Such bonding is the human glue of the Japanese workplace.

Socially, Masako had a busy time of it back in Tokyo – catching up with old friends like the singer Kumi Hara, drinking in the Green Room with her baseball idol Haruaki Harada, attending concerts and the theatre. There still do not appear to have been any serious boyfriends on the scene, however, though unsubstantiated rumours would later fly around that she had a fling with a married co-worker at the ministry. Recently the London *Sunday Times* magazine 'outed' him as Katsuhiko Oku, a rugby-playing Oxford-educated diplomatic high-flier. Oku, who was married with three children, was tragically killed in 2003 when his vehicle was ambushed while he was on a mission in Iraq. The magazine cited only anonymous sources and gave no authenticating detail for its scandalous accusation, and my own sources at the ministry say that their relationship was quite proper, Oku acting as Masako's friend and mentor. Yukie Kudo, who used to hang out with Masako at university, also doubts there was any romance – she formed the impression that she was 'rather prudish and not interested [in boys]'.

Now aged in her early forties, Kudo is two years younger than Masako. After graduating from the London School of Economics she took jobs in corporate finance for the JPMorgan bank and as an executive at management consultants McKinsey&Company, before doing a career flip and becoming an anchor for the Asahi TV network. But not the sort of bubblehead you find on US television – Kudo is an expert in such arcane fields as derivative pricing theory, has interviewed Margaret Thatcher and covered the Asian economic crisis of the late 1990s.

She arrives a stylish two hours late at the sky-rise apartment in fashionable Roppongi Hills where we are to do the interview, dressed in a smart linen suit with a long string of pearls twisted twice around her neck. Breathless apologies as she presses a copy of her latest book, about *kamikaze* pilots, into my hands and sips a glass of persimmon vinegar. She composes herself, poised and smiling this way and that as though to several hundred people in a TV studio rather than an audience of one. This is what she says about her friend Masako, in her perfect Oxford English:

She was full of zest for life was 'Owa'. But I don't agree with the assessment that she had become Westernised, strong-willed and outspoken. She is modest, she is passive, she was always the listener, we were always the talkers. She is like a typical Japanese woman of the 1950s or 1960s, perhaps because that is how she was brought up by her parents overseas. She had little exposure to how attitudes have changed in Japan.

The other Masako. And, indeed, that 'time warp' theory is borne out by the 'finishing school' skills Masako set about acquiring in her spare moments away from the office. Kazuhana Restaurant is in the heart of Ginza, perhaps the priciest restaurant district in the world, where a single pair of perfect sushi, made with the belly-fat of the black tuna from the Aleutian Islands, can set you back $50. It is a maze of tiny, discreet members-only clubs and bars where politicians and *yakuza* mobsters carouse and connive, hidden away behind the *shoji* screens. As I arrive, a powder-blue Rolls-Royce with a shadowy figure in the back concealed by smoked glass pulls out, attended by two bowing flunkies. It could be either of the above. Upstairs, in a minute restaurant which would sandwich no more than eight around the counter, and another six in a private cubicle, Hisao Yamada, a beaming chef in lunch-soiled whites, is waiting. Nearly 20 years before, Masako was his most famous student.

Trained in Osaka, which boasts it is the home of

Japan's greatest cooking, Yamada was then working at another high-class *ryotei* in Ginza called Harumi, and running a cooking school, which Masako's father had heard about. Once a week Masako would turn up to learn the finer arts of *kaiseki ryori*, traditional Japanese *haute cuisine*. And this was no technical college course – her seven companions in the class, photographed in their blue aprons on graduation day, included the future head of Japan's tax office, and Yoriko Kawaguchi, later to become the foreign minister. No curried rice, crumbed pork cutlets or *yakiniku* (barbecued beef) here. They learned to make their own *dashi*, the dried bonito-fish stock which is the essence of Japanese cooking. Masako was taught how to properly slice fish like Pacific saury – from the way she held the knife Yamada guessed she had not done much cooking before. The two favourites of the 22 dishes she learned were squid pickled with its innards and topped with shreds of *yuzu*, a type of citrus; and a dish of simmered *daikon* radish with *miso* (bean-paste) topped with a prawn and some stalks of *mitsuba*, 'Japanese parsley'. In each lesson they would create two or three dishes, then eat them, washed down with beer, for lunch.

Masako's goal, says the chef, was not what you might guess: to acquire 'wifely skills' to make herself more attractive to a future husband. 'She expected to be posted abroad [by the Foreign Ministry] and she wanted to be able to cook proper Japanese dishes when she was entertaining [foreigners],' says Yamada. As usual, she was learning to cook not for fun but for duty.

Back in October, a few days after learning that Masako had won a place in the Foreign Ministry, the Owada family had received a highly sought-after invitation, embossed with the imperial golden chrysanthemum. The Infanta Elena of

Spain was visiting Japan to help promote a travelling exhibition of paintings by the Spanish master Goya, and a reception was being held in her honour. The venue was the East Palace, home of Japan's then Crown Prince Akihito, Princess Michiko and their family. Could they come?

Just how the Owadas' name got on that list is a matter of great conjecture. As well as the usual clutch of diplomatic dignitaries, bureaucrats and worthies from the arts world, court officials had invited a number of eligible young women whom they thought Naruhito should meet. The prince was 26, and the pressure on the next-but-one-in-line to the Chrysanthemum Throne to marry and produce an heir was increasing. But Masako, for all her parents' samurai ancestry and her father's prominent position in the bureaucracy, did not come from the 'right' background for the snooty Men in Black. No royal connection; wrong school; too 'foreign'.

Some say her name was added to the guest-list by hand at the last minute, at the suggestion of Toru Nakagawa, a former Ambassador to the Soviet Union, who had known the Owadas in Moscow, and who had been one of the prince's minders when he attended Oxford University. That's the way Tokyo's old-boy network works. Either way, it was a date with destiny. Masako found herself one autumn afternoon wearing her smartest blue dress, being ushered with her parents into a spacious state room in the palace she now calls home. An ensemble of handbell ringers entertained the guests who were then handed drinks and hors d'oeuvres by white-gloved servants.

After the speeches Naruhito appeared and began circulating around the room. He stopped in front of Masako, she bowed, and he said, 'You must be Miss Owada. I am glad that you came.' He congratulated her on her recent appointment to the Foreign Ministry – it had been in the newspapers, and he would have been briefed on the guests by one of the palace officials. They chit-chatted for a minute or two before the young prince was urged on by an equerry to greet another guest. But that was enough. 'Something shot through me the moment I met her,' he confessed to some old school-friends later. Or, as we would say in the less inhibited West, it was love at first sight.

5

The Dreaming Spires

BARDWELL ROAD IS A PLEASANT, PROSPEROUS STREET OF
gabled three-storey houses, with gardens full of rose
bushes and lavender, a short bus ride from the historic
centre of Oxford. It runs beside playing fields fringed with
horse-chestnut trees where in winter Britain's brightest
young men do muddy battle for rugby glory, and in
summer haul their boats into the River Cherwell to
prepare for the annual grudge-match with arch-rivals
Cambridge. It is a street popular with university dons, and
in the 1980s it was the home of Charles Wenden, a historian and bursar of All Souls College, and his wife Eileen.
It was also where an ambitious young student named
Masako Owada came seeking refuge from the persecution
of the Press.

Since that reception at the East Palace two years before
when Naruhito had fallen for her, Masako's name and face
had with increasing frequency been plastered over the
covers of Japan's celebrity magazines, her comings and

goings dogged by paparazzi, her history, her interests and her intentions dissected on the afternoon TV 'wide shows'. Later, journalists were even to rifle through the glove-box of her car to find out what sort of tapes she played (Bach, Vivaldi), and fly to Boston on a fool's errand seeking those probably fictitious 'topless photographs' of her.

After that first meeting, the couple's courtship, such as it was, was conducted with chaperoned Victorian propriety. The breezy informality of the European royals would be unimaginable in Japan – the idea of Naruhito taking Masako grooving at a nightclub, which is how Denmark's Crown Prince Frederik met his Australian bride, Mary Donaldson, quite unthinkable. Naruhito had arranged to bump into her again a few weeks later at a formal function organised by the Japan–British Society where they had a polite chat. And then the day before New Year's Eve in 1986 he took the plunge and had his father invite the entire Owada family over to the palace for a get-together. One can only imagine the excruciating hour or two of genteel conversation over bowls of soba noodles and green tea that would have ensued as the two families sized each other up.

Their only trusted ally through the long and tortuous courtship was to be the prince's uncle Norihito, Prince Takamado – the 'Canadian prince' who was just five years older than Naruhito and whose charm and international outlook instantly attracted Masako. Norihito was also, incidentally, the only royal to hold down a 'real job', writing ballet reviews and working as an administrator at the Japan Foundation, a government organisation set up to promote cultural exchange with other countries. After his sudden and tragic death in 2002 the grief-stricken princess said that the prince and his wife Hisako had been 'truly caring persons' and Norihito 'like an older brother' to her husband.

It was at Norihito's official residence that the couple was able to meet alone for the first time. Naruhito brought out his photo album and showed her snaps of his travels the previous year – mountaineering in Bhutan, Nepal and India. He talked about his time at Oxford University – he had returned to Tokyo earlier that year after two years studying (no prize for guessing) medieval transportation, on the River Thames. A few months later, he invited her back to the East Palace one evening to meet a bunch of his male friends from university days for a meal and some drinks. They hung out for a couple of hours joking around and talking about their time at university, baseball (their beloved Giants were trailing the Hiroshima Carps that year) and mountaineering. In short, Naruhito was making it as clear as he could that he fancied Masako without actually saying so, said Masanori Kaya, an old school-friend who was there and noticed the glint in the prince's eye.

It was not as if he had not had a wide field from which to choose. The *Kunaicho* had been assiduously searching for a bride since the prince was in his teens. Royals marry early in Japan, especially crown princes on whom the dynasty depends. Naruhito's father Akihito had been 25 when he wed, grandfather Hirohito 22, great-grandfather Yoshihito 20, and great-great-grandfather the Meiji Emperor Mutsuhito married at just 16. That winter of 1986 Naruhito was approaching his twenty-seventh birthday, the oldest unmarried heir in the long history of the Chrysanthemum Throne. He joked that he and Britain's Prince Charles were vying for the Olympic gold medal for the oldest royal groom – eventually Charles, who was 32 when he married the teenaged Lady Diana in 1981, pipped him to the altar by more than a year. 'I am not doing the ox-walk,' he protested when journalists ever-so-politely nagged him about his search for a bride at his annual birthday press conference. The ox-walk is a peculiar foot-dragging tactic practised by members of parliament to show their disapproval for measures on which they are required to cast a ballot.

The tabloid frenzy had begun in 1977 when Naruhito was just 17. The weekly *Shukan Shincho* magazine splashed an article about the prince playing tennis with the granddaughter of a wealthy industrialist while holidaying at Karuizawa, which was how (the magazine heavy-handedly reminded readers) his parents had met. In the years that followed, Naruhito's name was linked romantically with 20 or 30 young women. Few, until Masako came along, had been identified by name. There was a 'royal relative', the 'daughter of an official at the grand shrine of Ise', a 'Seishin Women's University graduate', the 'daughter of an ambassador' and so on. But one by one the 'bride candidates', as the *Kunaicho* called them, disappeared.

Although the word 'candidate' implies that there was a queue of nubile young women jostling for the honour of being chosen by the prince, the opposite appears to have been the case. At least one woman fled the country to escape the unwanted attention; others hurriedly arranged marriages to other men to forestall a proposal from the prince; and a few threatened to have tattoos or body-piercings, believing that such 'mutilation' would make them ineligible for marriage to a royal. Public opinion polls gave a good idea why marriage into the Japanese royal family was not regarded as the glamorous fairytale it might evoke in the West. Two-thirds of young women questioned said that they could not bear the restrictions that would be placed on their lives. They had the cautionary example of the first commoner to marry a crown prince to justify their concerns.

The *Kunaicho* had opposed Akihito marrying Michiko from the start, delaying the marriage for two years before finally accepting that the prince would have no one else. She had been subjected to spiteful criticism – everything from her industrialist father having been a mere business-man, to her gloves not covering her elbows, as etiquette apparently decreed – by the families of the former aristoc-racy who thought Akihito should have chosen one of them, rather than a commoner. Her mother-in-law, the Empress Nagako – daughter of an old noble family and a distant cousin of the emperor – made no secret of her contempt for the low-born intruder into the imperial court. She was estranged from her family, whom she was not allowed to see for years on end – they were never invited to the palace, and magazines reported sightings of the lonely figure of her mother, Tomiko, lingering outside the gates, peering sadly into the grounds. In 1988 when Tomiko lay dying in hospital the only way Michiko could manage to visit her was to arrange to be secretly smuggled out of the palace.

As the years went by, this clever, vivacious woman – a linguist as well as an accomplished musician – slowly faded away, appearing nowadays as a stick-thin grey-haired wraith who, when she is not trotting dutifully behind her husband, spends her life feeding mulberry leaves to a collection of rare *koishimaru* silk-worms. She was hospitalised with the combined effects of a miscar-riage and a nervous breakdown early in the marriage, and spent months convalescing. Then, on the morning of her fifty-ninth birthday in 1993, it became impossible to conceal the gravity of her condition. Michiko collapsed just before she was due to give a press conference and could not utter a word for five months – a condition called idiopathic aphonia which can be triggered by stress. Even today, on those rare occasions when she is permitted to speak in public, it is in a barely audible whisper. Little wonder that when a Japanese magazine questioned 100 young women, 74 said that there was no way they would consider marrying Naruhito or any other royal. They typically gave the response 'I wouldn't want to join the rigid imperial family', or 'I would rather continue my career'.

When Naruhito turned 20 and was still a sophomore at Gakushuin University, the court began its search for a suitable bride in earnest. It was to be an arranged marriage, the idea of 'romantic love' having unpleasant overtones of something 'lax, loose, untidy and negligent' to older, traditional Japanese. Indeed, when Akihito's engagement to Michiko was reluctantly approved, the then head of the *Kunaicho* felt obliged to stand up in parliament and indignantly deny that it was a love-match. An *omiai* was the proper way to do things.

The marriage of Naruhito's grandfather Hirohito had been arranged in just such a way. According to the historian Jeffrey Taliaferro, in 1914, when Hirohito was still shy of his thirteenth birthday, his mother, the Empress Sadako, arranged a tea-party in the special concubines' pavilion in the grounds of the imperial palace. Sadako was especially fond of the boy because she was the first empress to give birth to a designated heir to the throne in 150 years, the rest being the sons of concubines. She invited a number of eligible young girls from the families of princes and the nobility and while they daintily sipped their bowls of green tea and nibbled sweetmeats, Hirohito, hiding behind a sliding *shoji* screen, cast his eye over the field and chose his pretty cousin Nagako, who was then just 11, as his bride-to-be. They did not actually meet until several years later when Nagako was ushered into his exalted presence with her eyes lowered, bowed, and exited without a word. Ten years after he chose her they were duly wed.

In the 1980s, the *Kunaicho* went about things in a rather more scientific way. A three-man committee was formed, which began by looking first among the ranks of the former nobility, who have their roots in the old imperial capital of Kyoto. Instead of sending emissaries with invitations to tea they sought the help of Kasumi Kaikan, an organisation representing the so-called 'floral families' which maintains a computer database of thousands of names which was combed to find eligible women of marriageable age. The vice-chancellors of respected universities such as Gakushuin and Seishin (Michiko's *alma mater*) were also sounded out. The word was put out on the old boys' network of serving and retired civil servants to discreetly inquire whether any of them had a suitable daughter.

It is officially denied that there are any hard-and-fast criteria for a royal bride, but authorities such as Toshiya Matsuzaki, a veteran correspondent who has been covering the royal family for half a century and who publishes a magazine devoted exclusively to the royals, believes the palace officials have some unofficial guidelines. I met Matsuzaki in his office in the backstreets of Yotsuya, a ten-minute walk from the East Palace. Hot rain was bucketing down from a black sky – typhoon Banyan had blown ashore, planes were grounded, highways closed, trains halted and the local bars and restaurants shuttered as Tokyo battened down for the storm.

Over sweet cakes and barley tea, with water sluicing down the windows, he talked about his years covering three generations of royals, particularly Naruhito, whom he has known since he was a child and often chatted with informally. Matsuzaki was a member of the imperial *kisha kurabu* – the 'club' of accredited journalists who document the doings of the royals – and until recent years had unprecedented access to them. However, most of these insights had to remain off-the-record – in 50 years his biggest published scoop, he boasts proudly, was spotting that the Emperor Hirohito had acquired a Mickey Mouse watch after a visit to Disneyland. Such is the media's obsession with royal minutiae. He also went mountain-climbing with the prince – in later years, as he puffed and panted up the slopes, Naruhito would always solicitously ask him how he was doing as he passed him.

Some of the 'bride criteria' are uncontroversial, some quaintly old-fashioned, some quite tendentious and offensive to Japan's minorities. Naruhito's bride had to be younger than the prince, shorter than him, well educated – and healthy. The Empress Nagako, for instance, almost didn't make the cut because of a family history of colour-blindness. Foreigners need not apply – unlike the European royals, who have kept their family trees vigorous by regular infusions of foreign genes, the Japanese imperial family is remarkably inbred, perhaps explaining the preoccupation with sound health, particularly mental health. 'Foreigners' includes Japanese citizens of Korean ancestry whose families may have been in the country for many generations. What is puzzling about this particular prohibition is that, as any serious scholar would know, Korean blood runs through the veins of the imperial family itself. During his annual birthday meeting with reporters in 2001, the current Emperor Akihito remarked that he felt a 'certain kinship with Korea' because the mother of his ancestor the Emperor Kammu (736–806) was Korean. The remark outraged Japan's xenophobic Right.

Families with a *buraku* connection are also out. Although indistinguishable from other Japanese, the three million or more *burakumin* are the classic shunned 'other' of Japanese society, the descendants of families which worked centuries ago in 'unclean' occupations like butchery, leatherwork or grave-sweeping. Today, they can be identified only because their family register records their household address as one of the former *buraku* ghettos such as the run-down Kyoto suburb of Sujin. The Ainu, the original Japanese, who were pushed into the wilds of the northern island of Hokkaido when modern Japanese arrived, are also banned, even though most have now successfully integrated into the broader community.

The list goes on. Relatives of politicians are frowned on – apart from their proclivity for corruption, the imperial family must be seen as being above politics. Tattoos and piercings are taboo – in fact, because of their association with *yakuza* crime gangs, tattoos will even get you banned from Japanese bath-houses. Baptised Christians (or Jews or Hindus, presumably) are out, because the empress is required to take part in Shinto religious rites. There must be no criminal record or hint of impropriety in the family going back three or four generations. And finally, a virgin is preferable – 'no one wants an ex-boyfriend leaping out of the woodwork one day with topless photos talking about the time he and the princess got into a threesome', as a Western journalist in Tokyo irreverently puts it.

Matsuzaki believes that, in spite of these restrictive criteria, over the years the *Kunaicho* eventually came up with the names of around 100 'perfect' young women. They had survived vigorous vetting by private eyes hired by an attorney, a former senior public prosecutor with offices in the Marunouchi business district, who could be trusted for his discretion and his thoroughness in plodding back through the family trees of the 'bride candidates'. Little can be hidden – the right to privacy is a relatively novel concept in Japan, and legislation upholding it was only passed in 2003 after much debate. The crown prince's chamberlain, Minoru Hamao, was frequently spotted by royal watchers arriving at the East Palace with a brown paper envelope in his hand containing the details of yet another approved candidate for the prince to consider as his bride.

What did the prince think of them? Naruhito himself had returned from Oxford with a new outlook on life. He declared, showing an unexpectedly independent streak, that he had decided to meet his bride 'in the natural way', rather than have one selected for him. And, all importantly, he seems to have had his mother's support in this. The prince was no longer going to be content with the sort of simpering young society soubrettes the *Kunaicho* had been parading past him, but was looking for someone with a stronger personality, perhaps someone more like his mother. He spoke publicly of his admiration for the English women he had met at university, who 'were graceful and not afraid to speak their minds'. At the press conference to mark his thirty-first birthday he gave this description of the kind of woman *he* thought would make a good wife. It should be someone who shared his hobbies and interests in music and sport, and:

I am not so concerned about height, education or family. I would like her to have a similar value system to myself, in the sense of abstaining from luxuries. I prefer someone who has the same plain tastes and modest money sense as myself. A cultured person who appreciates simple beauty, not a person who wants to buy this and that at, say, Tiffanys in New York . . . [someone] who speaks easily to people . . . who gives her opinion, where necessary.

The problem, of course, would be finding someone who matched those criteria and who was willing to accept the constrictions of a life inside the moat. 'Many of them rejected the prince,' says Matsuzaki. 'No one wanted to live the lifestyle of the imperial household. It is very isolated, very strict, you cannot meet your friends, you cannot travel, you cannot even see your own family. People watched Michiko suffer.' Even though he likes and respects Naruhito, Matsuzaki says that if one of his three daughters had wanted to marry him, 'I would stop her because I would see that she is going to suffer and get sick.'

Fate, however, would intervene before Masako had to make that call. Since she was a last-minute addition to the guest-list for that fateful reception for the Spanish Infanta, there had not been time to do the exhaustive background checks that protocol demanded. While the smitten Naruhito was telephoning and inviting her over, the Marunouchi attorney was busy digging into her past. Inevitably, he found the skeleton in the Owada family closet, and he passed on the intelligence to the Men in Black. Relieved – because whatever the prince might think, they did not believe a brainy, western-educated diplomat would fit in at the imperial court – they told the prince the romance had to end before it had really begun.

The problem was not with Masako's high-achieving but unpopular father Hisashi; it was on her mother's side of the family. Yumiko's father was a man named Yutaka

Egashira, who had risen through the ranks to become managing director of the Industrial Bank of Japan, the engine used by the government to finance the country's post-war reconstruction. So far so uncontroversial. But in 1964 the bank had imposed Egashira as president of a company called the Chisso Corporation, a major creditor of the bank which was on the brink of bankruptcy. His job was to save it from collapse.

Chisso's main factory is in the seaside town of Minamata on the southern island of Kyushu, a sprawling labyrinth of rusty pipelines, smokestacks and administration buildings. The place is referred to as 'Chisso castle town', because of the deference the citizens show to their economic overlord – the company is still the town's main employer. The factory was built in the 1930s with the support of the national and prefectural governments, and it made acetaldehyde, a toxic chemical used in the plastics industry, whose manufacture involves the use of the 'liquid metal' mercury. In the 1950s Minamata became known around the world as the site of the first, and greatest, pollution disaster of modern times.

First the residents noticed massive kills of fish floating on the Shiranui Sea, and beds of dead shellfish. Then seabirds began dropping from the sky. After that, the cats and dogs began running hysterically around in circles, foaming at the mouth and sometimes jumping into the sea. The strange and frightening phenomenon became known as 'dancing cat disease'. And then the people began to sicken and die like their pets – first of all fishing families living on nearby islands who depended on fish for their only protein, then the townsfolk. Women began miscarrying, and babies were born with dreadful physical deformities and intellectual deficits. The finger of suspicion began to be pointed at the

Chisso factory, which continued dumping tonnes of mercury effluent into the sea, but the company and the governments vehemently denied that there was any connection.

It took more than 20 years for the first successful class actions to grind their way through the glacial Japanese judicial system, and by then thousands had been killed or crippled. The courts found that the company had negligently and knowingly dumped the mercury into the sea, where it worked its way up the food-chain until it was consumed by humans. Two Chisso directors were convicted of 'voluntary manslaughter', though their punishment was merely a bond. The calamity became known around the world through the heart-rending photographs of the late Eugene Smith, and Minamata was for many years a rallying point for the international environmental movement, much as Chernobyl is today.

The latest official toll, according to Hideo Kitaoka, a Minamata activist I first met during a visit in the mid-1990s, is 1500 dead, and more than 14,000 suffering from incurable disabilities due to damage to the central nervous system, much of it caused by the mercury penetrating the placenta while the child was still in the womb. Damages awarded exceed $1 billion, and the company is technically bankrupt. However, the national and prefectural governments have come to the rescue, bankrolling the compensation payments and taking control of the victims' assessment procedure. The Chisso Corporation remains in business, and at the time of Masako's vetting Egashira was still listed as an 'advisor' to the company, although he was well into his eighties.

What was Egashira's role in this horror story? Quite obviously, he had nothing to do with the establishment of the factory or its industrial processes. He remained based in Tokyo, and his prime responsibility as 'outside' president and then chairman was to keep the company afloat, and protect the bank's and the government's investments. He was acting, if you will, like the receiver of a bankrupt business under the Australian Corporations Law. He did, however, through the 1960s and early 1970s, ignore the mounting evidence that Chisso's effluent was the cause of Minamata's suffering, and allow the factory to continue discharging the mercury. He also ensured that the victims were denied justice for more than two decades, by fighting every action to the death through the Japanese courts. Morally, if not legally, he bears a heavy burden of responsibility for the tragedy.

Having said that, if the Marunouchi attorney had telephoned Kitaoka down in Kyushu he would have learned that the victims bear Egashira no grudges. Their venom is reserved for the governments which bankrolled the litigation, and which imposed unfair and arbitrary restrictions on those seeking compensation. 'In reality, I don't think most Minamata disease patients even knew that Egashira-san existed,' he told me. So why did the *Kunaicho* so adamantly tell Naruhito to forget about his love? The only plausible answer is that the agency was opposed to Masako for other reasons – her 'foreignness', her non-aristocratic background, her brains and her fluency in half a dozen languages. All, a foreign observer would have thought, assets to be exploited, rather than deficiencies to be deplored. But no career woman had ever married into the royal family, and the agency was determined that none ever would.

As well, we now know that Masako's father was also opposed from the start to any idea that his high-flying daughter should truncate her brilliant career by marriage to anyone. The story that the prince had taken a shine to Masako had finally been leaked to the media in the summer of 1987, and the Owada household was under siege. An East Palace emissary was sent to the house in Meguro to press the prince's suite with Hisashi, asking him to 'think about it positively'. Without consulting Masako – perhaps he already knew his daughter was not interested – Owada explained, with pained punctiliousness, that Masako 'has to go overseas', and he asked the messenger to 'please make it so that such a thing never existed'. In other words, forget it.

Not long after this, Tomohiko Tomita, a senior official at the *Kunaicho*, summoned the love-lorn young prince, explained the 'Chisso problem' to him, and told him it would be inappropriate for him to continue seeing Masako. According to an account Tomita gave later to the *Shukan Asahi* magazine, Naruhito meekly replied *wakatta*, 'I understand.'

Masako was, by now, thoroughly fed up with being hounded by the Press. It's not that the Japanese media are as aggressive as, say, Fleet Street in full cry can be. They would certainly never install cameras in a gym to spy on Princess Diana, or attempt to infiltrate the palace itself, as two British tabloid journalists did recently. Being pursued by Japanese newsmen is more akin to being caught up in a flock of sheep softly nuzzling you to death. No matter how many times she snapped 'No comment – there is nothing for me to say', they kept coming back for more. Privately, she told her friends, 'How come there are all these head-lines when I haven't even been proposed to?' Not only was she not interested, she had a job to do.

The overseas trip her father referred to is a plum perk reserved for the highest achievers at the Foreign Ministry, those destined to become ambassadors, section heads, even the ultimate prize of head of the department. Those fortunate enough to be chosen are sponsored for two years' postgraduate study on full pay at a great overseas university, usually Harvard or one of the Oxbridge colleges. Hisashi Owada had studied law at Cambridge under this program, and was determined his daughter would follow suit.

Masako had applied herself diligently since she began work at the ministry early in 1987, working those gruellingly long hours. In spite of her father's senior position at the ministry (he had by then worked his way up to No. 2), Masako mucked in like any junior employee, doing the grunt work, volunteering to stay up late to liaise with Japan's missions overseas, often working 200 hours of overtime a month. When, the following year, it was announced that she had been selected to study for a Masters degree in international affairs at Oxford, few begrudged her the opportunity. As a bonus, she must have been feeling a tremendous relief at escaping from the prying eyes of the media, who had not given up on her as a 'princess candidate' even though Naruhito had – for the time being at least – stopped calling.

Which brings us back to that comfortable Victorian manor in Bardwell Road, Oxford. If Masako thought that moving across the world would put her beyond the reach of the Japanese media she had another think coming. She enrolled at beautiful Balliol College, one of the federation of 39 colleges that make up Oxford University, whose honey-coloured stone buildings are built around a grassy quadrangle in the heart of the old city, at the beginning of what is quaintly called the Michaelmas term in September 1988. Steeped in tradition, Balliol only admitted its first female student in 1979. It is one of the oldest colleges in Oxford (it was founded in 1263, less than 50 years after King John signed the Magna Carta) and the ministry favoured it for its fine reputation in international relations.

It is not hard to see why Oxford should be such a magnet for overseas students like Masako and Naruhito. It is the English-speaking world's oldest university – it celebrates its millennium towards the end of this century – and around a quarter of its 16,000 students are from overseas, including the annual intake of Rhodes scholars such as the former Australian Prime Minister Bob Hawke. Although it ranks behind Cambridge at No. 8 on the Jiao Tong University hit parade of the world's greatest universities, it claims among its alumni 46 Nobel laureates, 25 British prime ministers including Tony Blair and Margaret Thatcher, 86 archbishops, six kings – and now, most likely, its first emperor and empress.

As well as its heritage of great scholarship, the place drips with history at every turn. On the northern approach to the town stands a blackened stone monument to the sixteenth-century Anglican churchmen Cramer, Latimer and Ridley, burned at the stake for heresy; nearby is the chapel where John Wyclif campaigned against the Pope for the vernacular Bible. It was here that Edmund Halley predicted the return of the comet which bears his name, that Charles Wesley laid the foundations of the Methodist church, and Matthew Arnold penned the lines that still best describe this city of churches and colleges set in the midst of woods and pastures on the banks of the Isis, as the River Thames is known here:

And that sweet city with her dreaming spires,
She needs not June for beauty's heightening.

As a graduate student, Masako took up residence at Holywell Manor, a university boarding-house less than ten minutes' walk from Balliol. However, within a matter of weeks, Japanese TV crews arrived on the scene. They were obviously not buying the story that the affair was over. Masako could hardly walk out of her lodgings without finding a camera trained on her from the little park opposite, and she snapped. 'Regarding this issue, I think it's got nothing to do with me. If possible, I'd like you to leave me alone. When my training is finished, I plan to keep working as a *Gaimusho* employee,' she retorted when a reporter asked her about rumours she was to be engaged to Naruhito. Another news clip shows her striding along in a long trench-coat demanding to know a journalist's name, and what organisation he represented – most unladylike, they tut-tutted when the footage was shown back in Tokyo. Privately she told friends the media were behaving like 'grubs'. Masako turned for advice to her distinguished 'college advisor', Sir Adam Roberts, mountaineer, marathon-runner and for more than 20 years professor of international relations at Oxford.

For all his knighthood and his formidable reputation, Roberts is an approachable man, a lanky informal type whose casual manner masks a brilliant mind. In his mid-sixties, he has a floppy quiff of hair, a beaky nose, and is dressed in Oxfam chic when we meet in his cluttered office, up a spiral stone staircase. He is wearing black pants, a white open-necked shirt, a rumpled cream seersucker jacket, and clunky black boots which he seems not to know where to put – one minute they are parked on his desk, the next on the arm of a sofa. On the walls are photographs taken from the mountains he has conquered. Unlike Naruhito, Roberts is a serious 'technical' climber – ropes

and pitons – and has scaled peaks including the Matter-
horn in Switzerland, which has killed more climbers than
almost any other mountain in the world.

Roberts referred the troubled Masako to some friends,
and did not learn until years later that to escape the media
she had moved in with Charles Wenden, the famously
discreet bursar of All Souls, and his wife Eileen. They
became her minders, much as the Oldmans had when she
was attending Harvard years before. 'I told her "Please
don't tell me where you live. I don't give a toss whether you
are having an affair with, or are in love with, or engaged to,
or not engaged to the crown prince. Don't tell me. It's your
business. I don't want to know," ' says Roberts. Oxford
kept its secret, and Masako was allowed to continue her
studies without any more molestation from the media.

There has been much speculation about why Masako
never completed her degree at Oxford. Perhaps being kind,
perhaps just sloppy, Japanese journalists have reported this
was due to ill health – Masako has never been robust, and
she was occasionally laid low by colds or the flu. But this
was not the real reason for her lack of academic success.

She began studying for what is known as an M.Phil.,
a master of philosophy in international relations, but
switched to the less demanding M.Litt., a master of letters,
which also involves submitting a thesis, but not sitting
for term examinations. Perhaps she was finding it tough
going, perhaps illness exacerbated by that first dank
English winter forced her to make the switch. Either way,
Roberts had read her Harvard thesis, and says that he
had high hopes she would successfully complete her postgraduate degree. She made intelligent contributions at the
weekly two-hour seminars where students are required to
speak off the cuff for 15 or 20 minutes on subjects chosen

from the curriculum such as the causes of World War I, where the Paris Peace Accord of 1919 went wrong, or the Great Depression:

She's very able, very good at languages. She struck me as someone who was very articulate and quite subtle in her understanding. She was really a mature individual. There was something about her that made me think 'here is somebody with wit and humour'. She was quiet, and there was nothing brash about her. She certainly seemed to be a well-rounded person.

The real reason she did not, as Roberts had hoped, complete her thesis after she left Oxford? Well, it emerges that her studies were the first casualty of her eventual decision to marry the prince. She had been researching the sale of warplanes by the United States to Japan in the 1980s – probably the highly contentious decision by the US to license Japanese manufacturers to build the high-tech F16 fighter, rather than see Japan develop its own warplane. That, says Roberts, would have been much too controversial a subject for a royal-to-be: 'For the imperial family, it's got to be something pretty esoteric and harmless. What was it Hirohito was interested in? Molluscs or something.' Masako agreed to drop the thesis she had spent two years working on, to save the royal family any embarrassment. When Roberts was later invited to the East Palace during a visit to Tokyo he discussed with Masako completing her thesis on a more anodyne subject. 'There was a glint in her eye that she might embark on another thesis – she even got some books from the University of Tokyo library. But for one reason or another that never worked out.'

Naruhito's uncontroversial thesis, on the other hand, was successfully completed and is there for all to read. The prince's college was Merton, a favourite with Japan's royals, because as well as being historic (it was the first college to get its formal charter, in 1264) and having a good academic reputation, it is one of the smaller colleges where staff and students can get to know one another. It is a chocolate-box building of Jacobean stonework and stained glass, built around a grassy 'mob quad' where students perform strange rituals. For reasons lost in antiquity, at two o'clock in the morning of a day in November which is deemed to mark the end of summer, all the undergraduates walk backwards around the quad while drinking heavily, an activity Naruhito would no doubt have enjoyed immensely.

I took a tour of the building, along with a coach-load of Japanese tourists, and particularly admired the library where he would have studied, with its yellowing eighteenth-century globe depicting Australia as *Terra Australis*, seventh-century Assyrian clay tablets, ancient astrolabes and rows of leather-bound tomes chained to the reading desks to prevent theft. In an adjoining room there is a shrine to the college's most famous son, the essayist and caricaturist Max Beerbohm. Downstairs in a sunlit reading-room, the librarians are kind enough to bring me what they have referred to in emails as a 'small collection of ephemera' relating to Naruhito's stay.

There is a copy of a Japanese magazine article, an abstract of his thesis, and then the *pièce de résistance*: the leather-bound admissions book, embossed with a dragon motif and the college motto *Qui Timet Deum Faciet Bona* ('Who fears God shall do good,' whispers the librarian). The book is borne to me reverentially, as though a fragment of the True Cross, and opened on a lectern, with straws of soft cloth containing what seem to be small lead fishing weights to hold down the open pages. And there is the record, in October 1983, of Naruhito signing his name in English in a wobbly hand as he is admitted to the college by the warden, Sir Rex Richards.

There is also a *tanka* poem he composed:

As I approached my Oxford lodgings
The evening bell echoed through the town.

But perhaps it loses something more than its syllable count in the translation.

To read Naruhito's actual thesis you have to seek admission to the splendid Bodleian Library, founded in the seventeenth century by a pilchard magnate named Thomas Bodley. One of Oxford's most imposing buildings, it is familiar to fans of the TV series *Inspector Morse*. It is one of Britain's six national copyright libraries – it receives a copy of every book published, close to 1000 a day – and currently has more than seven million volumes, stored on shelves that would stretch to London, some 90 kilometres away, and back. Before you are allowed into its hallowed halls, you have to produce a letter certifying that you are a *bona fide* scholar, then stand under the stern gaze of Thomas Lockley BD (Librarian 1660–1665) and recite the following oath:

I hereby undertake not to remove from the library, or mark, deface or injure in any way, any volume, document or other object belonging to it, or in its custody; not to bring into the library or kindle therein any fire or flame, and not to smoke in the library; and I promise to obey all the rules of the library.

After all that it is almost an anticlimax when you climb the stairs to the great sun-drenched upper reading room, with its stained-glass windows and stern portraits of ancient scholars and writers, and are handed the slim, black-bound volume which represents six years of the prince's scholarship. '*A Study of Navigation and Traffic on the Upper Thames in the 18th Century*' is a worthy companion to Naruhito's earlier work on water transportation in the Seto Inland Sea.

It is actually little more than a compilation from various sources of long lists of commodities that were transported down the turbid Thames to London in 180-tonne horse-drawn barges: coal, cereals, malt, manure, wood, wine, cider, tin, salt, lead, ashes, paper, hemp, tallow, rags, horn-tips, vitriol and grease as well as manufactured items such as baskets of plumb bobs, scythes, gudgeons and mangles. While it no doubt did wonders for Naruhito's English vocabulary, the prince develops no real thesis and draws no conclusions from his research. He skirts around the conflict over water rights between the fishermen, the millers whose water-wheels were powered by the river, and the authorities building locks to facilitate transportation – too controversial for a royal to venture an opinion, even three centuries later. As his friend, Prince Takamado, once wrote of his ballet reviews: 'I never called my writing criticism because I could never write anything bad or nasty.'

The thesis concludes, rather lamely: 'Such a wide cross-section of goods, which a study of traffic on the Thames reveals to have passed along the waterway, raises as many questions as answers about the commercial enterprise and manufacture which gave rise to their existence, and the nature of the markets . . .'

I don't want to carp about this, because an Oxford degree of any sort is a fine achievement, especially when one's first language is not English. But there is a long gap between Naruhito's leaving Oxford in 1986, and his submitting the thesis three years later, with generous acknowledgement to four scholars at Oxford and Gakushuin University in Tokyo who in the meantime 'helped my research and made many helpful suggestions for writing this paper'. The prince's high-powered brains trust was: Dr Roger Highfield, Dr Kenneth Morgan, Dr Heita Kawakatsu, and Professor Takeshi Yuzawa. It would be unkind to suggest that Naruhito would have been lost without their help, but his scholarship is certainly not in the same league as Masako's. His thesis seems a team effort that went through many drafts and rewrites before it was finally signed off on by the economic historian Professor Peter Mathias. In 2003, for this contribution to Japan–UK relations, Mathias was awarded Japan's Order of the Rising Sun (with) Gold Rays and Neck Ribbon, with a citation saying that he '. . . earned the gratitude of the imperial family by serving as research supervisor to Crown Prince Naruhito'.

While Masako burned the midnight oil in her attic in Bardwell Road, Naruhito – who left Oxford two years before she arrived – seems to have had a more enjoyable time discovering the city's other attractions, particularly its pubs. And Oxford is a great town for the serious student of Britain's pub culture, as Bob Hawke discovered 30 years earlier when he achieved a world record for drinking two and a half pints of beer from an antique pewter pot in 11 seconds – something he says endeared him to more Australians than anything he ever did while prime minister.

In a book he penned some years later, catchily entitled *The Thames and I – a Memoir of Two Years at Oxford*, the crown prince writes fondly of sunny afternoons pedalling along for a pint at the Perch, the Trout Inn or the White

Hart, with his English police bodyguard panting in his wake. These are three of more than 300 pubs, clubs, bars and inns in the district – enough to support their own newspaper, published by CAMRA, the Campaign for Real Ale, which claims credit for saving characterful British beer from the bland conformity of the big multi-national lager-brewers. During term-time they are thronged by students and locals alike, the hub of Oxford's social life. Naruhito managed to visit 21 of these historic inns during his time at Oxford, he once told a reporter.

He would, without doubt, have downed a foaming pint or three at the Eagle and Child – known locally as the 'bird and baby' – a centuries-old Tudor-style pub with oddly-pitched wooden floors and low ceilings where the Inklings, a drinking club led by the author C. S. Lewis, once hung out. Perhaps he slipped across the road to soak up the atmosphere and enjoy a champion Cornish Betty Stogs in front of the open fire at the Lamb and Flag which – like the Eagle and Child – is actually owned by St John's College. Graham Greene once drank here, and the pub is mentioned in Thomas Hardy's novel *Jude the Obscure*. He and his college friends certainly did enjoy the cosy 'snug' at the Turf Bar, an ancient freestone pub hidden away down an alleyway so narrow you can touch both walls with outstretched hands. It has a wonderful array of hand-crafted beers pulled from wooden casks with names such as Morland's Old Speckled Hen, Mauldon's Mole Trap, and, when I visited (purely in the interests of research) a brew known simply as Village Idiot. Naruhito, disappointingly, appears to have preferred the lighter Japanese-style lagers to the rich, darkly intoxicating 'real ales'.

Naruhito's time at Oxford was very different from Masako's in other ways as well. The *Kunaicho* had arranged for an official, one 'Councillor Fuji', to look after his affairs while he was at Oxford. This Fuji, a graduate of Copenhagen University, by the way, who was an expert viola player and had a doctorate for the study of sea urchins, was to be the crown prince's main minder for two years. It seems to have been a cushy assignment. A former chamberlain to Emperor Hirohito, he set himself up for the duration in a rented rectory in the village of Bessels Leigh near Oxford, along with his wife, two children, and a niece. Naruhito's retinue also included two British policemen who worked shifts, sleeping in the room next door and accompanying him everywhere he went. And at any official function there was always a chauffeur and flunkies dispatched from the Japanese Embassy in London to make sure there was not the slightest glitch in protocol.

It was obviously hard for Naruhito to pretend to be 'just another student' with all this security. An account by a teacher named Joseph Lieberman published later in Japan gives an idea of the restrictions placed on the young prince. At the time, Lieberman was teaching English as a second language at the University of Kent in Canterbury, and was attending a Chaucer festival at nearby Chilham Castle at which Naruhito was to be the guest of honour. Police sirens heralded the prince's convoy, and he arrived at the reception 'sandwiched between a British bobby and a bodyguard built like a sumo wrestler'. After a cello recital and some speeches, Lieberman found himself chit-chatting to the prince for 20 minutes, about his studies, music, and his current movie-star heart-throb, Brooke Shields. Wrote Lieberman:

I felt a wave of sympathy for this altogether nice guy who was accompanied by bodyguards every time he stepped out of his front door, and surrounded by stifling rules and conventions for even the least public act or words. He had position and obligations, whether he wanted them or not.

Nevertheless, Naruhito says he enjoyed the relative anonymity he found at Oxford, and freedom for the first time in his life from the all-embracing clutch of the *Kunaicho*. He slipped, incognito, into a British guest-house one night, signing himself 'Hiro' and enjoying eggs and bacon for breakfast. He writes with mischievous delight of meeting someone who asked where he came from. 'Tokyo,' replied the heir to the Japanese throne. 'Whereabouts in Tokyo?' 'From the centre of the city,' said the impish young prince. 'It is really important and precious to have the opportunity to be able to go privately at one's own pace where one wants,' he writes.

Japan's royals all enjoy the relative freedom they are allowed while overseas. Hirohito said he felt 'like a bird released from its cage' when he spent six months travelling around Europe in the 1920s when he was crown prince. And Naruhito, the first heir to be allowed to study overseas, was no exception. He was amazed at the relatively relaxed security and informality enjoyed by the British royals. Queen Elizabeth II, he noted with surprise, poured her own tea and served the sandwiches. He shared the royal box at Ascot, where he had his first (unsuccessful) £1 wager, and he spent three days holidaying at Balmoral Castle in Scotland where he had a barbecue with the Queen and Prince Philip, and Prince Charles taught him to fly-fish for salmon. When he returned to Tokyo, Naruhito tried to melt a tiny piece of the permafrost of palace protocol by asking the imperial police to stop their practice of disrupting traffic flows throughout Tokyo every time he went out in a car by programming the traffic-lights to green for the royal cavalcade. Even that small gesture would not be possible, he was told.

At Oxford he mucked in with the chores like any other student, wearing a smart/casual uniform of slacks, roll-necked jumper and jacket. He lugged his own suitcase up to his room, which overlooked the beautiful Christ Church meadow where Naruhito liked to jog, served himself from the buffet in the dining-hall, and washed his own clothes, including a highly publicised incident when he flooded the laundry with suds. His police escort had to show him how to iron a shirt. At the age of 23, this sheltered young man went to a bank for the first time in his life, got an electric blanket when he found his third-floor room too cold, and enjoyed the freedom of being able to wander around Oxford's wonderful antiquarian bookshops, buying old maps and books with his first credit card. He even has a delightfully backhanded way of praising Britain's infamous boarding-school catering: 'I particularly liked the almost over-cooked brussels sprouts [though] the tea was very strong and the same colour as the coffee.' His only complaints were the draughty college corridors and the fact that the water ran cold in his bath when it was only one third full – all Japanese, not just the royals, love a long, luxurious soak. 'Did the custom of enjoying hot baths leave Britain with the Romans?' he asks, rather plaintively. Well, actually, yes.

Naruhito seems to have made a few friends at Oxford, though, unfortunately, they are identified in his book only by their initials. He seems surprised by the freewheeling conversations they had over beer and sherry in the college common-room, though he steered clear of anything remotely smelling of controversy, such as the angry debate then raging over the awarding of an honorary degree to Baroness Thatcher. He learned how to take a joke – his friend 'P', a student of the *shakuhachi* flute, nicknamed him *denki* (light-fitting), a play on his title *denka* (majesty). He joined (of course) the Japan Society, but also the karate and judo clubs (as honorary president, not a competitor) and the dramatic society. He was taken on a pub crawl, defined at Oxford as downing a punishing pint of beer in each of ten pubs. And he tried unsuccessfully to get into a disco, wearing jeans and a T-shirt. The heir to the Japanese throne was refused admittance by the bouncers, explaining typically, 'While I was at Oxford I tried as far as possible to be like other students and certainly did not explain who I was. So I gave up and went weakly away.'

And his time out wasn't just beer and skittles. The prince played inter-college tennis, seeded No. 3 in the Merton squad of six, and seems to have made up in deter-mination what he lacks in height and strength. His attitude to the game shows again that the mild-mannered prince has a stubborn streak: 'Even when I was clearly weaker than my opponent, there were times when I returned all the balls, using every ounce of strength in my arm, and my opponent became tired or irritated and lost his poise. I was then eventually able to win the game.'

He was not so successful in other sports. He tried rowing, but caught a crab and hit himself in the stomach with his oar, a manoeuvre he calls, rather gruesomely, *hara kiri*. And his golf doesn't seem to have progressed much since he sneaked out onto the course at Point Lonsdale a decade or so before. He took lessons from a pro, but 'I felt pretty wretched when I missed the ball or my club tore up a piece of turf'. And he found some friends who shared his passion for mountain-climbing, or should we say hiking up hills. In his three years at Merton he added the scalps of the three highest peaks in Great Britain to his growing collection: Scotland's Ben Nevis, England's Scafell Pike, and Mount Snowdon in Wales. Though, on each occasion, Britain being Britain, it was either raining or so foggy he couldn't see a thing when he got to the top.

His travels through Europe sound more like a nineteenth-century Grand Tour than anything the normal visitor will encounter. He indulged his passion for the classics, sharing the royal box at Covent Garden with Prince Charles and Princess Diana for a performance of Mussorgsky's *Boris Godunov.* He tortured 'Bruce', his police escort for the night, with a performance of Wagner's opera *Meistersingers von Nürnberg* that lasted six interminable hours. He played on Mozart's viola at the house where he once lived in Salzburg, and visited Beethoven's birthplace in Bonn, Dvořák's house in Prague, and Elgar's in Worcestershire.

Naruhito seems to have met most, if not all, the remaining crowned heads of Europe – indeed, that would not be hard since after a century of republicanism and revolution there are now only 30 monarchs left. They are the world's most exclusive club, and the last whose membership is based on heredity rather than ability or money. He homestayed with the Windsors – Prince Charles was kind enough to say, in the forward to Naruhito's book, that he shows '. . . a keen eye, a delicate sense of humour, and an enviable desire to be involved in a wide range of activities'. He went skiing with Hans-Adam II, now the ruling prince of the minute, mountainous principality of Liechtenstein. He holidayed on the Mediterranean island of Majorca at the villa of Spain's King Juan Carlos I, and in the chalet of then Grand Duke Jean of Luxembourg. He sailed the fjords of Norway with Harald and Sonja, now the king and queen, spent time with the Belgian royals and cruised the canals of Holland with the chain-smoking Queen Beatrix of the Netherlands, whose mother Queen Juliana began the tradition of 'bicycle-riding royals'. One only wishes Naruhito had recorded his impressions of Holland's popular 'people's monarch' who – in stark contrast with Japan's cloistered royalty – holds regular public audiences which any citizen may attend, and is not afraid to speak out on public issues.

Although his social life sounds great, back at Oxford, Naruhito struggled with his studies. Before entering the university, he was given an intensive three-month English course at the country house at Chiselhurst, near Oxford, of a Colonel Tom Hall. As well as having a royal connection – Hall was 'a gentleman at arms in the Queen's bodyguard', whatever that may mean – he owned a language school in Japan, and organised tutors for Naruhito. The prince studied for four hours a day in a basement classroom, and in his spare time took dips in the heated swimming pool, and tried to pick up some of the finer points of croquet. Unlike Masako, he still had great difficulty with his English, and had to resort to tape-recording his lectures for later transcription. Indeed, it's surprising his police escorts do not rate a credit in his thesis – they frequently had to decipher musty tomes for him as, sneezing with the dust, he ploughed through the archives in the County Record Office for his thesis.

With less time for fun, the diligent Masako buried herself in her studies. Oxford was not, I can reveal, her first choice of university – she desperately wanted to go back to Harvard to do her masters. According to Oliver

Oldman, she tried to re-enrol to work towards an advanced degree called a JD, Juris Doctor. However, Harvard's bureaucrats would not give her credit for her study-time at the University of Tokyo, so she was obliged to fall back on her second choice.

Unlike Naruhito, one cannot imagine Masako enjoying the Oxford pub scene – she did learn a little about wine, but being a very moderate drinker was more often seen sipping soft-drinks at the parties and receptions she attended. She also played tennis, she swam, she popped across to Paris to see her family and practise her French – her father had wangled himself the plum job of Ambassador Extraordinary and Plenipotentiary to the OECD. Dr David Morris, a Japan scholar and director of Oxford University's Development Office in Tokyo, knew Masako at Oxford and remembers that 'she was always helpful in promoting Japanese activities'. On one occasion she helped put up posters advertising a lecture by an influential Japanese politician who was visiting. As at Harvard, she supported the university's Japan Society, promoting cultural exchanges such as screening a movie by the left-wing avant-garde Japanese film-maker Nagisa Oshima, *In The Realm of the Senses*, which was banned in Japan for many years because of its explicit depiction of sexual penetration, fellatio, sado-masochism and penis amputation.

As far as her own love life is concerned, Oxford added little to the rumour-mills. No ex-boyfriend has emerged from the shadows, with or without topless pictures to flog, and from the little we know, she does not appear to have any romantic entanglement. At a party in Tokyo before she left, she gave the impression that nothing could be further from her mind. 'I was warned by my mother recently that I have been off my guard,' she joked to a friend. ' "You have to tighten your loin-cloth," she told me. Unfortunately, I didn't have one, but I bought one to take to Britain.'

Nor does Naruhito refer, even obliquely, to any affair, although as we have seen he was impressed with the forthrightness of the English undergraduates he met, in contrast with the coy and deferential Japanese girls to whom the *Kunaicho* had been introducing him. But he does seem to have had some admirers, as evidenced by this cryptic, and rather dismissive, reference buried in his book: 'On Valentine's Day there were cards from various unknowns.' Perhaps those outspoken English girls were just a bit too much for the shy and sheltered lad. On his very first night at Merton, he writes, 'Attracted by the smell of beer, I soon found myself in the bar. The first girl to whom I was introduced was wearing a straw hat, despite the fact that we were indoors, and had a silver star on her forehead. I wondered what sort of strange place I had come to.'

As for Masako, another who remembers her well is the then master of Balliol, the distinguished American Nobel laureate Baruch Blumberg. According to his former colleague, Sir Adam Roberts, Dr Blumberg 'has probably saved the lives of more people than anyone alive'. In 1971, screening a blood sample from an Australian Aborigine, he discovered an antigen for Hepatitis B (a potentially fatal blood-borne disease which can cause liver cancer) which became known as 'the Australian antigen'. This led to the world's first method of screening against hepatitis, and the development of the first anti-cancer vaccine, which has been used to protect tens of millions of people, particularly in Asia and Africa.

'Barry' Blumberg told me that when reports of Masako's engagement first circulated, he asked her about it and: 'She assured me that it was not the case. She had no plans to marry, and she seemed set on following her career.' He was surprised when, a few years later, the wedding was announced, and wondered what had occurred in the meantime to persuade her to change her mind. Like many who met her at Oxford, Masako came across to him as 'modest, quiet, thoughtful and intelligent'. Blumberg, too, says that she was a very good student, and 'it was a shame that she did not complete her degree'.

And so, in the summer of 1990, as the mulberries ripened on the trees along the Isis where Masako and Naruhito each used to stroll, watching young couples punting past in hire-boats, Masako packed her bags once more and prepared to head back to the grindstone in Kasumigaseki. The Foreign Ministry, which had paid for her expensive education, now wanted its money's worth; and Masako was keen to prove that she had what it takes to carve out a career in the male-dominated world of the Japanese bureaucracy.

In the two years that she had been away, there had been no contact from the prince. The reporters had lost interest and were hounding other 'bride candidates' back in Tokyo. No doubt she was hoping that Naruhito had forgotten all about the diplomat's daughter he had fallen for and taken the advice of his courtiers to choose someone else.

But nothing could be further from the truth.

By Royal Appointment

Not long after Masako joined the imperial family, so the story goes, she decided that she should learn a musical instrument so that she could join in their classical musical soirées. She had learned the piano as a child, but this was deemed inappropriate – her mother-in-law, the Empress Michiko, is a dab hand at the ivories, and it would be a grave social solecism for Masako to be seen to be trying to upstage her.

Eventually, she decided to learn the flute, a tutor was engaged, and the search began for the right instrument. But, of course, Masako, being a royal princess, couldn't simply send a courtier to a music shop to pick a Yamaha off the shelf. Nothing but the very finest of craftsmanship is suitable for the imperial family. So the Imperial Household Agency approached the venerable Muramatsu company, established nearly a century ago, and the makers of 'the most revered and sought-after flutes in the world . . . the standard against which all professional flutes are measured', or so it boasts. James Galway, the legendary Irish flautist, uses one; so does Marcel Moyse, the French genius; and so should Masako.

These exquisite flutes come in a range of models, starting off with the basic EX, which retails for a little over $3000. But this would not do for Masako, the company decided. Not the solid silver model, nor even the gold-plated one, would be good enough. Eventually Muramatsu produced a hand-crafted flute made of solid platinum which was delivered to the palace in a leather case, wrapped in a fleece-lined nylon cover, with a rosewood cleaning rod. 'Price on application,' says the company's US website, but there would be little change from $100,000 for this masterpiece.

No doubt Masako would have been deeply embarrassed if she had known the trouble, and the expense, involved in catering for her little hobby. The royal family, after all, prides itself on its frugality and lack of ostentation, and is always wary of any extravagance which could arouse public jealousy or criticism. However, there are certain standards which one must uphold – especially when entertaining foreign dignitaries is part of the job description. And to ensure the very highest quality is maintained, an unofficial system of royal patronage exists, the gold standard to which every Tokyo social-climber aspires. Life within the moat does have its little consolations. The cigarettes in their silver boxes are made with Turkish tobacco and lit by servants using wooden matches; the wines are French, the cars by Rolls-Royce, the horses Arab bloodstock.

The royal appointment system began during the time of the Meiji emperor in the late nineteenth century, with the first official blessing bestowed on a Kyoto kimono-maker called Kawashima Somemono. It persisted through until the 1950s when it was officially abolished, although in practice little changed apart from a ban on the overt advertising of imperial custom. But, of course, news of where the royals shop continues to be passed by word of mouth around Tokyo's wealthy society matrons. They know which pork butcher in Azabu-juban provides the imperial sausages and which 300-year-old store in Nihonbashi puts aside its very best *nori* seaweed in which to wrap the imperial sushi – much as New York socialites know where to get their Manolo Blahnik shoes, Parisiennes their Hermès 'Kelly' handbags, and Sydney advertising men their Bathing Ape T-shirts.

For those who are interested, here is a short-list of some of the royal suppliers – although be warned that many of them have waiting lists years long, and the royal cachet means you will pay the earth:

Yamada Heian-do makes the imperial family's lacquerware, especially the gold and black soup bowls, hand-painted with the chrysanthemum motif, which cost $3280 for a set of five.

Miyamoto Shoko in Tokyo's Ginza department-store district began by making ornate samurai swords, but now is official purveyor of silverware, including tableware, goblets and bonbonnières. Empress Michiko has a tiny hand-made silver pillbox which cost $2600.

Koiwai Shoten in Tokyo's Setagaya district is the royal sandal maker – they make the golden open-toed sandals, as well as the red and gold clutch-bag that Masako carried for her wedding ceremony.

Hashi Katsu produces the hand-made cedar chopsticks which the royals use for special occasions, and **Kitorinson** the bathtubs made of Japanese cypress in which the royals relax at night.

The **Mitsukoshi** department store supplies the imperial family with its mercery, including 'velvety towels made using the finest thread over a gas flame [which] are 1.5 times as absorbent as ordinary towels'.

Kako Shirts makes the emperor's shirts of the finest cotton, with buttons made of New Guinea mother-of-pearl. The company cuts the top button slightly thinner than the others to make it easier to close.

Maehara Kouei Shoten is the place to go for an imperial umbrella. The company studied videotapes of Emperor Akihito opening and carrying an umbrella to produce the optimum design, incorporating 16 ribs.

6

The Pledge

W HEN MASAKO RETURNED TO TOKYO THE LAST thing on her mind would have been marriage. 'I am so busy I need a wife myself,' she joked to friends as she threw herself into her tough and demanding schedule at the Foreign Affairs Ministry. Her father, back from his plush posting in Paris, was about to achieve his life-long ambition to become head of the ministry, and Masako was keen to impress him with her dedication.

Masako had been reassigned to the ministry's most important division – a job that most of *Gaimusho*'s 5000 employees would have given their eye teeth for – at one of the most crucial moments in its history. The Second North American Division was in charge of Japan's most vital economic relationship at a time of boiling trade tensions. Ezra Vogel, Masako's one-time mentor at Harvard, had just shocked America to the core with his book *Japan As Number One*, raising the prospect of the end of half a century of US global hegemony. Japan's surplus with the

US had ballooned 100-fold to more than $50 billion since the mid-1960s, and American manufacturers were screaming at President George Bush Senior to negotiate more favourable access to Japan's protected and cartelised markets.

American computer-chip makers wanted their chips in Japanese laptops, steel-makers wanted their steel in Japanese shipyards, lawyers wanted to be able to set up their practices in Tokyo, car manufacturers, having belatedly discovered that Japanese drive on the 'wrong' side of the road, wanted better access to their showrooms. And this, hardly coincidentally, was the area of Masako's greatest expertise – she had spent four years at Harvard studying Japan–US trade, and developing just the sort of arguments that would be useful to try and fob off the Americans at those sweaty late-night meetings where the deals would be done.

Over the following two years she took on increasingly more important tasks, often working until the wee hours of the morning. With her language fluency – she could even switch from American English to the Queen's English when required – she was in great demand as an interpreter. She took minutes and translated for government heavyweights and former prime ministers Yasuhiro Nakasone, Noboru Takeshita and Sosuke Uno; she was there for top-level trade talks between Foreign Minister Michio Watanabe, US special trade negotiator Carla Hills and Secretary of State James Baker; she attended economic summits in Houston and Hawaii; she was even at the famous State banquet in Tokyo when, just as the *wagyu* beef was being served, George Bush vomited into the lap of Prime Minister Kiichi Miyazawa – surely the messiest diplomatic rebuke of all time.

Even those across the table from the Japanese negotiators came to know and respect her. 'She was known from the American side as an expert on foreign lawyers and semi-conductor issues,' said Roger Masasu, who was then a lobbyist with the Japan office of the American Semi-Conductor Association. A semi-conductor is not, as one web wit has it, 'a part-time employee on a street-car' but a computer chip component. 'At the summit in 1991 she showed acute understanding as a tough negotiator [and was] meticulous, outgoing and charming.'

Another American, Louis Cohen, then with the US Trade Representative Office in Tokyo, was even more besotted. When Masako's engagement was announced he was quoted in the Tokyo Press as saying:

She is living proof that typifies Japan's progress in the education system, and the increase in women's status in the past 30 or 40 years. You would not have been able to meet someone like her before.

But she was not all work and no play. A former senior colleague of hers says that 'in the office she was serious and sombre, but away from work she could be fun'. She and her work-mates went occasionally on office skiing trips, or visits to *onsen*, hot spring hotels in resort towns such as Hakone and Atami, where in between bouts of soaking in scalding mineral waters – a favourite Japanese pastime – Masako would join in singing popular karaoke numbers such as 'From Canada', and 'I Start the Journey One Fine Day'.

And so the months turned to years, her thirtieth birthday loomed, and one by one her girlfriends from school and university left their jobs to marry – Masako was in great demand as a speaker at their wedding parties, but there was still no sign of anyone special in her own life. She 'tightened her loin-cloth' and worked even harder.

Naturally, not everyone had the same high regard for the bright young diplomat in her uniform of black suit, white blouse clasped at the neck, and bobbed hair. Conspicuous success always breeds jealousy. Off the record, some of her former colleagues said that they felt that Masako had been put on a 'super fast track' because of her influential father. One of her more outspoken critics, Eric Johnston, the *Japan Times* correspondent, who is now the paper's deputy editor, describes Masako as 'very, very highly-strung, with zero tolerance of any criticism of herself, her work, her ability or of *Gaimusho*'. He says that when Masako eventually left to get married 'some of her colleagues were virtually dancing in the halls . . . they found her aloof, impersonal, and not very competent. She was given too much responsibility too soon'.

Johnston relates a story which I also heard second-hand from another Western journalist. They say that Masako was summoned one day to a meeting at the US Embassy in Tokyo for talks on computer-chip imports with a negotiator who had flown over from Washington. Masako arrived poorly briefed, and the US negotiator 'tore into her'. She responded by bursting into tears, walked out of the meeting and left the embassy. Later, Japanese diplomats had to apologise for her behaviour to the then US Ambassador, Michael Armacost. This incident seems out of character, and may be coloured by the fact that, as we have seen already, Masako and the media do not get on. I tried to contact the former ambassador at Stanford University, where he is now teaching, to ask him to confirm or deny the story, but could get no response.

Yukie Kudo, the economist-turned-TV-anchor, also

thinks Masako's talents have been exaggerated by a fawning media. 'Her real nickname was "black box" because you could never tell what she was thinking, when her work was going to be finished, or what form it would be in,' she says, in her cut-glass English. 'She was a very gentle, kind, sensitive person, but she did not strike me as having any interesting insights or ideas. She was a nice lady to talk to at a party or a reception, but you didn't get a lot back.'

While Masako was making a name for herself in the Foreign Ministry, Naruhito seems to have whiled away his time in the big, empty palace which he now had to himself, doing very little. In January 1989 Hirohito died at the age of 87, after reigning for 62 years – the longest of any non-mythological emperor. He was posthumously given the name of *Showa* or 'radiating peace', which many thought quite Orwellian considering his role in the world's most devastating war. He died of cancer of the duodenum from which he had been suffering for several years, but until his death neither the emperor, nor the public, was told – a practice still common among Japanese doctors who believe it causes the patient unnecessary anxiety.

Akihito became the new emperor and he moved with Michiko and their two younger children, Prince Akishino and Princess Sayako, up the road to the imperial palace. Japan's monarch, incidentally, has neither a throne nor a crown, and his succession ceremony is as shrouded in secrecy as his marriage. It involves a solitary all-night vigil communing with the ghosts of his ancestors in a Shinto shrine.

After their departure, Naruhito was left to his own devices, surrounded by his chamberlains, equerries, chefs and maids in the East Palace. In 1991 he was officially proclaimed heir to the throne, and was invested as crown prince. At the age of 31 – a year beyond the marriage deadline he had publicly set himself – he became the oldest single heir to the throne in history. He was unmarried and unhappy, with his parents and courtiers increasingly thinking the unthinkable: that he might one day die without an heir, bringing down the curtain on a dynasty that had lasted for more than 2600 years.

The bride-hunting committee kept pushing brown envelopes into his hand, and Naruhito dutifully agreed to meet some of the young women they were proposing. 'The daughter of a friend of (Akihito)' was the magazines' hot tip for a while. 'The pretty and talented daughter of an ambassador' rejected his advances. The family of 'an heiress to the Mitsui fortune' said no. Then there was an 'academic from Gakushuin University'. The prince met her four times for cakes, tea, and *soba* noodles, the peeking tabloids reported, before she, too, faded from the scene. Some blot on the family escutcheon, it was whispered.

Some of those *omiai* were held at the home of Isamu Kamata, the prince's trusted friend and fellow musician. 'After Masako said "no", the *Kunaicho* suggested many names, and so did I,' he told me. 'There were lots of very nice girls in the [Gakushuin alumni] orchestra, but either he was not interested, or they said "no". Their fathers would say "If he was not the crown prince I'd agree to the marriage". It is nothing like Snow White; they know that their daughter would become like a prisoner, she would lose her freedom. If she wanted to come to a club like this [he gestured around the Foreign Correspondents' Club] or go to a beauty shop or a department store it would not be possible.'

As each birthday went by, the prince had to endure the same gentle grilling at his press conference – phrased in exquisitely polite language pre-approved by the *Kunaicho*, but inescapable: when was he going to get married? On one occasion, a reporter coyly invited the prince to compare his search for a bride with climbing Mount Fuji, the sacred peak west of Tokyo that Naruhito had scaled more than once. Entering into the spirit of things, the prince estimated that he was at the 'seventh or eighth' of the ten way-stations that break the steep, shaly ascent. 'I can see the top of the mountain, but I cannot get there easily,' he said. But it was becoming increasingly apparent to observers such as the veteran royal reporter Matsuzaki that the prince's heart wasn't in it. His thoughts were elsewhere.

As crown prince, Naruhito began performing some official duties – receiving ambassadors, attending functions, taking an occasional overseas trip. He laboured over his Oxford thesis. Sometimes, he would kit himself out for a solitary climb up a mountain, his only companions his official minders and a straggle of out-of-breath journalists. It was through this hobby that he met Gregory Clark, the former Australian journalist and long-time Tokyo resident. Clark is also a keen mountaineer, and around 1990 had written an article about a particular climb for an obscure mountaineers' journal. To his surprise, he received a phone call from one of Naruhito's minders who asked whether he and his wife would mind popping over to the East Palace for a chat.

The prince, Clark discovered, wanted to climb a peak called Kitadake in the Southern Alps, taking a little-frequented route up the back of the mountain which Clark knew about. After they had discussed the climb, the prince seemed in no hurry for them to leave, so they remained chatting about the great time the prince had at Oxford. This was the impression Clark came away with:

He came over as a pretty boring sort of guy, nice but boring. All the effort to make conversation had to be on my part, not his. You wondered what he does all day. He was surrounded by men, valets and so on who kept poking their heads around the door. They seemed to control his life . . . they [the royals] have almost no independence – they can't even see their parents when they want to. They just sit there like shags on rocks. I felt sorry for the guy. He really was like a bird in a gilded cage.

The years dragged by. In the summer of 1990 the prince's younger brother Akishino, the moustachioed, catfish-loving good-time boy of the royal family, married his girlfriend Kiko Kawashima, the daughter of a Gakushuin University professor, becoming the second prince to take a commoner as his bride. This was a shattering breach of imperial precedent in more ways than one. Protocol dictates that the older brother marry first. But this was not entirely the fault of Naruhito, the reluctant bridegroom. Akishino's carousing around the nightclubs of Tokyo and the flesh-pots of Bangkok had become the talk of the town. According to the journalist Edward Klein, he had earned the nickname 'Fast Hands'. Kenichi Asano, a professor of journalism at Doshisha University and a long-time critic of the royal family says he knows two of the women the prince had affairs with, one the daughter of a personal friend. The Kawashimas were also insisting he make an honest woman of their daughter. So it was decided that the prince had to be taken out of circulation before any more permanent damage was done to the royal reputation.

None of this scandal, it goes without saying, has been

reported in Japan. The Japanese media have a respectful, almost reverential, attitude towards the imperial family, unlike their counterparts in Britain and Europe. In part, says Asano – who was a bureau chief for Kyodo, Japan's national news agency – this reflects the *kisha kurabu* system where reporters are assigned to a particular round, and become beholden to the organisation they are covering. 'Political reporters are mostly the lap-dogs of prominent politicians,' he is fond of lecturing his students. 'Police reporters are police officials with pens. Ninety per cent of the output of Kyodo is press releases.'

And the 300 or so journalists officially accredited to the imperial press club are not only under the thumb of the *Kunaicho*, they also exercise an unusual degree of self-censorship. I met a member of the club for coffee one morning in a grand hotel across the road from the palace, an earnest young newspaperman in a black suit who was waiting for his big assignment of the day – a photo opportunity of Princess Sayako admiring some cherry blossom. What would happen, I asked him, if he got a real royal scoop – for instance, incontrovertible evidence that Naruhito and Masako had a test-tube baby. He would try and ask them if it was true, said the journalist. And if he could get no confirmation? 'I could not report it – as a man, I could not disturb their happiness.' Another club member interviewed on condition of anonymity by David McNeill, the Japan correspondent for the *Irish Times*, said royal reporters were further constrained by having to get their stories '120 per cent' accurate. 'If I make a mistake in a business or a crime story I have to apologise,' he explained. 'But if I make a mistake in a story about the emperor, the head of the newspaper [company] has to apologise.'

Members of the club are housed on the second floor of the *Kunaicho* building inside the palace grounds, where they mostly hang around waiting for a press release or a photo opportunity. One word out of place, one tiny breach of etiquette, and they will find themselves on the outer – or worse. The press corps is still aflutter about the photographer who took a perfectly innocuous but 'unapproved' picture at Prince Akishino's wedding (his bride was brushing a stray quiff of hair from his forehead), who was subsequently sacked. They have to abide by several pages of rules setting out their code of conduct – for instance, it is forbidden to walk down the middle of the red carpets in the corridors of the palace. That is the 'royal road' reserved for the emperor – everyone else must skulk along the edges, as David McNeill discovered a couple of years ago when he was allowed into the palace to cover Emperor Akihito receiving the Irish Prime Minister, Bertie Ahern:

> We were met by . . . a superbly unpleasant and sniffy bureaucrat, who did not feel the need to smile or even greet us in the usual formal Japanese way . . . He complained that it was 'rude' to turn up in informal clothes to meet His Majesty [and] then berated me for walking in the centre of the long hallway leading to the meeting room. 'Only His Majesty walks in the centre,' he said, banishing me to the edge of the carpet . . . We were told we would have only 90 seconds to [take the] photograph. We should be careful not to make any noise when we entered the room. We would leave directly afterwards.

My own close encounter with the Men in Black is somewhat of an anticlimax. It has taken two months of rebuffs by telephone and letter to arrange this meeting, and a second meeting will be required before the *Kunaicho* is satisfied with my credentials. Arriving at the nearest subway station, Nijubashimae, I step past an orderly row of homeless men sleeping on pieces of cardboard with their shoes removed and neatly placed nearby. The palace is a short walk away, over a bridge which spans the turbid green 'inner moat' where Australia's swimming champion, Dawn Fraser, took a dip during the Tokyo Olympics, before shinning up a flagpole to souvenir a flag – and getting herself banned from international competition. Today there are only white swans to be seen gliding about.

Even though it is a steamy summer's day, I am sweating in a business shirt and tie and a black suit, which I imagine – based on David McNeill's experience – to be the correct uniform for those seeking an audience with the *Kunaicho*. At the gate-keeper's lodge, I am given a visitor's pass embossed with an imperial paulownia blossom, and a guard points me towards a gloomy-looking building of grey stone where the imperial press officers are housed. Climbing three floors on a rather worn pinkish-red carpet, I glance into offices and notice, among the standard-issue government furniture, sacks of soft-drink cans, chopsticks and paper plates, the garbage from a party.

I am met by three unassuming middle-aged men, all comfortable in open-necked shirts. The Men in Grey and White. My attempt at formality has been foiled – since I was last in Tokyo, trendy Junichiro Koizumi, the prime minister, has launched a catchy campaign called 'Cool-biz' to encourage Tokyo's regimented *sararimen* to conserve energy by cutting back on the air-conditioning and dressing more appropriately for the climate. Tie manufacturers are screaming blue murder. After a round of bowing and the ritual of the two-handed exchange of business cards, I ask whether my request for an interview with the royal couple has been granted. That would be 'difficult', they say – code for 'no'. May I ask why? 'It has never been done before,' says one of them. Has my request even been passed on to Naruhito and Masako? They look at each other in silence. It's pretty obvious that I haven't even penetrated the outer defences of the *Kunaicho*, so what's the point of being here?

'Well,' suggests one of the officials, 'perhaps we can help with photographs for your book.' This is actually one of the more subtle ways in which the agency manages the image of the royal family. News agency photographs can cost $200 or $300 each, but *Kunaicho*'s official pictures are available for about $10 a pop, to approved clients, and have a quaint, stilted charm in their 'look at the birdie' naïvety. To gain approval, I have to sign two letters – one in Japanese, one in English – in which I solemnly swear that this book will not contain anything scurrilous, and will not defame anyone. Fortunately there is no definition of either term.

The pictures eventually arrive, and the *Kunaicho* is also happy to answer questions of fact which arise while I am putting this book together. It would be churlish to say that they have not been helpful, although I am dealing with low-level officials in the media office, not the haughty heads of household whom McNeill and others have encountered. The *Kunaicho* is also not a monolithic organisation, and within it are competing factions, some seeking to gradually modernise the monarchy, others fighting tooth and nail to preserve the *status quo* unchanged.

Unlike, say, Thailand, Japan no longer has an actual law of *lèse majesté*. Criticising the royal family will not get you locked up, although it might not so long ago have got you murdered. As well as the agency's formal restrictions on media coverage of the imperial family, there is widespread fear that any criticism of the royals, no matter how mild, may attract the wrath of Japan's right-wingers, ageing ultra-nationalists who drill in uniform with wooden rifles in the grounds of Yasukuni Shrine, Japan's controversial war memorial, where the country's war dead, including 14 hanged for war crimes, are honoured.

These right-wing groups have links with the *yakuza* crime syndicates, and many make a living out of petty extortion and blackmail – for instance charging companies protection money for not disrupting their annual meetings, the speciality of niche crooks called *sokaiya*. Back in 1960 one of these gangs of self-styled patriots took violent exception to a parody by a radical writer named Shichiro Fukazawa, in which he depicts leftists storming the imperial palace and beheading Akihito and Michiko. In retaliation, a teenage fanatic invaded the house of the president of the publishing company, Hoji Shimanaka, hacked his maid to death with a sword and wounded his wife. Even nearly 50 years on, the case is still cited with a shudder by writers and publishers to justify the kid-gloves treatment accorded the royal family.

These days the right-wingers mostly make a nuisance of themselves driving around in black-painted omnibuses adorned with rising sun flags bellowing patriotic slogans through megaphones. Or, at least, they used to until the local authorities found a cunning way to shut them up by banning diesel-powered trucks from central Tokyo. 'Return the Northern Territories!' used to be a favourite – referring to the Kurile Islands, seized by the Soviet Union in the dying days of the war. Occasionally one of the more rabid of them will take exception to something on TV or in one of the newspapers – recently, for instance, there were threats against the left-leaning *Asahi* newspaper over something as minor as getting Masako's honorific wrong, referring to her as Masako-*san*, rather than the more respectful Masako-*sama*. But it is many years since the last major outrage when, in 1989, right-wing thugs shot and nearly killed the Mayor of Nagasaki, Hitoshi Motoshima, for suggesting that Hirohito bore responsibility for Japan's involvement in World War II.

There is also a strong current of self-censorship in coverage of the royal family. Japanese media tend to regard themselves as part of the Establishment, and thus rarely need reminding what is 'appropriate' to publish. But this self-regulation does not apply to the more irreverent foreign language publications in Tokyo which can find themselves the victims of heavy-handed black letter censorship when they dare to show disrespect towards the monarchy.

Greg Starr was editor of a lively news-and-entertainment publication called the *Tokyo Journal* in 1993 when it tried to publish an issue spoofing the wedding of Naruhito and Masako with *origami*, board games, puzzles and cryptic crosswords. Their publisher, a company called Toppan, flatly refused to print something so disrespectful, and negotiations went back and forth for days before a sufficiently bowdlerised compromise was agreed on. As Starr remembers it the main points of contention were a veiled hint that the emperor was responsible for the war, and a pictorial makeover of Sayako, then the unmarried 'ugly duckling' of the royal family, in which her hair was remodelled to look like Madonna's. Others believe it was a reference to the size of the crown prince's penis in a board-game that was the problem.

With such a docile media, it came as no surprise in February of 1992 when the Japan Newspaper Association, the organisation representing Japan's 150 or so daily newspapers, news agencies and broadcasters, was summoned to a meeting with *Kunaicho*'s top brass. There was, they were lectured, too much publicity being given to the crown prince's long and futile search for a bride – it was putting the girls off. While such an approach is not unheard-of in the West – there was an unofficial and rather leaky Fleet Street agreement not to intrude on Prince William's schooling, for instance – one cannot imagine any British editor agreeing to suppress reporting on the courtship of their own crown prince, Charles, and Lady Diana Spencer. Not so in Japan. Just as things were about to get interesting, a total blackout descended on all the 'princess candidates' 'in line with their human rights and privacy'. It was time for Naruhito to make his move.

The crown prince was by now finding excuses to avoid meeting any more potential partners, says Kamata. When Shoichi Fujimori, a palace official, asked him what the problem was, Naruhito replied, not for the first time, 'I see that Owada-san is still single.' In spite of the stilted circumlocutions of the court, the message was lost on neither the Imperial Household Agency nor his parents. The prince was making it clear that that he was not interested; if Masako could not be his, then he would remain a bachelor, no matter the consequences. In this he seems to have won the all-important backing of his mother, who had been urging her favourite son from the start to follow his heart. Accepting the inevitable, the *Kunaicho* reluctantly fell into line.

Disposing of the 'Chisso Problem', which had been used as an excuse to derail the romance five years before, was relatively simple, since, as we have seen, there was never really a problem from the start. The Marunouchi lawyer promptly 'discovered' that Masako's grandfather had played no part in the mass poisoning of the people of Minamata. However, two apparently immovable obstacles remained. The first was that Masako's influential father remained opposed to the match, and without his consent she would never agree. The second was Masako herself – she was adamant that she did not want to get married just yet, to Naruhito or anyone else. She had her heart set on a career that she hoped would lead her within a decade or so to becoming an ambassador, only the third or fourth woman to hold such a distinguished position. If that meant her being jeered at as a 'Christmas cake', the Japanese term for a single woman approaching 30 who is 'past her use-by date', then so be it.

It was not revealed until nearly a decade later that, deeply concerned about the impasse, Akihito himself intervened. According to a tape-recorded diary made shortly before his death, Tametoshi Irie, a distinguished old retired palace grand chamberlain and confidant of the emperor, received a phone call from him one night. 'I need your help,' he said. Naruhito was in love – but the Owada family was resisting the idea of him marrying Masako.

Whatever their failings, the men of the *Kunaicho* are not without influence and connections in the backrooms of Kasumigaseki, Tokyo's bureaucratic bee-hive. Irie set about finding intermediaries who could exercise leverage on Hisashi Owada – or, as he would prefer to put it, remind him of his 'duty as a Japanese'. The name he came up with first was that of Kensuke Yanagiya, a 68-year-old public service mandarin, a former Ambassador to Australia and top bureaucrat at the Foreign Affairs Department, who was

then serving as head of the Japan International Cooperation Agency, a foreign aid organisation. For a bureaucrat,
Yanagiya is surprisingly forthright, and had been forced
to resign from the ministry after offending China with
remarks critical of the Chinese leader Deng Xiaoping.
More importantly, he was seven years Hisashi's senior at
Gaimusho and had a *sempai/kohai* relationship with him,
the strong senior/junior bond which Japanese form at
school and in the workplace which binds both in a complex
web of lifelong obligations, responsibilities and rights.

A phone call was made, and one day in May Yanagiya
knocked on the Owadas' door in Meguro with the unwel-
come news that 'Naruhito is saying that he wants to
welcome Masako as [his] princess'. Yanagiya has down-
played his role in the delicate dance that followed, saying
publicly only that he was 'one small cog in the wheel', but
few underestimate the influence he brought to bear. His
visit was just the start of weeks and months of subtle
pressure and inducements to persuade Masako's parents,
principally her domineering father, to change their minds.
During the negotiations, Hisashi would have been left in
little doubt that the future of the monarchy was in the
balance, a quite unbearable burden for a loyal public
servant. 'Of course there was a lot of pressure, but also
there were advantages,' says Matsuzaki. 'If the marriage
went ahead it would be very prestigious for *Gaimusho*,
and also for Owada personally.'

It took three long months for the parties to reach the
consensus required by Japanese social etiquette. Owada
dropped his opposition to the courtship; he told his
daughter that it was her decision. Now it was up to
Masako.

On 16 August 1992, a humid, cloudy Sunday, an

unmarked station-wagon with curtains drawn across its back windows pulled out of the East Palace gates. It was to be a real cloak-and-dagger rendezvous, the first time the love-lorn prince had seen the woman he had pined for in five years. Although the media had agreed to continue its self-imposed blackout on news of the royal romance, Naruhito was taking no chances. Only a couple of his most trusted aides had been told of the assignation; the rest of the gossipy palace staff were kept in the dark.

The vehicle pulled up outside Yanagiya's house in Tokyo's Chiyoda district and the crown prince went inside. Masako had already arrived, driven there by her sister Setsuko in her blue Honda Inspire. There for four hours, the two chatted alone in Yanagiya's lounge room. Naruhito told friends he sympathised with Masako over her having been hounded by the media. 'It must have been an ordeal,' said the prince. It was getting dark when they said their goodbyes, exchanged phone numbers, and slipped away into the summer evening.

It is pretty obvious that Masako was still not convinced. Although she had done much of her growing-up overseas, she would have well understood the restrictions that would be placed on her life as a royal. She still had a lot to prove to herself – and her father – at work. And maybe she simply didn't fancy the diminutive self-effacing prince. But Naruhito insisted he had to see her again. 'Whatever you do, don't propose on the phone,' his mother had scolded him. So six weeks later Masako agreed to meet him once more, this time at the unlikely venue of the royal duck-pond.

Among the vast estates which the imperial family once owned are several choice pieces of real estate which they were allowed to continue using when the emperor's assets were confiscated and transferred to the State after the war, some 25 square kilometres of properties in total. Among them are holiday homes they decamp to by special train for weeks on end – in the forest at Nasu, at Shimoda on the Izu Peninsula where there is a private beach reserved for the royals, at Hayama in Kanagawa Prefecture, and in Tochigi Prefecture where there is a royal horse-stud. Life as a member of the Japanese imperial family does have its compensations. And then there is the duck-pond, actually more of a lake, on three hectares of land at Shin Hama, near Ichikawa City, on the boggy shores of Tokyo Bay.

Established nearly a century ago on the lines of the estates once patronised by fox- and grouse-hunting European royalty, this was where the emperor and his guests used to go to shoot wild ducks. These days, however, it is a place for kinder, gentler pursuits. A white wooden decoy is used to lure the ducks to the lake, which are then captured in hand-held nets a bit like large lacrosse sticks, banded, and released. On the first Saturday in October, Naruhito again smuggled himself out of the East Palace behind the curtains of the station-wagon, unbeknown to most of the servants who brought lunch of fruit and noodles to his room believing the prince was still there. Another car picked up Masako, and they rendezvoused at the duck-pond.

Goodness knows what Masako thought of the venue, but it was here, amid the quacking and splashing, that Naruhito chose to pop the question. They strolled around the lake, played a game of quoits, and then he plucked up the courage to ask her to marry him. Masako must have known what was coming, and worried about finding a formula to politely refuse – saying 'no' to a crown prince would be a serious solecism. According to friends in whom

Pomp and circumstance . . . Naruhito, decked out in a traditional *oninoho* outfit, is escorted into the sacred shrine where the secret wedding ceremony will take place.

Here comes the bride . . . With attendants carrying the train of her 16-kilogram robe and led by a shrine high-priest, Masako enters the 'awe inspiring place' where she will be admitted to the imperial family.

The official wedding photo . . . Naruhito and Masako decked out in elaborate costumes modelled on those worn in the Heian court 600 years ago.

The happy couple . . . Naruhito and Masako wave to the crowds as they drive to their palace after the wedding.

Attending to formalities . . . Flanked by chamberlains and ladies-in-waiting, Naruhito officially presents his bride to his parents with the requisite 60-degree bows before their first formal lunch together.

A ray of sunlight in the midst of economic gloom . . . Tokyo celebrates the nuptials with a street procession.

Meeting the in-laws . . . Masako (*centre*) with (*from left*) former Princess Sayako, Emperor
Akihito, Crown Prince Naruhito, Empress Michiko, Prince Akishino and his wife,
Princess Kiko.

BEN HILLS

Prisoners of the palace . . .
Iron grilles, guard-posts and
armed police surround the
East Palace, home to Masako
and Naruhito.

Getting away from it all, not . . . Masako and Naruhito are never far from the prying eyes of the paparazzi, even on a mountaineering outing.

HARUMI KOBAYASHI

HARUMI KOBAYASHI

Official duties . . . Masako gives the crowd her special wave at the royal family's New Year's appearance.

The ultimate in tackiness . . .
A saleswoman holds up a special
version of Rika-chan, a popular doll,
made to commemorate Masako's
pregnancy. A turn of a key returns the
stomach to 'normal'.

A child, at last . . . Nearly nine years after their marriage, Masako and Naruhito
welcome Aiko into the world.

Smile for the birdie . . . The royal couple puts on a brave face for the fans when they arrive for a holiday in the country.

BEN HILLS

IMPERIAL HOUSEHOLD AGENCY

The little girl some wanted to be the next emperor . . . Aiko gardening with her mother in the East Palace grounds.

All smiles on the outside, but after ten years of marriage Masako is secretly suffering from depression.

she confided, she replied, 'I will reply to you properly later, but would it be all right if the answer was "no"?' After Masako spent days and sleepless nights talking it over with her family and friends, her father telephoned an inter- mediary and said that Masako was 'unable to decide' – the closest he could manage to 'no'.

But Naruhito turned on his stubborn streak. He tele- phoned Masako several times asking for another date, and eventually she succumbed. They met again three weeks later, this time in his quarters at the East Palace. According to the unofficial *Kunaicho* history of the affair – the agency had been briefing reporters in the imperial press club, even though they could publish nothing – Masako 'for the first time had a full, personal talk with the crown prince'. Again he asked her to marry him, and again she begged for time to think it over. Masako was later to say that she 'agonised considerably' over whether to accept the proposal and abandon the career for which she had fought so hard. Under the strain of it all, she fell sick, and had to take a fortnight off work. The leaves on the birch trees around the palace turned lemon and fell to the ground as the dark winter nights closed in and Naruhito burned with unrequited love.

Eventually the emperor and empress themselves had to intervene again. There are various versions of what happened. Most well-connected sources say that Michiko made a personal telephone call to the Owadas, in which she assured Masako and her parents that she would do her best to protect their daughter if she would agree to marry her son. According to one account, by Edward Klein in *Vanity Fair* magazine, Michiko actually arranged a secret face-to-face meeting with Masako at the home of Isamu Kamata, the royal family's musician friend, driving there in the familiar curtained car. There she offered Masako – who had 'dark splotches under her eyes and looked as though she hadn't slept for days' – her personal promise of protection.

This version of events is impossible to verify. It has been officially denied by *Kunaicho* (though they would, wouldn't they) and Kamata refuses to comment. As well, I am always suspicious of what purports to be a verbatim transcript of a private conversation between two people, neither of whom has ever discussed it publicly.

What seems to have tipped the balance, according to well-informed palace observers such as Akira Hashimoto, is that Naruhito himself, head over heels in love, made promises to Masako – promises he could not keep. Hashimoto is a small, neat man with a blotchy face and a 'lazy' eye who looks closer to 50 than his real age of mid-seventies. He is another veteran of the imperial beat who went to school and university with Emperor Akihito. One of his claims to fame is that, as schoolboys, he and Akihito played hooky one night, scoffing cakes and coffee in the bright lights of Ginza shopping district while police frantically searched for the missing prince. We meet in the boardroom of a borrowed office on the thirty-fifth floor of the Green Hills office tower in inner-city Kamiyacho, overlooking the dense white cloud of photochemical smog, pierced with the surrealistic ceramic-clad spires of municipal garbage-incinerators, that shrouds Tokyo in summer.

Hashimoto believes that Masako tried to fob off Naruhito's advances by telling the prince that she wanted to devote her life to public service, particularly to improving Japan's relations with the rest of the world as a diplomat. Naruhito countered by saying that if she married him:

... she would become a kind of royal diplomat, accompanying him on overseas trips. He used [the promise of] a diplomatic role as a wooing tool, and that was a great mistake. The royal family are just symbols, they are not part of the diplomatic service . . . it could not happen. He made a promise he could not keep. He was stupid to make it, and she was stupid to believe it.

Perhaps Masako was also now starting to realise, after three years in the job, that carving a career for herself in the foreign ministry was a far more formidable task than even she had expected. According to Irie, the emperor's ageing confidant, '. . . she began to sense that the reality of the life of a foreign bureaucrat was somewhat different from what she imagined . . . [that] the Foreign Ministry was the type of organisation that would not elevate a woman higher than section-manager level no matter how talented she was.'

Most likely it was a combination of all three factors that finally persuaded Masako to change her mind. Her father – whose approval she valued above all else – was no longer opposed to the marriage. Indeed, while dreading the media circus, he must have been quietly proud that he was restoring the family's honour, languishing since his samurai ancestors were turfed out of their castle in Murakami. As far as her career was concerned, Masako may have genuinely believed that, with her husband's help, she could modernise the monarchy and carve out a useful role for herself. Finally, the prince was a charming, educated man with whom she shared many interests. He was madly in love with her, he had promised to protect her . . . and he wasn't *that* bad-looking.

On 12 December 1992 she went to the East Palace, bowed deeply to the prince, and gave him the news he had been waiting for since they first met more than five years before. To a Western ear it sounds strangely strained and subservient, but this is the language of respect that a commoner must use to address a royal in Japan: 'If I can be of support to you, I would like to humbly accept. Since I am accepting, I will work hard to make Your Highness happy, and also to be able to look back on my life and think "It was a good life." ' In return, Naruhito pledged: 'I will be by your side and will do everything in my power to protect you from any possible hardships throughout my life.' No prize for guessing from whom – the crown prince was promising to shield Masako from the bureaucrats and others who had made his mother's life so miserable, driving her to a nervous breakdown. Hashimoto was the third person to whom Naruhito broke the great news, after his parents. 'It was a long road,' sighed the persistent prince.

There were still weeks of planning before the engagement could be announced, and six months of formalities leading up to the wedding itself. On Christmas Day Masako returned to the East Palace to see the prince once more, and to meet the future in-laws again. On 8 January a grand steward, stiff in his morning-coat, rapped on the Owadas' door to formally propose the betrothal. On 19 January an august body known as the Imperial Household Council, which includes the prime minister of the day, the speakers of both houses of parliament, the chief justice of the Supreme Court, the head of the *Kunaicho* and the emperor, convened to formally approve the engagement.

With all these comings and goings the Men in Black

would have been the only ones surprised that they were unable to keep a lid on things. The timing of the announcement was taken out of their hands. As a final indignity, the Japanese media, which had been faithfully keeping their promise not to report on the prince's romance, got scooped on the story – by a foreign newspaper. The media organisations had all agreed to simultaneously break the news, and had huge teams of reporters out gathering background material for the coverage, which they were ready to run whenever the *Kunaicho* gave the nod. However, Tom Reid of the *Washington Post* got a tip-off from one of his contacts and broke the story on 7 January 1993.

It only made a small item on an inside page of the paper, but when wire services relayed the news back to Japan all hell broke loose. If you think the West is celebrity-obsessed you should see the Japanese media in full cry. The six Tokyo TV networks broke into their normal daytime schedule of talk shows and corny samurai dramas to air endless hours of footage and commentary. Every aspect of Masako's life was turned over, from her Moscow kindergarten days to her battered grey Foreign Ministry desk with its telephone stained with inky finger-prints, the pedigree of her pet terrier Chocolat to her liking for *ma po dofu* (spicy Sichuan bean curd), her softball prowess to her taste in Hermès silk scarves – one channel devoted an entire program to a demonstration of scarf-tying, Masako-style. Even the financial press got in on the act, printing a summary of her Harvard economic thesis. Friends and relatives suddenly found their houses under siege. Kumi Hara, Masako's old school-chum, came home to find her house surrounded by black media vehicles, with reporters shoving microphones and cameras into her face. She called Masako who said: 'Yes, it's amazing. There are helicopters hovering over our house. Chocolat wants to go to the bathroom but we can't get out of the house.'

Newspapers and magazines rolled out special editions with adulatory commentary. Masako was 'Japan's new sweetheart', gushed *Newsweek* magazine. 'This is the greatest news of the century,' enthused Rokuro Ishikawa, chairman of the Japan Chamber of Commerce. Equally over-the-top comments came from Masako's friends, colleagues and teachers overseas. In *Vogue* magazine, Susan Pharr, a Professor of Japanese Studies at Harvard and a friend and mentor of Masako's, was quoted as saying: 'Japan never had a Jackie Kennedy or a [Winston] Churchill. When we think of Japan we think of faceless, colourless bureaucrats. Masako will change that.' Once again Masako was being weighed down by expectations. Hardly surprisingly, in view of the way things actually turned out, an obviously embarrassed Pharr declined to revisit her comments when I contacted her. In the same article, Kumiko Inoguchi, a friend of Masako's at Harvard now teaching political science at Sophia University in Japan, was quoted as saying:

> *Prince Charles married a good-looking virgin [who was] interested in tap-dancing and discos. He had nothing in common with her, and look at the mess they are in. You've got to hand it to our prince – he's chosen to have a truly modern marriage.*

Amid the euphoria I found a few more moderate and measured comments in the files, although they appear to have been drowned out by the cheer squads. The *Asahi* newspaper editorialised: 'If she ends up politely smiling "royal smiles" then the crown prince's choice of bride will not have been put to good use.' Precisely what Masako herself must have been thinking as she prepared for her marriage.

To begin with, Michiko went out of her way to make Masako welcome. In her new life as crown princess, this was to be her most important new relationship – and not only because of Michiko's influence over her devoted son. Getting on well with the mother-in-law is an asset in any marriage in the West. In Japan, where aged care is not well developed, it is essential as it is still widely regarded as the duty of the daughter-in-law to care for her husband's parents in their old age.

Japanese princes do not give engagement rings, so Michiko presented Masako with an heirloom platinum ring set with a seven-carat ruby which had belonged to her own mother-in-law, the Empress Nagako. More importantly, she welcomed Masako's family to a private banquet at the palace, something her own family, ostracised by the sniffy Nagako, had been denied. The media drooled over the menu: soup, smoked salmon and sea scallops arranged in the shape of a heart, oyster fritters and strawberry *bavarois*, washed down with fine wines from the imperial cellars. What a glittering night it must have been for the socially ambitious Owadas as they sat there dining with the royal family at a table spread with starched napery and heavy with antique silver, with five wineglasses lined up at every place, and the menus embossed with the imperial chrysanthemum, the ultimate seal of social success. How full of hope they must also have been that their misgivings about the marriage would prove unfounded.

The months went by and wedding plans proceeded apace. Masako flew through her indoctrination lessons by aged court scholars at *Kunaicho*'s quaintly named

Archives and Mausoleums Department, brushing up on such imperial know-how as calligraphy, poetry and the religious rites of the royal court, but excused English and French because she was already fluent. The engagement gifts were presented – the sea-bream, silk and *sake* delivered to the Owadas' home. Masako's wardrobe underwent an overhaul. Out went the smart suits, bright silk scarves and sensible shoes – she now began to appear in public in dowdy pastel dresses and pillbox hats in girly pinks and yellows. Her steps became shorter, her eyes downcast, her hands folded together in her lap. She even occasionally spent hours kitting herself out in a kimono, the 'special occasion' garment which has fallen out of fashion since the war (except among *geisha* and others in traditional occupations) because many younger women find it expensive, constrictingly uncomfortable, and symbolic of the old-fashioned subservience of women. The *Kunaicho* was recasting a crown princess more to their liking. Masako, brilliant scholar and high-flying career woman, was being made over as a *ryosai kenbo*, a 'good wife and wise mother', said the commentators.

Although all the polls showed that the public was overwhelmingly in favour of the marriage, as the wedding day approached, amid all the enthusiasm, there were some – mainly foreigners – bold enough to say they thought Masako was making a terrible mistake. William Bossert, her old house-master at Harvard, was stunned: 'Why would such a bright woman as Masako do such a thing?' he wondered when he heard about the engagement. Kumi Hara was '. . . very shocked. I know how much effort she put into becoming a diplomat and I could not imagine that she would quit'. Hara was so dismayed that she fled Masako's 'hen's night' to hide in the toilets and cry, and boycotted her old friend's wedding by going to stay with an aunt in New York. Tim Olewine, Masako's English tutor when she joined *Gaimusho*, said: 'I was very sad when I heard about her marriage. She was very down to earth – smart, vivacious, outgoing. You look at her now – three steps behind, no personality, sacrificed for her country.'

Newsweek magazine epitomised the difficulty. Its American edition highlighted the obstacles faced by Masako in joining the imperial family with the headline '*The Reluctant Princess*'. In Japan the magazine ran the same story, but rendered the cover as '*The Birth of a Princess*'. A Japanese editor denied this was censorship, explaining rather feebly that the word 'reluctant' was 'too difficult to translate'. Anna Ogino, an award-winning author and professor at the prestigious Keio University, put her finger on the dilemma facing the commentators: 'It is a turning point for the royal family – whether a talented woman like Masako will be buried under the stereotypes, or become a stimulus to opening up the royal family.'

So who would prove right? Could Naruhito deliver on his promise, and persuade the *Kunaicho* to allow his princess to redefine the role of the monarchy, to devise a meaningful future for herself? Or would she suffocate under the layers of tradition, suffer like Michiko, and end up a royal cipher?

7

Heir Unapparent

'I WANT TO BE FRANK,' SAID THE GRAND CHAMBERLAIN of the East Palace, Tsuyoshi Soga, in a magazine interview a couple of years after the wedding. 'I have plenty of opportunities to see them together. They show their affections so openly it makes me blush.' It was three years after the wedding, and Naruhito and his princess were, to all outward appearances at any rate, blissfully happy. At a press conference, the doting prince confessed that when he was with Masako, 'She is so pleasant [to be with] she makes me unaware of the passing of time.' The naysayers who predicted that Masako would never be able to adjust to the life of rigid protocol behind the Chrysanthemum Curtain looked as though they would have to eat their words.

In private, though, it was a different story. As so often in Japan, there is a gulf between the *tatemae*, the outward façade, and the *honne*, the inner truth. Masako had been trying hard to play the dutiful consort, dressing in those dowdy pastels, walking three paces behind her husband, smiling, waving, and speaking softly if at all. How she must have loathed it. After the debacle of her engagement press conference, where she dared to speak for longer than the crown prince, she had been given precisely one opportunity to speak in public in three years – a few carefully scripted platitudes at a charity function. The Associated Press wire-service dubbed her 'the quiet princess', although by the standards of her predecessors she was positively garrulous. Her mother-in-law Michiko, palace-watchers pointed out, had not been allowed to speak in public at all for the first seven years of her marriage.

Inside the palace, after the giddy whirl of the wedding and the weeks of formalities which followed, life had settled down to a routine. Garden parties were hosted (the annual cherry-blossom viewing is Tokyo society's must-be-there event), ambassadors were welcomed, students on community-work-abroad projects were farewelled, schools and homes for the handicapped and the elderly were visited.

There were regular meetings with the in-laws – informal meals, as well as the grand state banquets and mysterious religious ceremonies – though Masako had lost almost all contact with her own family, as her sad pre-wedding Christmas card had predicted. In her first three years of marriage she was to see them only five times, said the Owada family maid. Friends made appointments for tea, though less and less frequently as time went by – palace officials discouraged such 'personal contacts', and in any case Masako's Japanese friends felt awkward having to address her with the new vocabulary of respect which was required. The newlyweds played tennis, they took summer breaks at one or other of the imperial holiday retreats, Masako dutifully kitted herself out in boots, windcheater and camera and stumped up and down mountains with her husband. Gradually she was losing contact with the world beyond the moat.

Sir Adam Roberts, Masako's old mentor from her Oxford University days, admits to having had 'mixed feelings' when news of her engagement was announced, because of the demands, the protocol and the isolation involved in joining the imperial family. He consoled himself with the hope that '. . . although it was taking out a talent, there was a potential for her to transform the monarchy'. He did not attend the wedding festivities because of other commitments, but over the following decade stayed in touch and visited Masako and Naruhito for tea or dinner at the palace whenever his lecturing duties took him to Japan. As the years went by, he saw her change from 'the old Masako that I remembered, with her quick wit and her very nice sense of humour' to someone quite different:

I would not necessarily say bored but isolated, seriously isolated . . . that business of not being able to go out, to go shopping, to go to exhibitions, to get on the tube [train], to just be yourself. The isolation is a lot to do with the lack of relatives. I don't fully understand that. The imperial family don't have the hinterland of masses of cousins, sisters, aunts and in-laws that, for example, the British or the Dutch or the Norwegian royal families have.

There was an endless round of official duties to keep the couple busy – good training for the day when – if – Naruhito inherits the throne. The emperor is said to have more than 1000 engagements a year, almost three a day, though all are undemanding formal appearances at un-controversial events such as National Arbor Day (a tree-planting ceremony), disabled sports carnivals, and the 'Cherished Sea Festival', which is dedicated to marine conservation. It would be inconceivable for the Japanese royals to be associated with anything as controversial as Princess Diana's championing of land-mine clearing, the AIDS Trust, and the Leprosy Mission. In contrast with Mary Donaldson, who became patron of 17 organisations tackling issues such as mental health and child victims of violent crime during her first two years as Denmark's crown princess, Naruhito and Masako are barred from taking any active role in a charity, with the sole exception of the Red Cross, which the royal women have patronised since Meiji times. The *Kunaicho* must figure that their mere presence at ceremonies promoting blood donation or at the National Convention of Agricultural Youths adds sufficient *kudos* to the cause.

And as for that role of a royal diplomat which her husband had dangled in front of her, in their first five years of marriage, Masako got to visit the VIP departure lounge at Tokyo's international airport, Narita, just twice. On both occasions it was for trips to the Middle East – Oman, Saudi Arabia, Qatar, Bahrain, Jordan, Kuwait and the United Arab Emirates, countries where the influence of women on public affairs is even less than in Japan. All are men-only monarchies of varying degrees of absolutism. By a terrible accident of timing, their second trip, in 1995, had to be abandoned when Japanese television showed the couple watching camel-racing while rescuers battled to recover more than 6000 bodies from the ruins of the port city of Kobe after what became known as the Great Hanshin Earthquake. They had to cut short their trip and rush home so that they could be seen comforting the victims of Japan's greatest disaster since World War II.

It did not take long for the racier magazines to put two and two together. Fuelled by leaks from the *Kunaicho*, they began speculating that Masako had been 'grounded' until she produced an heir. A pointed comparison was made with Akihito and Michiko who, when they were crown prince and princess, had visited no fewer than 37 countries. Naruhito's brother Prince Akishino and sister-in-law Kiko, having produced the requisite child within a couple of years of their wedding, were travelling abroad more often; so even was young sister Sayako. 'Is Masako under house arrest?' asked a contributor to one of the new chat-rooms springing up in cyberspace, unfettered by the constraints of the mainstream media. The agency did nothing to dispel the story, and years later, when he resigned, Toshio Yuasa, grand steward of the imperial household, confirmed that the gossip was true. 'It was painful not to be able to meet the wishes of their majesties regarding overseas trips,' he said. 'I believe my predecessors, too, naturally became cautious due to hopes for the pregnancy of Her Majesty.'

It is about time we digressed here to examine precisely how officials like Yuasa came to wield such power, how the inmates came to be running the asylum. Minoru Hamao, the prince's curmudgeonly former chamberlain, once actually boasted that of all the 'requests' made by the royal family, the *Kunaicho* only 'granted' about ten per cent. Every time Masako wants a new dress, needs a haircut, feels like a drive, wants to meet a friend or take a trip, the officials first have to give their approval, then require days or weeks to make the proper arrangements. Even a visit to Disneyland requires a detail of 1000 security men. She cannot meet her parents without their say-so, nor can Naruhito pop over to the palace to meet *his* parents without an appointment. Everything has to be done according to protocol. Japanese royals, for instance, cannot go to the shops – their purchases have to be handled by special department-store liaison officials who visit the palace with their wares. 'If she wants a book, it will be delivered tomorrow,' says Isamu Kamata, the emperor's friend, 'but she wants to go down to a bookshop in Marunouchi and spend a few hours browsing. That is impossible, they say. And it's not just Masako – the *Kunaicho* will not even listen to the emperor.'

To understand the source of *Kunaicho*'s power, you have to travel back into Japan's dreamtime and learn a little of the traditions and beliefs that underpin the country's identity. The modern agency is the descendant of the ancient imperial court and has been around for more than 1300 years. They were the officials who managed the affairs of the god emperors who claim to descend in an unbroken line from the first emperor, Jimmu, great-grandson of the sun goddess Amaterasu Omikami. The Japanese for Japan is Nippon, 'origin of the sun', and the national flag, the *hinomaru*, is a red disc on a white background. Claiming the authority of the sun is not, incidentally, unique, as Japanese would have the world believe. The Egyptian pharaoh Akhenaton proclaimed the sun to be the sole deity and was named after it. France's Louis XIV was called the Sun King, while the Aztecs made human sacrifices to their sun god.

According to the classic texts the *Kojiki* and *Nihon Shoki*, Japan's earliest written histories, Jimmu became emperor on precisely 11 February 660 BC, which remains a public holiday. This would make the Japanese throne the oldest inherited job in the world – almost three times as ancient as the British monarchy. 2007 marks its 2667th year. But modern scholars debunk these early records as myth, not least because of the improbable longevity of those first emperors. Jimmu allegedly lived to 126, and nine of the next dozen emperors to beyond a century, topped by the lucky Emperor Suinin who died at the ripe old age of 139. The grassy knolls of their enormous supposed 'tombs' dot the landscape around the imperial capital of Nara, though the *Kunaicho*, their custodian, never allows any serious archaeological excavation, for obvious reasons. The first emperor of whom there are more-or-less reliable records is Kimmei (539–571 AD), whose reign saw the official introduction of Buddhism to Japan. However, Japan's ultra-nationalists, along with the Shinto priesthood, insist on the accuracy of the ancient texts, in much the same way as Christian fundamentalists defend the literal truth of the Old Testament. The *Kunaicho* is the guardian of that legend, and woe betide those who dare to dissent.

In 1942 a historian named Sokichi Tsuda was jailed for 'insulting the dignity of the imperial family' by questioning whether the first nine emperors were actually historical characters. This crime of *lèse majesté* was abolished after the war, and nowadays most historians quietly accept that the Yamato people, the ancestors of modern Japanese, did not arrive from the north-east Asian mainland until many centuries after the time of Jimmu. They settled on the fertile plains of central Honshu, Japan's main island, cultivating rice which they had imported with them, and later adopting Chinese as their written language, and establishing their first capitals at Osaka, Nara (710–794 AD) and then Kyoto (794–1868 AD). With them they brought a system of government common in ancient times, consisting of a sovereign/priest whose job was to intercede with the gods, and a secular general/administrator who defended and ran the realm.

Likewise the claim of unbroken male lineage withstands little scrutiny, in what the historian Kenneth Ruoff calls Japan's manufactured tradition. According to the ancient texts themselves, in 592 AD the Emperor Sushun was assassinated leaving no obvious heir; in 858 AD a dispute over succession was decided by a wrestling match. For much of the fourteenth century there were rival dynasties in northern and southern Japan. Eventually the legitimate 'southern emperor' Go-Kameyama surrendered – he journeyed to Kyoto from his capital of Osaka and yielded the sacred insignia, the sword, mirror and jewels, to the 'northern emperor', Go-Komatsu. This rendered all subsequent emperors up to the present day illegitimate, as proud Osakans are fond of pointing out. 'Down here people aren't that interested [in the imperial family],' says Eric Johnston, the Osaka-based journalist. 'They think of them as just a bunch of spoilt aristocrats.'

This system – an emperor who reigned in name alone and left the actual ruling to the *shoguns*, those 'barbarian-subduing generalissimos' – continued right up until the arrival of Commodore Perry's warships in the middle of the nineteenth century. Unlike European monarchs, Japan's emperors did not lead their troops into battle, levy taxes, proclaim laws or form alliances with other countries. The only emperor to break with this tradition and attempt to seize real power was Go-Daigo (1288–1339), who mounted a rebellion which overthrew the Kamakura shogunate. But he was eventually driven into exile in the Yoshino mountains, where he founded the ultimately unsuccessful rival southern dynasty.

What token authority the emperors had was under-mined by the fact that many were enthroned as children as young as eight, with regents ruling in their name. Others were ciphers for their predecessors, who issued their pronouncements from monastic retreats, a system known as 'cloistered rule'. The succession was manipulated by the barons, particularly the powerful Fujiwara clan, who infil-trated wives and concubines into the court. The emperor was little more than a sacred symbol to legitimise the rule of the *shoguns*.

In fact for many centuries most Japanese had never heard of the emperor, and took their orders from the *daimyo*, the *shogun*'s local lord. Foreigners thought the *shogun was* the emperor. When America's first consul, Townsend Harris, arrived in Japan in 1856 he was unaware for more than a year of the existence of the Meiji Emperor and supposed the *shogun* to be the sole ruler. Behind the granite ramparts of his castle in Edo, as Tokyo was then named, Yoshinobu, the fifteenth and last of the Tokugawa *shoguns*, ruled the land – at least until his over-throw – while Mutsuhito, the Meiji Emperor, held court in his secluded palace in Kyoto. Murray Sayle described it thus:

> *The first Westerners who met Meiji in 1867 found a youth of fifteen with a shaved head, blackened teeth, and long, lacquered fingernails – the standard outfit of an Oriental priest/king.*

With the overthrow of the *shoguns* and the installation of a new class of secular rulers to 'advise' him, the role of the emperor took on a new significance. Mutsuhito moved from the obscurity of his palace in Kyoto to the *shogun*'s

great moated castle in Tokyo. While adopting a constitution, a peerage system and a two-tiered parliament from
the West – the grey monolith where Japan's Congress
meets is still called the *Diet* – the emperor became for the
first time in history, at least nominally, a real ruler with
almost absolute power. Under the constitution adopted in
1889, he was both *genshu*, the head of the empire, and
daigenshu, supreme commander of the armed forces. He
had the power to convene and dissolve the parliament,
issue ordinances, and appoint ministers and military
commanders. In 1900, the foundations were laid for 'State
Shinto' with the emperor elevated to a living deity at its
head. A government ministry for the country's 80,000
shrines was established, and all citizens were required to
enrol in a Shinto parish.

But in practice, Japan had changed little. Instead of the
bakufu, the 'tent government' of the military shogunate,
there was now an inner court of elder statesmen, the
genro, drawn from the ranks of those *daimyo* warlords
who had backed the restoration, and the old samurai class.
These were the puppetmasters, the men who – in the name
of the emperor – actually made the decisions that were to
drive Japan's breakneck modernisation. Within half a
century this feudal backwater, where warriors with top-
knots used matchlock rifles and waddled around with their
kimonos tucked between their legs because they had never
heard of marching, underwent a belated industrial revolution which saw it defeat, in short order, both of its mighty
neighbours, China and Russia, and seize vast territories,
from Taiwan in the south to Sakhalin Island in the north
and Manchuria on the Asian mainland. The Korean peninsula was conquered, its last monarch, King Kojong, forced
to abdicate, and his ten-year-old son and heir abducted to

Tokyo where his bloodline was extinguished by marriage into the Japanese nobility. The last sad pretender to the Korean throne died alone and almost unnoticed of a heart attack in a Tokyo hotel room in 2005. After two millennia, the emperor at last had an empire. Japan's economic and military might seemed unstoppable.

While his empire was expanding abroad, the Meiji Emperor was acquiring enormous tracts of land at home, particularly on the northern island of Hokkaido. In 1945, the Americans audited his estates and revealed that the imperial family was Japan's biggest landholder, owning an extraordinary one sixth of the entire land area of Japan. The emperor was the richest individual in the country, and one of the wealthiest in the world, with a fortune in stocks, bonds, bullion and treasure. In today's terms, only the great corporations like Toyota and Mitsui would be in the same league as the Japanese royal family.

And administering this far-flung empire – which included farms, forests, mines and manufacturing, as well as palaces, shrines and those burial mounds – was the *Kunaicho*. In its heyday, the ministry had more than 10,000 employees, and the imperial family which it served numbered close to 100 princes and princesses, each with his own palace and retinue.

When General MacArthur arrived in devastated Tokyo in 1945 to take charge of the country's postwar reconstruction he found the imperial institution battered – the palace had been bombed – but intact. He persuaded President Harry Truman that the monarchy had to be preserved, arguing – in the face of demands from the Allies for the trial of Hirohito for war crimes, and from Japan's radical Left for the abolition of the entire imperial system which it held responsible for the war – that it was essential to retain the emperor if Japan was to survive. He feared that without the legitimacy conferred by the support of Japan's ruling class, the US would have to commit 500,000 men indefinitely to administering the country. As well, Stalin's Soviet empire now stretched to within sight of Hokkaido Island, and the Americans needed Japan as their 'unsinkable battleship' against the advance of Communism.

But there had to be a radical restructuring.

While MacArthur decided that, on practical grounds, the 'emperor system' had to be maintained, its excesses deeply offended his republican sentiments. After all, America fought a war to win its independence from the yoke of British sovereignty. He and his advisors negotiated a new constitution which was duly adopted by the *Diet* in 1946. It established Japan as a Western-style democracy, abandoned war, and defined the role of the emperor – who renounced his divinity – as merely '. . . the symbol of the State and the unity of the people, deriving his position from the will of the people with whom resides sovereign power'. Although he retains a symbolic authority, the only practical impact the emperor has on the life of most Japanese today is that, instead of the Roman calendar, Japanese still count their years from the date of the emperor's accession. 2007, for instance, is Heisei 19, the nineteenth year of the reign of the Heisei Emperor Akihito.

The emperor's authority was curtailed to 'matters of State approved by cabinet'. His sole function was to be ceremonial, to 'promulgate' decisions of the three branches of government: the legislature, the executive and the judiciary. There were other changes. Before the war, teachers had died trying to rescue the emperor's portrait from blazing schools where it had been on display. Today his image does not appear on stamps, bank notes or coins, for the curious reason that this would render it liable to be defaced. The emperor is no longer even the head of state – that function falls to the prime minister – though in practice Hirohito and now Akihito acted as if they were, opening parliament, receiving ambassadors, appointing the Chief Justice of the Supreme Court, awarding honours and so on. As always, the sources of power in Japan remain enigmatic.

In practice, many of MacArthur's reforms failed to take root. Instead of a Western-style democracy, Japan's political system remains a stunted parody, with one party, the conservative Liberal Democratic Party, holding almost unbroken power since the war. Emperor Hirohito, who was supposed to be quarantined from any role in the political process, was found to have been receiving regular secret briefings from his ministers, who still reverentially approached him sideways with their eyes averted, the so-called 'crab walk'. The media continued for years to take his photograph only from a respectful 20 metres away, never while he was smiling, and preferably only showing the upper half of his body and never his back because Hirohito was both bow-legged and stooped.

Next, MacArthur took an axe to the imperial family, declaring:

> For many generations these families have enjoyed privileges and have been accorded honors and dignities to which they had no legal nor moral rights. There are, no doubt, thousands of persons in Japan and other countries who have descended from royal families in the last 500 years but they earn their livelihood and make no ridiculous claims to imperial dignity.

Eleven branches of the family, some 51 princes and princesses, were stripped of their royal status and evicted from their palaces. Hirohito threw a farewell banquet for them at which red and white wine was quaffed one last time, before the crestfallen royals trooped off to join the ragged ranks of the common folk queueing in the ruins for ration-books. Today, their children and grandchildren work in corporations and academic institutions around Tokyo, indistinguishable from other *sararimen* except to those in the know. Princes, and there were several of them, who had served as officers in the military were banned from ever again holding public office. The five-tiered peerage, modelled on that of Prussia, was abolished entirely – more than 900 noble families were no longer allowed to call themselves prince or duke, marquis, count, viscount or baron and lost all their privileges. And there was one other important change: in future, princesses who married would have to leave the imperial family (and the public payroll) and would forfeit any claim to the throne for their children.

The imperial estates, enterprises, palaces and treasures were confiscated and transferred to the State. Many were turned into museums and opened to a curious public for the first time. From now on the remaining royals were to be subject to direction from the Prime Minister's Department, their budget dependent on a grant from parliament. The Imperial Household Agency was decimated, its ranks reduced to the 1100 or so public servants who remain today.

Paradoxically, as *Kunaicho*'s influence on the outside world withered, MacArthur's root-and-branch reforms had the effect of enormously increasing its power over the few remaining royals. Of the dozen or so of Hirohito's brothers, uncles and their wives and children permitted to stay in their palaces, none now had independent wealth or income. This is in stark contrast to most other monarchies around the world. Britain's Queen Elizabeth II, for instance, is still one of the world's wealthiest women, with a fortune estimated by *Forbes* magazine at $650 million, even after her courtiers persuaded the magazine not to count her palaces, which are owned by the State. Her son and heir Prince Charles – Naruhito's counterpart – owns a 58,000 hectare estate, the Duchy of Cornwall, and his Duchy Original organic products business turns over $82 million-worth of oaten biscuits, sausages and ale a year.

And even the British royals are small beer compared with the wealth of other monarchs, led by the oil-rich states of the Middle East and Asia. King Abdullah bin Abdulaziz of Saudi Arabia is the world's wealthiest monarch, and fifth wealthiest man, with a fortune estimated at $27 billion; Sultan Haji Hassanal Bolkiah of Brunei was not far behind on $26 billion; and the reigning Prince Hans-Adam II of Liechtenstein, Naruhito's one-time skiing companion, inherited $5 billion in palaces, real estate, art and even an investment in a US producer of hybrid rice when he took over the throne of the miniscule alpine tax haven.

But the Japanese became royal paupers, dependent on the taxpayer for their living, and thus delivered into the hands of the *Kunaicho* bean-counters. When he died Hirohito left a personal estate worth a mere $25 million, but much of this is believed to be in family artworks and heirlooms rather than stocks and bonds. The imperial family has been whittled down to an inner core of five who own next to nothing in their own right – the Emperor Akihito and Empress Michiko, Naruhito and Masako, and their daughter Aiko. There are 12 other royals and their children on the so-called 'civil list', including Prince Tomohito of Mikasa, a cousin of the emperor, and his family who receive an allowance of almost $700,000 a year, although their royal duties are undemanding, and few Japanese even know who they are. Increasing their dependence, Japanese royals are discouraged from earning anything on the side – the idea of endorsing Weight Watchers for $2 million a year, the way the brassy Sarah Ferguson, Duchess of York, earns a living, would be anathema. Anything they do earn – for instance by writing books, as the Empress Michiko has done – is taxed.

This reliance on the taxpayer also exposes the imperial family to criticism, particularly from the still-noisy Communist Party which believes that the monarchy should be abolished altogether. Japan's imperial family, says Yohei Mori, is not good value for money, costing – per head – almost twice as much as the British royals. Mori is an assistant professor of journalism at Seijo University, a concrete complex on Tokyo's urban fringe. His tiny office, down a corridor of ancient but gleaming lineoleum, is furnished with typical Tokyo academic grunge – grey metal bolt-together shelving and cupboards. Mori was for four years a member of the leftish *Mainichi* newspaper's imperial household press club, but it was only after he left that he was allowed to put the inside knowledge he gathered – together with using Japan's new freedom-of-information law – to good use, publishing a best-selling book which documents the waste and extravagance of the palace establishment.

'If this was a corporation, it would have been restruc-tured long ago,' says Mori. 'They could get by on half the staff they have now.' Let's run the numbers. To look after the 23 members of the imperial family, the *Kunaicho* had a staff of 1080, or 47 servants for every royal. There are 25 chefs, 40 chauffeurs, 30 gardeners, 30 archaeologists (to protect the 895 imperial tombs), and four doctors. There are 13 full-time scholars who, 17 years after his death, were still engaged in writing the official history of Hirohito's reign for the secret archives of the imperial palace. There is a *gagaku* orchestra which is wheeled out for special occasions, with 24 richly costumed players of thousand-year-old instruments such as the *koto* and the *sho*, a 15-reed bamboo flute. There are four white-robed vestal virgins still on the payroll to attend to ceremonial duties, and a royal silkworm-breeder. The position of imperial stool-inspector was only abolished when Akihito came to the throne in 1990.

As for the imperial estates, there was a staff of 78 to look after a palace in Kyoto that no one occupies, and 67 to care for the horses at the Tochigi ranch, as well as scores more to staff the summer palaces on the beach and in the mountains where the royals drop in for a week or two a year. The main imperial palace alone has 160 servants. Staff numbers are inflated by absurd demarcation rules – for instance, if a royal spills something, two servants are required to mop up, one to clean the floor, the other the table. The steward in charge of silverware would not dream of handling the crystal.

As for the image of frugality and modesty he tries to convey, Mori discovered that the emperor recently spent more than $300,000 building a wine-cellar which holds 4500 vintage bottles. When South Africa's President Thabo Mbeki visited Japan in 2001 he was served a 1982 Château Mouton Rothschild, a *premier cru* Bordeaux which retails today at more than $900 a bottle, and a 1992

Dom Pérignon Champagne. Mori puts the real annual cost of running all this, including off-budget items such as the 1000-strong special imperial police force, at $325 million, the budget of a medium-sized Japanese city. This does not put a huge dent in Japan's national accounts. But it does give critics of the monarchy an axe to grind – especially when, again unlike the British royals who throw open Buckingham Palace to visitors in summer, the Japanese imperial family lives in seclusion behind the Chrysanthemum Curtain and contributes nothing to attracting foreign tourists.

All royal families struggle with this dilemma of how to remain aristocratic and special, while trying to accommodate middle-class notions of decency and restraint. But in Japan the idea of a royal on a bicycle pedalling along the esplanade calling out *'Bonjour!'* to passers-by, as Monaco's Princess Grace liked to do, would be quite incompatible with the emperor's exalted status. Someone actually dared to ask Empress Michiko about this once, and got this diplomatic response: 'I like riding a bicycle, but the traffic in Tokyo is so heavy that I think I'd be scared, and it would make people around me nervous too.'

There was one other unforeseen consequence of MacArthur's re-writing of the constitution defining the role of the emperor, and the law governing succession, which would have a direct impact on Naruhito and Masako. Under the Imperial Household Law of 1947 – and in conflict, incidentally, with the equal-status-for-women clause which the redoubtable Beate Sirota Gordon had written into the new constitution – succession to the throne is restricted to the oldest 'male descendant in the male line of imperial ancestors'. And, unlike its 1889 predecessor, which gave priority to 'full blood' over 'half blood' children, the straight-laced Americans made no provision for the offspring of concubines to inherit the throne, nor for adoption.

As for women, in ancient times Japan did have a number of female emperors. But all of them were 'pinch hitters', to use the baseball expression – emergency players brought in to break a deadlock when there was no obvious male heir, says Professor Hidehiko Kasahara, a law professor I called on at Tokyo's Keio University and an authority on imperial succession. Japan produced no female ruler with a shred of the historical importance of Britain's queens Boudicca or Bess, or Russia's Catherine the Great.

In all there have been eight females on the Chrysanthemum Throne, though just to confuse matters two of them reigned twice under different names. Typically, they were the daughters, sisters or widows of male emperors. Only one, the Emperor Saimei, was succeeded by her son – and that was because the child's father was the Emperor Jomei. The first female emperor (an empress is the wife of an emperor, not a ruler in her own right), a nun named Suiko, was brought in as a temporary compromise at the end of the sixth century to avoid a showdown between rival warring clans. The sixth, Shotoku, almost brought the entire dynasty to an end when she tried to abdicate in favour of a charismatic Buddhist monk who cured her of an ailment. It would be more than eight centuries before Japan's king-makers would trust another woman on the throne. The last female emperor was Go-Sakuramachi, who filled in for her nephew until he turned 14 in 1770 and was judged old enough to reign, whereupon she abdicated in his favour.

So, the Meiji law of 1889 made women ineligible to succeed. The American-dictated law of 1947 kept the ban on women emperors, and further curtailed eligibility to inherit the throne by implicitly ruling out the traditional source of half of the Japanese sovereigns, concubines, or *karibara*, 'wombs for hire', as they were known. MacArthur had stripped three-quarters of the imperial family of their royal status, and banished married princesses from the court. A genealogical time-bomb was ticking away. It was only a matter of time before Japan began to run out of heirs to the throne.

Many other countries are spoilt with choice when it comes to succession. Of the 191 members of the United Nations, 46 are still monarchies of one sort or another, although 16 of these, like Australia, have a monarch by default because of the historical accident of having been colonised by Great Britain, Denmark, Holland, Spain and so on. In fact, there are only 30 monarchs left in the world, less than a third the number of a century ago, and many of these reign over pocket-handkerchief kingdoms such as Andorra, Liechtenstein, and Vatican City. Of these, almost all – apart from the Islamic States of the Middle East and North Africa – now allow women to accede to the throne, thus doubling their chances of finding an heir. In 2006 three of Europe's thrones were occupied by women – the United Kingdom, the Netherlands and Denmark – and the heir to Sweden's throne was a fourth, Crown Princess Victoria Ingrid Alice Désirée.

As well, many monarchies maintain elaborate orders of succession going back centuries which allow for recruitment from distant 'cadet' branches of the family – as, indeed, Japan used to do before MacArthur changed the rules. In Great Britain, for example, successors are decreed under the Act of Settlement of 1701 to be all descendants of Sophia, the Electress of Hanover, who was the granddaughter of

James I of England. Women are, of course, allowed – but not Roman Catholics nor bastards. Prince Charles is first in line – and after him princes William and Harry, the 'heir and a spare' he and Diana produced. After them, at last count, there were no fewer than 4360 names on the list of possible successors to Queen Elizabeth II, and of the top 35 seventeen were women. Holland's royal website lists ten possible successors to their bicycling Queen Beatrix, Spain's 11 in line of succession to King Juan Carlos I, and Denmark has eight royals eligible to succeed King Christian X, now that Crown Prince Frederik and Mary have produced a child.

Some countries are even better off. Thanks to the astonishing fertility of Abd al-Aziz Al Saud, the first king of Saudi Arabia, who travelled around the Arabian deserts in the 1920s and 1930s, pausing at oases to father up to 200 children by nearly as many mothers, Saudi Arabia will never run out of rulers. The country's greatest budgetary headache is too many chiefs and not enough indians. Even with a ban on women rulers, the kingdom has 3000 to 4000 royal princes, who negotiate murky deals behind closed doors to decide which one of them will become the next king. In 2005, Swaziland's King Mswati III, Africa's last absolute monarch, married his thirteenth wife – a 17-year-old high-school beauty queen whom he chose from 50,000 bare-breasted virgins vying to catch his eye at the annual reed dance ceremony. This was even though, at the age of 36, he already had 24 children. Swaziland's succession problem, like the House of Saud, will be an embarrassment of heirs, not a shortage.

So, few, if any, countries have been faced with the royal succession crisis that confronted Japan in the summer of 1993 when Crown Prince Naruhito finally married

Masako. Seven girls, but not a single boy, had been born into the imperial family since Akishino was born in 1965. The imperial family was down to its last two 'breeding pairs' – the newlyweds, and Akishino, who was next in line to the throne after his brother (see pages viii and ix). There were four other males in the line of succession, but all were too old for children. Fourth in line to the throne, for instance, was Hirohito's brother Takahito, Prince Mikasa, who served as a cavalry officer in World War II and who turned 90 in 2005. Akishino and his wife Kiko had produced two children, in 1991 and 1994, but both were girls and will be turned out of the palace when they marry. So it was up to Naruhito and Masako. If they did not produce a boy, unless the rules were changed the Japanese imperial dynasty would come to an end.

From day one, the media had been speculating about an heir. In fact, even before the marriage, at that famous press conference to announce their engagement, they were asked about their plans for a family. Naruhito coyly replied, 'Let's say it's up to the stork.' Masako then smiled and revealed that they had rehearsed their answer to that question before the press conference. She had urged her eager royal groom-to-be not to blurt out what he had told her in private – that he wanted 'enough children to form an orchestra'. At that, Naruhito also grinned.

But it was not to be that easy. For a start, like an increasing number of Japanese couples, they were marrying rather late. Naruhito was 33, Masako would turn 30 at the end of the year. Obstetricians understand well that fertility declines from one's teens, and that after the age of 40, in spite of great advances in pre-natal care, the chances of giving birth to a healthy child are dramatically reduced. Those who expected the couple to produce a squawking heir to cheering crowds within a year, as Charles and Diana had, were forgetting that Diana only turned 20 a few weeks before her wedding.

As well, just imagine the difficulty of achieving intimacy while surrounded by prying courtesans, and in the full glare of an expectant media. Rihachi Iizuka, a fertility specialist at Keio University's school of medicine, was quoted as saying: 'Being a wife in the imperial family has got to be the number one cause of stress. That's why caged animals like monkeys and pandas in zoos don't have as many babies as the ones out in the wild.'

On top of all this there was the princess's public, who after their initial wild enthusiasm for the match, were feeling let down by Masako's increasingly rare and unpredictable public appearances. There is a small band of 50 to 100 fans, many of them middle-aged housewives, so-called *okake*, who follow Masako around like groupies stalking a rock star. One of the keenest is Harumi Kobayashi, a struggling mother-of-two from Chiba Prefecture who calls herself Masako's number-one fan. 'From the moment I first saw her I admired her . . . she looks cool, she's an educated woman . . . she's a star,' Kobayashi told me when we met in a snack-bar at Tokyo's central train station. She has taken thousands of photographs of the couple, amateur snaps refreshingly different from the stilted official portraits, and published them in two unauthorised best-sellers.

Everywhere Masako goes Kobayashi tries to follow, toting her trusty analogue Nikon with a 300–500 mm zoom lens to capture those intimate moments. She has snapped Masako and Naruhito climbing mountains, arriving at train stations, appearing for their New Year's wave to the crowds from their glassed-in reviewing box. But it has become increasingly difficult for Kobayashi to track her idol, because the *Kunaicho* has stopped giving out Masako's itinerary, except to members of the imperial press club. So she and the other fans have resorted to an only-in-Japan strategy. Every time the royal couple plans to make a trip – for instance, to Karuizawa, where the royals sometimes holiday at a secluded hotel – the local police responsible for their security notify the neighbourhood associations, a sort of Neighbourhood Watch which keeps an eye on all Japanese communities. Kobayashi has built up a network of informants/fans who pass the information back to her. She says the royals are very nice to her and sometimes say hello, but you can imagine how Masako and Naruhito must feel when they finally get away from it all on top of Mount Kuruma in the Japanese Alps, only to find a chubby Chiba housewife/*paparazza* popping up from behind a rock hoping to snap the first picture of a pregnant princess.

One year became two, and two became three. 'Third Year Without Pregnancy – Masako's Crucial Year', blared a women's magazine bold enough to give the couple a deadline. The magic rice-cakes which had been placed in their wedding chamber were not working, nor was the ritual with the bran. At his birthday press conferences, the prince pleaded with the media to stop badgering them: 'The stork needs some peace and quiet.' And behind the scenes, Emperor Akihito and Empress Michiko were also becoming concerned. There is no way to verify the following, and one should always treat with caution unsourced transcripts of conversations. In an on-line account of the marriage, Lesley Downer – a writer on Japanese history and culture and author of books on *geisha* and Japanese cooking – painted this picture of a humiliating monthly ritual she claims Masako was obliged to endure:

According to well-placed palace insiders, every month since her marriage the princess has been summoned to the imperial presence. Using the politest and most formal of language, the emperor enquires as to whether she has had a period that month. Each time she has to lower her head in shame and confess that, sadly, she has failed yet again to conceive a child. They also point out that she has effectively been grounded until she does her duty and produces an heir.

The *Kunaicho* seems to have decided that overseas travel was the problem three years after the wedding. In May of 1997 a trip she must have been looking forward to, the opening of a Japanese cultural centre in her beloved Paris, was cancelled at short notice, and her sister-in-law Sayako was sent in her place. It was to be another two years before this talented and well-travelled one-time diplomat was allowed abroad again, apart from a flying visit to attend a funeral in Jordan. I leave it to the reader to judge whether the Men in Black genuinely believed that getting on a plane or sleeping in a strange bed interferes with procreation – or whether there was an unspoken understanding that overseas travel was a 'privilege' being withdrawn until Masako 'cooperated'.

Either way, it had no effect, other than to drive an increasingly rancorous wedge between the couple and their staff, who began leaking spiteful stories to the media. She was said to have harangued one official on the phone, hanging up with the threat that if things did not improve she was going to 'resign' from the royal family. At her first solo press conference at the end of 1996 she felt obliged to deny that she was 'in a state of depression' though she candidly admitted: 'At times I experience hardship in trying to find the proper point of balance between [imperial] tradition and my own personality.'

Finally, six years after the wedding, the journalists at the *Kunaicho* press club were called to a briefing at which they were given the news Japan had been waiting for: Masako might, just might, be pregnant. They were told to keep it under their hats until medical tests could confirm the happy event, but inevitably the story was leaked, and Japan's royal-watchers rejoiced.

But the celebrations were short-lived. In January 2000, Masako, several months pregnant, was admitted to hospital for 'surgery to remove the [dead] foetus of her unborn child', announced Dr Takashi Okai, chief of obstetrics and gynaecology at Tokyo's Aiiku Hospital. He said he did not believe the stillbirth was the result of a trip Masako had finally been allowed to take – to Belgium, for the wedding of Crown Prince Philippe and his aristocratic speech-therapist fiancée Mathilde d'Udekem d'Acoz. He also denied that the miscarriage was caused by 'the stress of the speculative Press frenzy'. However, later that year, Masako told journalists: 'Honestly speaking, it is a fact that I was disturbed by the overheated coverage in the mass media from the very start.' She had obviously still not adjusted to life in the royal goldfish bowl.

In spite of this, the in-laws, the officials of the Imperial Household Agency and the public were not satisfied. Masako was now approaching 40 and the heir apparent was still without an heir. It was time for extraordinary measures.

8

The Hand of God

H IS COLLEAGUES, STAFF, AND STUDENTS AT TOKYO University's elite medical school called him simply *sensei*, master. But his patients and the public at large came to know him as something far grander, 'The Hand of God'. Professor Osamu Tsutsumi, a solid, square-jawed man in his mid-fifties, is one of Japan's leading obstetricians and gynaecologists, a world-renowned scientist with a book and scores of learned papers to his name. More importantly, at his university clinic he was one of the pioneers in Japan of the technique of *in vitro* fertilisation, more popularly, if inaccurately, known as test-tube baby-making.

By the summer of 2000, Masako and Naruhito must have been despairing of ever having one child, let alone the 'orchestra' Naruhito had joked about before their engagement press conference. Seven years of marriage had resulted only in the heartbreak of a failed pregnancy the year before. Naruhito's brother Akishino and his wife showed no inclination to help out by producing a son and heir – in spite of some heavy-handed hints from palace officials. Akihito and Michiko were said to be 'gravely concerned', not only as parents, but as custodians of the ancient dynasty which now faced an unprecedented crisis. It was time to call in the experts.

The royal couple was not, of course, alone in having trouble conceiving. Infertility is a rapidly growing problem around the world in the dawning decade of the twenty-first century, affecting around one couple in six. There are lots of causes, real and speculative, ranging from the prevalence of sexually transmitted diseases which can damage women's reproductive systems, to the supposed effect of urban pollution in reducing men's sperm count. Japanese men, in particular – perhaps because of their gruelling work and commuting hours – are the least sexually active in the world, according to a survey by the Durex condom company. They have sex, on average, less than once a week, 45 times a year, compared with the champions, the Greeks (138), Americans (113) and Australians (108). But fertility specialists I interviewed in Australia, the US and Japan agree on one thing: the major cause of couples being unable to conceive is their age, particularly the age of the woman.

Japan is no exception to the universal trend to later marriage and older would-be mothers. Masako and Naruhito were typical of their generation. Between 1971 and 2003 the average age of brides rose from 23 to 28, and it is now hovering at just under 30. According to Sydney IVF, one of Australia's leading fertility clinics, at the age of 22 a woman having unprotected sex has one chance in four of falling pregnant each month; at 31 this falls to one in five; at age 38 it is one in eight, and then the odds drop off the edge of the cliff until at age 45 the chances are only one in 40.

At the turn of the millennium, Masako had just cele-brated her thirty-seventh birthday, and Naruhito was approaching 41. There was increasing concern in the royal household, and speculation in the media, that one or the other had a serious infertility problem. Royal watchers like Matsuzaki recalled that, when he was a schoolboy, Naruhito had a severe dose of mumps which put him in bed for a week. Mumps can cause permanent damage to the reproductive organs, leading to infertility, although Matsuzaki would be far too polite to write such a thing. It was left once again to the foreign media, in this case the Munich newspaper *Süddeutscher Zeitung*, to carry an outrageous and unsourced article illustrated by a picture showing the crown prince with the caption *Tote Hosen* (Dead Trousers) across his groin. The paper later apologised.

In fact, according to Dr Devora Lieberman, a fertility specialist at Sydney IVF, it is statistically just as likely that Masako was the one with the problem: in 25–30 per cent of cases it is the man, in 25–30 per cent the woman, in 10–20 per cent it is both, and in 25 per cent the cause remains a medical mystery. Sydney IVF is the largest and (it claims) the most advanced of the 57 IVF clinics in Australia, occupying five floors of consulting rooms and laboratories where gowned technicians operate monitors, microscopes and incubators in a tower block in the city's financial district. The head of the clinic, Dr Robert Jansen, is Professor of Reproductive Medicine at Sydney Univer-sity. In his best-selling guide *Getting Pregnant – a Compassionate Resource for Overcoming Infertility* he suggests that with a couple aged under 35 it is usually a problem with the man's sperm; when they are over 35 it is more often a problem with the woman's eggs.

The stress of her life in the royal court and the intense pressure being put on Masako to have a child would not have helped. Although it is medically controversial, at least one international authority, Dr Alice Domar at Beth Israel-Deaconess Hospital in Boston, says that the association between stress and infertility has been known since Biblical times. A major study in 2004 which she cites found that of 112 infertile women, an extraordinary 40 per cent met the criteria for a psychiatric illness – anxiety disorder, followed by a major depressive disorder. At her Mind/Body Center for Women's Health, Domar is doing ground-breaking research developing innovative programs to help infertile women reduce their physical and psychological symptoms. It is a scientific approach to a phenomenon many women having trouble conceiving will understand. How often does pregnancy follow a relaxing holiday? How many frantically worried couples who believe themselves infertile conceive shortly after adopting a child?

Their discovery that pregnancy was not going to be as easy as waiting for the stork to drop by must have devastated Masako and Naruhito. Even with 'normal' couples, writes Dr Jansen, the initial reactions include '. . . surprise, disbelief and denial of the problem; anger with the partner and medical attendants; resentfulness of the need to participate in infertility tests; feelings of depression, loss of self esteem, marital disharmony and temporary sexual problems such as loss of interest and poor erections'. In other words, the stress makes it harder to conceive, failure to conceive increases the stress – a black spiral of negative biofeedback.

There is no doubt the couple was showered with traditional advice from day one. Japan has as many old wives' tales associated with falling pregnant as any other country – 'avoid eating eggplants', her mother-in-law Michiko might, for instance, have advised her. The older generation still places a lot of faith in *kampo*, traditional roots-and-bark medicine, and in practices such as moxibustion in which cones of powdered mugwort are placed on the body's 'acupressure points' and set alight in the belief that this will 'improve the circulation'. We do not know which remedies the royal couple tried, apart from the business with the rice-bran on the belly and those tiny nightly rice-cakes on their silver salver. That none of the nostrums had worked is obvious.

In the West, the couple would have been advised to seek professional help after a year of unsuccessfully trying for a child. So why did it take Masako and Naruhito seven? First of all they would have been reluctant to consult a doctor over such a delicate matter, especially the conservative old fogies favoured by the *Kunaicho* as the official palace physicians. Masako is known to have been furious that news of her earlier, failed, pregnancy had been leaked to the media, and suspected her medical team.

As smart, English-reading, Western-educated people they would also have been aware that Japan tends to lag in adopting the latest medical technology, drugs – and ethics. 'National health' doctors have to churn through more than 100 patients a day to make a living; many refuse to tell patients, even royal patients, what drugs they are prescribing, nor when they have a terminal disease. The contraceptive pill was banned in Japan for more than 30 years (largely to protect the condom and abortion industries), lepers were still banished into exile on remote islands until the 1990s, and the first doctor to perform a heart transplant, in 1968, was threatened with prosecution for manslaughter. 'First world country, third world medicine', patients' advocates often complain.

And so it is with fertility treatment. In 1978 Britain's Dr Patrick Steptoe delivered the world's first test-tube baby, Louise Brown, with 'the biggest yell you ever heard from a baby'. That cry echoed around the world, bringing hope to infertile couples everywhere. Australia, now one of the world's leading nations in IVF, was especially quick off the mark, producing 12 of the world's first 15 test-tube babies, beginning in 1980. But Japan, although it had the technology, became mired in debate about the ethics of the treatment, and the first test-tube baby was not delivered there until three years later.

The techniques have been considerably refined since those pioneering days, but the principle remains the same. Most often tests find that the partners produce viable eggs and sperm – the problem is bringing them together to create a new life. After a complicated and – for the woman – a physically invasive process involving hormone treatments, egg extraction, external fertilisation of the eggs with the man's sperm, and embryo implantation, a 'normal' pregnancy should follow.

Of course, it is rarely as straightforward as this. The patient advice books I flick through in waiting rooms warn that the drugs used can cause headaches and mood swings. The woman's ovaries swell from their normal walnut size to the diameter of oranges. There is a stressful regime of injections and ultrasound examinations. Many women find some of the procedures physically painful, and the whole process emotionally draining. Even advanced clinics such as Sydney IVF only claim that a live birth follows about one-third of embryo implants. If the woman has to return for a second, third, or subsequent treatment the effect is often compared to being on an 'emotional roller-coaster'. IVF is not a procedure to be undertaken lightly, particularly in Japan.

As a result of its reluctance to embrace what is now scarcely a new treatment – Australia's first and the world's fourth test-tube baby, Candice Reed, turns 27 in 2007 – Japan now lags behind most developed nations in offering couples fertility treatment. Worldwide more than a million IVF babies are now estimated to have been born, though only a tiny fraction of these are Japanese. Denmark leads the world, with more than three IVF babies in every 100 births. Australia is not far behind, with one child in 35. In Japan the latest figure is one in 75, or just 15,000 IVF births out of a million babies born a year. Among developed countries only the United States does worse, most likely because – like Japan, but unlike Australia and the Scandinavian countries – the national health scheme does not pay for the treatment, which there averages $50,000 to $175,000 for a 'take home' baby, depending on the age of the woman.

Japan's slow uptake of IVF is particularly surprising considering the official hand-wringing over the country's ageing, declining population. The country's birth-rate has fallen by more than two-thirds since the war, and has been below what demographers call the replacement rate of 2.1 children per family for a generation. Only the fact that Japanese live longer than any other people on earth has propped up the tottering inverted demographic pyramid. The number of active workers peaked in 1998. In 2005, for the first time in a century, its population began to shrink from a peak of 127 million and is expected to decline by a third over the next 50 years. Japan running out of Japanese? A tongue-in-cheek projection by the *Nikkei*

Business magazine predicted that at this rate by the year 3300 there would be only one Japanese left alive. Prime Minister Koizumi, only half jokingly, ushered in the Chinese Year of the Dog in 2006 urging his fellow citizens to 'breed like dogs' to stave off a population crisis. The alternative, increasing Japan's miniscule migrant intake, is apparently politically and socially unacceptable.

To try and find out why Japan is so unwilling to accept a treatment that offers a modest contribution to population growth, and so much to childless couples like Masako and Naruhito, I took a train 90 minutes from the centre of Tokyo, out beyond the urban fringe where grey stucco buildings give way to rice paddies and rows of pole-beans. I was bound for the Saitama Prefecture Medical School Hospital, a huge tile-clad complex which is one of Japan's most advanced centres for the treatment of infertility. There I met Professor Osamu Ishihara, the chairman of the hospital's department of obstetrics and gynaecology, a personable man with excellent English who has studied at London's renowned Hammersmith Hospital and has an international reputation in his field.

Dr Ishihara explains that, although it is more than 20 years since the first IVF birth in Japan, the medical establishment is still wrestling with regulating the field, and specialists like himself are operating in a vacuum. IVF is in a medical twilight zone, where there are restrictions, imposed by the Japanese professional association of obstetricians and gynaecologists, which would be regarded as absurd in other countries. There is a ban on donor eggs, a ban on donor embryos, and restrictions on the use of donor sperm. This pretty much confines IVF to a husband-and-wife affair; those couples where the woman cannot produce eggs, or the husband viable sperm, are effectively barred from the benefits of IVF, forcing them to go to more relaxed countries like South Korea or Taiwan for the procedure.

Three years ago the government appointed a specialist committee to sort out the mess, but it was unable to reach the required consensus because, rumour has it, one of its members, a paediatrician, is a Roman Catholic (the Catholic Church officially opposes IVF), and another, the consumer representative, is against IVF because she had a bad outcome when she was treated herself. As a result, IVF in Japan 'is underground . . . it is neither legal nor illegal. It is quite ridiculous', says Ishihara.

The best clinics, like the one in Saitama where between 360 and 470 'cycles' or attempts to implant an embryo are performed each year, are 'well run and something like world class', he says. But there are 10 to 20 smaller clinics which operate on the fringes of the law where he says bluntly the medicine is 'rubbish'. In recent years at least two doctors, one in Nagano Prefecture and the other in the port city of Kobe, had been deregistered for contravening the medical association's rules on IVF.

On top of all these restrictions there is the cost, not that this would have deterred Masako and Naruhito. A private clinic in Tokyo will charge around $5000 for each attempt to implant a fertilised egg – and, typically, it takes three or four attempts to produce a viable pregnancy. The doctors who own fertility clinics drive Rolls-Royces and regularly appear on the published lists of the biggest taxpayers in Japan. In hectic Shinjuku, for instance, Dr Osamu Kato, director of the Kato Ladies' Clinic, is open 24 hours a day, seven days a week and claims to perform 6000 to 7000 'cycles' a year.

But the most important reason for the slow take-up of

IVF in Japan, says the professor, is that in Japan there is a social stigma about the whole procedure. Admitting to using it would be seen as an admission that something is 'wrong' with one of the parents. There is an irrational but deeply rooted cultural belief that such children are not 'natural', do not really carry the family bloodline, and will be more prone to birth abnormalities. This, of course, is not borne out by nearly three decades of clinical experience – the greatest risk associated with IVF is that of multiple births. But the prejudice persists. Ishihara fondly remembers a newspaper photograph of a recent reunion of hundreds of young people born as a result of fertility treatment at Bourn Hall Clinic, a stately Jacobean mansion in the Cambridgeshire countryside which claims to be the birthplace of IVF, to mark the twenty-fifth anniversary of the technology. 'That would never happen in Japan,' he says, shaking his head. 'Here people would never admit that they use IVF.'

Indeed, it wasn't until 2005 that a member of parliament named Seiko Noda became the first high-profile woman to write a book and speak publicly about her experience with IVF. Like so many women, Noda, a former government minister who was once cited as the best prospect to become Japan's first female prime minister, postponed having children while she pursued her career. At the age of 44 she and her husband, Yosuke Tsuruho, found that they could not conceive and sought help from a fertility clinic. Ignoring the stigma, she persisted with eight treatment cycles in an unsuccessful attempt to fall pregnant, and had a number of 'spare' embryos frozen. And then, in the autumn of 2005, Prime Minister Koizumi called a snap election and she had to put the IVF on hold while she went off campaigning. 'I'll have to put off becoming a mummy until after the election,' she said. Noda was re-elected, but at the time of writing had made no announcement about whether she was continuing with the treatment.

In another life this might have been Masako, boldly defying convention and taking charge. But how, from the isolation of the palace, was she to seek help from those best qualified? One can only imagine the debate which must have gone on within the top ranks of the *Kunaicho* over who, and how, best to tackle the crisis. It had to be someone pre-eminent in the field of fertility, it goes without saying. But also someone with tact, diplomacy and sensitivity – someone who could avoid treading on the toes of the palace staff, win the confidence of Masako, and negotiate the exquisitely delicate task of asking a crown prince for a sperm sample. Above all, it must be someone of impeccable discretion. Not a word must be allowed to leak to the media. Eventually, the name Osamu Tsutsumi came up.

A quick scan of some of his published papers leaves no doubt that the professor is that rarity in Japan, a medical expert with a real international reputation. As well as being an authority on IVF, his expertise extends to such esoteric surgical feats as constructing an artificial vagina out of freeze-dried pig skin for a patient suffering from the rare Mayer-Rokitansky syndrome, a world first. Some time in the summer of 2000 he began clandestinely visiting the East Palace to begin his consultations, usually at night when he was less likely to be spotted by the ever-watchful media hacks. There was a low-key reception for him at the palace hospital at which he took everyone aback by boasting: 'One day in this hospital I am looking forward to the crown princess having a baby.' Unseemly self-confidence, scolded the official palace doctors, who for seven long years had been unable to offer the couple any help themselves.

In March 2001, when Masako had already begun a cycle of fertility treatment, Tsutsumi's appointment was officially announced. The *Kunaicho* did later refer obliquely to 'hormone treatment' but if anyone put two and two together – that preparations were being made for the birth of a child who could become the world's first test-tube emperor – no one published it, at least not in Japan, and not until much later. Even today, reactions range from tittering embarrassment to outraged denial when it is suggested that Masako may have been Japan's – perhaps the world's – first royal to receive IVF treatment. But why else would Tsutsumi, an IVF specialist, have been called in? What else could the 'hormones' have been for, other than to stimulate the production of eggs? I attempted to clarify this with Tsutsumi, but after initially indicating that he would be happy to talk, he said he would have to get *Kunaicho*'s approval. That, of course, was never forthcoming.

Round about this time, curious reporters noticed that Masako had stopped playing tennis and riding horses. She raised eyebrows by cancelling engagements including a lunch with the president of Lithuania, Valdas Adamkus, and a visit to the southern island of Okinawa. In an earlier era the *Kunaicho* would have simply lied – when Michiko first fell pregnant with Naruhito they declared that her indisposition was due to 'a cold'. But on 16 April Kiyoshi Furukawa, Grand Chamberlain of the Crown Prince's household, decided he could no longer keep it quiet and called a press conference to announce that Masako was 'showing signs' of pregnancy. One hundred reporters grabbed for their mobile phones, and TV stations broke into their normal programming with the news. A month later and it was official: the princess was in her third month of pregnancy and the baby was expected towards the end of the year.

Prime Minister Koizumi sent his congratulations, the media burst into excited speculation about whether it would be a boy, who could carry on the imperial line, and toymaker Takara Corporation set a new low in tackiness by offering, for $25, a maternity edition of its famous Rika-chan doll (a sort of Japanese Barbie), complete with a key so that its pregnant tummy could be returned to normal after Masako's child was born. Almost 2000 people were invited to a celebratory garden party at the Akasaka Palace. But in general, people heeded Furukawa's call to 'exercise restraint'. The media, in particular, did not want to be held responsible, however unfairly, for causing another royal miscarriage.

Masako gave up most of her royal duties for those anxious months, staying in seclusion at the palace, attended by Tsutsumi and her other physicians, including his disciple Dr Miyuki Sadatsuki of the Gunma Prefecture Medical School, a US-trained hormone researcher and specialist in older pregnancies. She busied herself designing a new nursery for the child – the first to be born in the East Palace for nearly 40 years – with cork floors, cream walls and a nice view over the gardens. Masako and, unusually for Japan, Naruhito, read up on childbirth. Masako did the exercises; no doubt Michiko lent her a copy of her book on child-raising. The empress began to knit tiny white socks, and to make baby-clothes embossed with the imperial chrysanthemum from silk spun from silkworms she raised herself.

And, of course, Masako was not allowed to neglect the

obscure ceremonials that attend a royal birth. In the fifth month of her pregnancy, on the so-called Day of the Dog, she was swathed in a traditional broad white ceremonial *obi* to ensure a safe pregnancy and a labour as easy as a bitch's is supposed to be. In her ninth month a messenger arrived from the palace bearing a pinewood box decorated with gilt cranes and pine trees. Inside was another special *obi*, a ceremonial four-metre-long crimson and white silk sash, which had been blessed at the three Shinto shrines in the palace grounds. Her chief lady-in-waiting wrapped it around Masako's waist, leaving Naruhito, dressed in a morning coat, to tie the knot. This time the magic worked – the pregnancy went like clockwork, although, as often happens with a first child, it was a couple of weeks late.

On the evening of 30 November Naruhito arrived home after attending his brother's thirty-sixth birthday party. Masako had stayed home on medical advice, but now she felt her time had come. It was getting on for midnight, with a full moon hanging in the winter sky, when their chauffeur-driven car pulled out of the East Palace, and they were driven across the moat to the hospital in the imperial palace grounds. Masako, dressed in a blue suit, smiled and waved to a few curious passers-by – and the media, who were already setting up TV cameras in a nearby car-park. Staff ushered the couple inside, where the *Kunaicho*, no doubt at Tsutsumi's insistence, had been busy installing a modern new labour ward for the princess – an American-designed 'LDR suite' to make the birth a 'family-friendly experience' with labour, delivery and recovery all catered for in the same room.

Naruhito's presence at his wife's side would be unremarkable in most parts of the world, but in Japan – especially for a member of the royal family – it was unusual to say the least. Most Japanese hospitals still do not allow fathers to be present for the birth of their babies. Naruhito's own father, Akihito, had stayed home at the palace waiting for a messenger to bring him the news while Michiko laboured alone with her medical attendants. It was designed to show the public quite clearly that the crown prince – whatever his other shortcomings – was determined to set an example and break with tradition, sharing responsibility for his child's upbringing, rather than leaving it all to his wife.

He went home that night, but returned the following day and was in an adjoining room when, at 2.43 in the afternoon, a cry from the delivery room heralded the baby's arrival. It was a girl, 3200 grammes and 49.6 centimetres long, announced the palace. The birth had been 'relatively easy', with no surgical intervention. Mother and daughter were doing well. The Owadas visited them in hospital. Masako was later to say that the baby 'had a placid character very much like that of [her father]'.

A royal birth of any sort is a joyful occasion. There were fireworks again in the Owada home-town of Murakami. 'I feel like I saw a flash of light in this age of war and economic downturn,' said an excited Shohei Kondo, president of the local chamber of commerce. Fire-fighting ships on Tokyo Bay put on a display with their hoses. Trestle tables were set up on the lawns of the imperial palace, where tens of thousands of people thronged to sign congratulatory books, and bow towards the palace with their arms above their heads shouting 'banzai'. That is not a war-cry, incidentally, but a cheer that literally means 'ten thousand years', and in practice is used where Australians would call out 'Hurrah!' On 7 December three scholars decided on a name for the child, which Emperor Akihito

approved and wrote with black brush-strokes on a sheet of
paper to be placed on the baby's pillow. The little girl was
to be called Aiko – the Chinese *kanji* characters stand for
'love' and 'child'. A floral emblem was chosen for her – the
white azalea, symbolising a pure heart.

Like Naruhito, Aiko was to be raised by her mother,
rather than a wet-nurse. In that respect at least the palace
had changed forever, and for the better. At the press
conference they gave to introduce the baby to the world,
the beaming new father said that Masako was breast-
feeding, supplemented by powdered milk; she was bathing
the child herself, and changing its nappies. 'I'd like to
thank the stork,' he said, tongue in cheek, understanding
that both he, and the smarter members of the media, knew
full well that it was Tsutsumi and his 'hand of God' who
was responsible – but that no one would let on, at least not
in Japan.

There are, of course, any number of alternative scenar-
ios gossiped about behind the fans in Tokyo's notoriously
bitchy circle of former aristocrats. If it was an IVF baby,
whose sperm was it *really*, is one of the favourite themes.
Akishino's? Akihito's? Another is even more far-fetched.

One of the most colourful characters I met while
researching this book was 'Princess' Kaoru Nakamaru,
who claims to be a granddaughter of the Meiji Emperor
by one of his more obscure concubines. She is a buxom
woman in her fifties who arrives for lunch in a frilly
aqua dress with huge turquoise rings on her fingers. The
business card she offers says she is the chairperson of
the International Institute for World Peace, and she has
travelled to 182 countries in that quest. Over a plate of
delicious deep-fried *matsutake* mushrooms, she explains
that Masako did not have a baby at all – the deception was

accomplished by her servants wrapping thicker and thicker layers of cloth around her waist as the phony pregnancy progressed. When the time came, a changeling baby was smuggled into the hospital – Aiko, she whispers, is actually the illegitimate child of the mistress of a prominent politician.

'How can you possibly know this?' I ask.

'We royals, we communicate with the gods,' she says, casting her eyes towards the ceiling.

I should have known it was tempting fate to laugh. Namazu, the giant catfish which legend says lies curled on the ocean floor with the islands of Japan resting on his back, stirred. A series of violent earthquakes shook the building, and Tokyo ground to a halt. Thankfully there was no major structural damage – the city's more modern skyscrapers have elaborate hydraulic systems to stabilise them built into the foundations. But the quake knocked out lifts, power, and the underground railway network for hours, leaving millions of people wandering the streets searching for a taxi, or crowded into bars and coffee shops waiting for emergency crews to get things running again. It was a reminder that life in one of the world's greatest cities is in the lap of the gods. It is only a matter of time before the Big One hits.

The baby celebrations continued for months and marked a new high point in Masako's popularity with the public. In May, Aiko was taken to the imperial holiday home in the mountains at Nasu to see her birth-flowers, the white azaleas, in bloom. A crowd of 1500, including Harumi Kobayashi, the royal groupie, met the family at the railway station, cheering, waving and snapping photographs. Perhaps, with the long-awaited birth of a child, Masako's years of unhappiness were over.

Somehow, of course, modern parenting was going to have to learn to live alongside ancient ritual. Aiko had to be formally presented to Emperor and Empress, and introduced to the spirits of her ancestors at the three imperial shrines. She was presented with a hand-forged ritual sword and a *hakama*, a wide, pleated pair of pants. In a ceremony most Japanese found especially inscrutable, the baby was bathed in a wooden tub while a 91-year-old scholar recited verses from the *Nihon Shoki*, a descendant of the Tokugawa shogunate cried 'Oh!' to drive out evil spirits, and an arrow was fired into the ground. Not for the first time, the very modern Masako must have been bemused by proceedings.

But as time passed and even the women's magazines tired of baby news, the doubts began to surface. Aiko might have been welcomed with due pomp and circumstance into the imperial family, but everyone understood that she could never, at least under the existing inheritance laws, accede to the throne. In the old days, news of the birth of a royal child would be broadcast by a one-minute blast from every siren in the land; if it was a boy that would be followed by a one-minute silence, then a second blast, at which the real jubilation would break out. While Masako and Naruhito were obviously enjoying sharing the parenting for which they had waited so long – the prince astounded the older generation by taking turns carrying the child in public, even allowing Aiko to pull the princely hair – there was still no heir. And adding urgency to the debate, the following winter it was confirmed that the world's only reigning emperor was suffering from prostate cancer, and had to undergo surgery. Palace-watchers let it be known that Akihito was deeply distressed at the prospect of dying without knowing whether the imperial line would continue, or end with one of his sons as Japan's last emperor. There would have to be a boy.

At the end of 2002 – after many requests to travel abroad had been rejected by the *Kunaicho* – Masako and Naruhito were allowed a week in Australia and New Zealand. It was not just that she wanted to get away from the pressure-cooker atmosphere of the palace, though who could blame her for that. Some of her critics, says Eric Johnston, '. . . portrayed her as a whining, spoilt bitch who just wanted an overseas holiday. It just made her sound childish'. But her friends leapt to her defence. 'It is not simply a matter of craving overseas trips,' said one. 'Ever since the princess was a young girl she has dreamed of serving her country in the international realm. To deny her that ambition is tantamount to denying her whole identity.' Not to mention the promise the prince had made when he proposed nine long years before.

That trip to Australia, we now know, was to be her last overseas sojourn for at least three years, and perhaps the last time she would feel truly relaxed and happy. The prince still remembered Australia fondly from his home-stay nearly 20 years before, and had stayed in touch with some of his Australian friends. No doubt he chatted to Masako about his schoolboy pranks – disappearing from that farewell dinner at Queenscliff to play pool, the forbidden game of golf. They went to Sydney's Taronga Park Zoo where they were photographed cuddling a wombat, laid a wreath at the Tomb of the Unknown Soldier at the Australian War Memorial in Canberra, shook hands with lines of officials – and found time to catch up with some old friends.

Colin Harper received a phone call from the Japanese Embassy to say that the prince and princess would love to see him, and he flew up to Canberra for tea and cake with them at the Hyatt Hotel. Unlike the last time he saw Naruhito moping around the palace, the couple was animated and cheerful as they chatted and reminisced. Masako he found to be a 'charming young woman', showing no sign of the strain she had been under. He gave them a gold chain with a koala charm as a present for Aiko. Instead of the scheduled half an hour they stayed for 45 minutes, ignoring the equerry who kept dashing in and out looking pointedly at his watch.

Back in Tokyo the warm afterglow of a Sydney summer soon faded. The pressure was intensifying on Masako to undergo a new round of IVF treatment, and relations with the *Kunaicho* had not improved. Magazines began carrying articles quoting palace staff making petty complaints about Masako – she made them stay up late ironing her clothes, she would ask for ramen noodles or a peeled apple at one in the morning, she 'raises her high-pitched voice and gets angry with staff'. Even more seriously, there had been a complete breakdown in relations between Masako and the in-laws – Michiko was said to be nagging her to try for a boy.

Akira Hashimoto, the royal-watcher and friend of Akihito, says that the relationship had deteriorated to such an extent that the only time Masako and Naruhito now saw his parents was for official receptions, when they stood 'like pillars of ice' in the imperial presence. They had abandoned the weekly family dinner, a practice dating back to Hirohito's days. Masako was also neglecting her formal obligations, often unable to attend the arcane Shinto rites associated with commemorating the emperor's ancestors. One reason may have been that women who are menstruating are deemed impure and not allowed to enter shrines. Previous crown princesses, who spent most of their fertile years either pregnant or lactating, would not have had this problem – for Masako, trying to synchronise her cycle with imperial anniversaries must be a nightmare. And on top of all this, the ailing emperor was now well into his seventies – he wanted to pass some of the burden of his official duties on to his son, but without Masako's cooperation that would be impossible.

Another royal correspondent was even blunter about the breakdown in the relationship. Quoted anonymously in an article by the London *Times*'s respected Japan correspondent, Richard Lloyd Parry, he said this:

> *Masako has become an imperial drop-out. She is hostile towards the emperor and the empress and is . . . waiting for them to die. It sounds horrible and shocking, but this is the truth of what's happening inside the crown prince's household and the public doesn't know about [it].*

A rift had even developed with the prince's younger brother Akishino, who had always had a serious case of sibling rivalry. Now, even though he and his wife had two children of their own who enjoyed playing with Aiko, there were fewer and fewer visits. When not engaged on their round of official commitments, or holidaying at one of the imperial country-houses, Masako and Naruhito lived a low-key life in the East Palace, listening to music, reading, walking their two dogs Pipi and Marie, painting and 'enjoying astronomical observations'. Very occasionally Masako managed to escape for lunch with a friend, dodging the media by using unmarked cars. The only regular visitor appears to have been Setsuko, Masako's younger sister, who lives in nearby Aoyama.

Masako's sense of isolation was increased by the dispersal of her family and friends. Her parents were soon to move across the world yet again, this time to Holland, where Hisashi Owada had been made a judge of the International Court of Justice. Her sister, Reiko, a political science graduate who had once worked for UNESCO in Vietnam, had married a lawyer and settled down in the suburbs of Tokyo where she was raising her own family. Reiko's twin, Setsuko – also a graduate of the University of Tokyo, in English, who had once roared around Tokyo on a motorbike – had also married and was living with her husband in Switzerland. Many of her old school-friends, like Kumi Hara, had been discouraged by palace officials and no longer called. Her former university colleagues were all overseas.

One can hardly blame Masako for alienating the in-laws by refusing to go through the ordeal of another round of IVF treatments. By now she was almost 40, and the odds of a successful pregnancy were receding rapidly – in some Scandinavian countries women over 37 are refused government-funded treatment because of its unlikelihood of success. As well as this, the high-flying Tsutsumi had found himself embroiled in – of all things – a money scandal. In June 2003 the University of Tokyo announced that it was suspending him for 'inaccurate or improper' accounting of almost $300,000 of government funds which had been funnelled into his own bank account. Although the university did not find that he did it for personal gain – the money was spent on laboratory equipment, office refurbishments and travel – and in spite of the fact that the professor apologised and promised to repay the money, he was disgraced and forced to resign as Masako's fertility physician. 'The hand of God' was gone, and after all she had been through Masako was apparently not prepared to start over again with someone new.

Against this backdrop, imagine how she must have felt when she picked up the newspapers a few days after news broke of Tsutsumi's resignation to read this gratuitous advice from Toshio Yuasa, then the top bureaucrat at the *Kunaicho*. 'Frankly speaking,' he expounded, 'as grand steward of the imperial household I want them [Masako and Naruhito] to have another child.' In December, when Masako had not obliged by falling pregnant, he turned his attentions to Akishino and Kiko. 'Out of consideration for the well-being of the imperial household, I would strongly hope for their third child,' he told the media. Whether or not he was speaking with the authority of the emperor, as some speculated, it is an indication of the arrogance of the *Kunaicho* that they would tender advice like this in such a public way.

By that autumn the pressure had built to such an extent that Masako began cutting back on her public engagements, often upsetting palace officials by cancelling at the last minute. Ambassadors were being stood up. Red Cross worthies had to find someone else to present their Florence Nightingale awards. Then she dropped out of sight completely – Naruhito was left to attend to their official duties on his own. Rumour swirled around the palace corridors and spilled over into the media. In December the *Kunaicho* was finally forced to admit that there was something seriously wrong. Masako had been admitted to hospital with shingles, a debilitating condition characterised by a painful rash and blisters on the skin, along with a fever, chills, headache and an upset stomach. Reporters consulted their medical texts to discover that shingles is caused by the chickenpox virus, *varicella zoster*. After people have chickenpox, usually as a child, it lies dormant in the nervous system until an outbreak is triggered 'through other infections, stress, being generally run down, or occasionally when the body's immune defences are affected by certain drugs or other immune deficiencies'.

In Masako's case there seems little doubt that it was the stress of palace life which had finally taken a devastating toll on her health. She had an agonising rash on the back of her head and under her chin, which failed to respond to treatment. Normally shingles will clear up spontaneously in a week or so, but in Masako's case the condition was so chronic she had to be admitted to hospital, where she spent a month receiving intravenous medication three times a day. When she was finally discharged, the *Kunaicho* announced that she was cancelling all her official engagements and going to the countryside to try and recuperate. A German television station later reported that Masako had attempted suicide, a report picked up by a Korean newspaper, *Chosun Ilbo*, though by no Japanese media. Again – what is it about German reporting out of Japan? – there was no evidence produced to support such a serious and scandalous claim.

In a quite unprecedented breach of protocol, Masako's mother Yumiko decided to take personal charge of her rehabilitation. Worried sick that her daughter would never recover if she did not escape from the palace, she insisted that Masako and Aiko go with her to the family *besso*, the holiday home among the hills and woods of Karuizawa, where she had enjoyed such good times as a child. Here, away from the media, the in-laws, and the bullying of the palace officials, she spent the spring in total seclusion trying to regain her health. But although he must also have been terribly concerned, Naruhito was not allowed to neglect his official duties – he remained in Tokyo, visiting his princess only for a few days, when he had to be put up at a local hotel rather than stay at the Owadas'.

March turned to April and April to May. The lemon-scented blossom on the dogwoods withered and fell and it was time for Yumiko to leave – once again, her husband was dragging her halfway across the world. Hisashi Owada had been sidelined after the wedding because it was considered unseemly, if not exactly unconstitutional, for the head of one of Japan's great departments of state to have such a close connection with the supposedly apolitical emperor. Instead of ambassador to the United States, the Foreign Affairs Ministry's most important posting, for which he had been angling, he had to be content with the low-key position of ambassador to the United Nations, back in New York again.

That job took him through to retirement age. But in Japan bureaucrats who have toed the line regard retirement as the opportunity to begin a new and lucrative career, a murky influence-peddling process known as *amakudari* or 'descent from the heavens'. Hisashi was quietly welcomed back into the back-rooms of Nagatacho, Tokyo's parliamentary precinct, where he became 'special advisor' to a succession of green new foreign ministers – in effect, for five years he was the shadowy *éminence grise* steering Japan's foreign policy. As well, he was rewarded with other lucrative sinecures – president of the Japan Institute of International Affairs, professor of international law at Waseda University, and 'senior advisor' to the World Bank. The gossips winked knowingly and whispered that this was his reward for delivering the reluctant Masako to the palace.

And then, in 2003, came a further honour – on the recommendation of the government which he had served so loyally, Owada was appointed a judge of the International Court of Justice. He gets to parade the marbled halls of the United Nations' 'world court' in The Hague in his black robe and white lace jabot until 2012, when he turns 80. It is an eminent, well-paid post, carrying a handsome salary, and it is not, one has to say, the world's most taxing job. Between them, according to the court's website, the 15 judges issued just four judgements in 2003, one of which ruled illegal Israel's construction of a wall partitioning Palestine, to which the new Judge Owada's contribution was a comment about 'the *so-called* terrorist attacks by Palestinian suicide bombers against the Israeli population', which enraged Jews. In 2004 the court's productivity dropped to just one case. In 2005 it also managed to make just one judgement, on a dispute between Costa Rica and Nicaragua over navigational rights.

So Yumiko went to join her husband, and Masako returned to the palace and the prince with her little girl, still wan and weak, though no doubt feeling better after her long convalescence in the countryside. The palace let it be known that she was 'slowly recovering'. But within weeks of her return there was a new and far more ominous crisis brewing.

9

The Black Dog

THE CROWN PRINCE WAS LATE. THE JOURNALISTS gathered in the conference room of the East Palace were getting restless. It was a late spring afternoon in May 2004 and the *Kunaicho* had scheduled a routine press briefing before Naruhito and Masako winged off on their first overseas trip in 18 months, with the usual scripted answers to the usual carefully vetted questions. The newspaper reporters might make an inside page; the story would be lucky to make the TV news bulletins at all. But as the minutes ticked by and there was no sign of the prince the room began to buzz. What was going on? The imperial press club was about to get its biggest story of the year.

Finally, half an hour late, Naruhito, dressed in a grey suit and a sombre tie, took his seat at the microphone beside a huge display of seasonal flowers, and began to speak carefully from prepared notes. He was 'very grateful' for the invitation to attend two royal weddings in Europe – that of Crown Prince Frederik and Mary Donaldson in

Denmark, and Crown Prince Felipe de Borbon y de Grecia to a TV newsreader, Letizia Ortiz, in Spain. He waffled on about Denmark being well-known for Hans Christian Andersen's fairytales, the statue of the Little Mermaid, and Kronborg Castle, the setting of Shakespeare's *Hamlet*. He made a few anodyne remarks about Granada's Moorish masterpiece the Alhambra, and the paintings of Velasquez and El Greco, and he sympathised with the Spanish over the recent Madrid railway station bombing. And then he was asked by one of the journalists about the last-minute decision by Masako to cancel her trip.

He began by reading from the script. The princess 'has not fully recovered her health, and after consulting with doctors it was decided that I would make the visit alone'. Masako was 'sincerely regretful' that she could not make the trip. Naruhito was 'wrenching myself away'. Then the prince put down his notes, his face flushed with anger, and launched into an unprecedented and unscripted attack on the *Kunaicho* that electrified the royal-watchers. The innocuous press conference was suddenly front-page news. These are the highlights of what he said, according to the translated transcript on the imperial website:

> *Princess Masako has worked hard to adapt to the environment of the imperial household for the past ten years, but, from what I can see, I think she has completely exhausted herself in trying to do so. It is true that there were developments that denied Princess Masako's career . . . as well as her personality . . . I believe that much tact and effort will have to be expended for Princess Masako to recover her original full spirit and strength, which are required to return to her official duties.*

By Western standards it was pretty innocuous stuff. Certainly nothing like the infamous BBC interview in which Princess Diana accused Prince Charles of adultery, revealing that 'There were three of us in this marriage, so it was a bit crowded.' But by Japanese standards it was a shocking breach of protocol for the prince to allow his emotions to show, let alone to criticise the mandarins of the Imperial Household Agency. Because there was no doubt to whom he was referring when he talked about Masako's spirit and personality having been crushed – he was laying the blame squarely at the feet of the Men in Black. Minoru Hamao, the prince's former chamberlain, commented that Naruhito had 'declared war' on the agency.

The commentators concluded that Naruhito, having found it impossible to protect Masako as he had promised when they got engaged, was now appealing over the heads of the royal court to the public. And it worked – for a while. Within hours of the news breaking, there was an overwhelming tide of public sympathy for the princess, with more than 2000 emails bombarding the *Kunaicho* website alone. Talk-back hosts, TV chat-shows and newspaper and magazine columnists almost unanimously sided with the royal couple. 'Why Was Masako's Personality Stamped Out?' demanded a headline in the big-circulation women's magazine *Josei Seven*. The liberal *Asahi* newspaper editorialised 'Can't the Imperial Household Agency give them a little more freedom?' *Kunaicho*-bashing, for a change, became the flavour of the month – journalists revelled in the opportunity to revenge themselves for the haughty disdain with which palace officials had treated them for all those years.

The remarks turned the rift between the royal couple and the rest of the imperial family into a ravine. The emperor let it be known that he was 'crestfallen' over the remarks and 'very worried' about Masako and Naruhito. Younger brother Akishino said the comments were 'regrettable' and implied that the princess was shirking her official duties – *he* did what he was expected to do, and did not attempt to define his own role, said the prince. A few months later at her birthday press conference, the Empress Michiko made a comment that some saw as a rebuke, saying that the princess must be '. . . feeling [great] pain in her extended period of rest'. In the face of the criticism, Naruhito eventually backed down and apologised; but the damage had been done.

The very private palace feud that had been simmering for years over Masako's failure to follow the script was now a very public debate that struck to the heart of the Japanese people's relationship with their monarchy. Did they want a remote and revered demi-deity, even if that meant sacrificing Masako in the tradition of the old Japanese saying 'the nail that sticks out gets hammered down'? Was it worth preserving a monarchy which the heavyweight historian Herbert Bix describes as 'totally out of sync with the times' and which 'can no longer function as a model, let alone a symbol, of national unity'? Or was it time to bring the royal family into the twenty-first century – perhaps not as liberated as Europe's bicycling, nightclubbing, toe-sucking royals, but allowed a more relevant role in public, and some freedom from the shackles of protocol in private? Polls showed that the public overwhelmingly favoured the latter, though the Imperial Household Agency remained as impervious as ever to popularity.

The agency was initially taken aback by the prince's attack and the groundswell of support for Masako. But a fortnight later its head, Toshio Yuasa – the one who so upset Masako when he, in effect, told her that a girl was not good enough and she should try for a boy – went on the offensive. He had no idea what Naruhito was talking about, he told the *kisha kurabu* hacks, but he would have a word with him. And then he dropped a bombshell. It was 'difficult' – read 'impossible' – for the agency to help Masako recover because her problems were 'not physical'. It would not be long before the dark secret of what was really ailing the princess would be out.

All the important stories of what was rapidly turning into a royal romance gone wrong have been broken by foreign news media, from Masako's engagement to her IVF pregnancy, to her fights with the palace bureaucracy. So few were surprised when it was Richard Lloyd Parry of *The Times*, who first dared to write what the royal reporters were only whispering. In an article a couple of weeks after the prince's press conference headlined 'The Depression of a Princess', he revealed that Masako had suffered a mental breakdown.

Agency officials, predictably, tried to hose the story down by denying that anything was wrong with the princess, just as a few years before they had publicly announced that Hirohito's cancer was 'pancreatitis'. The report was 'factually incorrect' and 'indecent', they said – a curious use of an adjective which says a lot about Japanese prejudice towards mental illness. Journalists covering the imperial beat were equally dismissive, probably still smarting from having been scooped yet again. One said the story had been 'invented', another that it was 'laughable'. But then, as spring turned to high summer and the princess remained out of the public eye, the agency reluctantly confirmed that Masako had been receiving drug therapy and counselling. She was suffering from what they called *tekiou shogai* or 'adjustment disorder'.

After her return from Karuizawa, Masako did initially look as though she was on the mend. She took up horse-riding, and was often seen cantering around the palace grounds, or visiting the imperial horse-stud. She began to go out a bit more, accompanying Naruhito to a performance of *bunraku*, Japan's traditional puppet theatre, and resuming some of her other official engagements. A video was released showing little Aiko playing with her toys while the family, seated stiffly in a row, looked on. Masako's mother, who had flown back to The Hague, told friends 'her heart is healing'. The *Kunaicho* briefed the royal hacks that she was 'preparing to return to public duties'.

But, in private, as soon as she returned from the mountains to her palace prison, Masako's condition began to deteriorate. Foreign friends who visited say that she put on a brave face, but 'she was not well, anyone could see that', says Andrew Arkley, the prince's old school-friend. She did turn out for the 'New Year's viewing' at the imperial palace, the most important public event of the year, an annual ritual in which the entire imperial family waves to the crowds from a glassed-in royal box – but she stayed only for the morning session. More and more often Naruhito was left to shoulder the official schedule alone – welcoming ambassadors, visiting schools and old people's homes, shivering on a dais amid the snow-drifts of the Japan Alps to open the Winter Olympics in Nagano.

In the summer of 2005, Masako did pluck up the strength to travel to the industrial city of Nagoya, south of Tokyo, to attend the opening of the Aichi World Expo, as a special favour to her husband who was the honorary president of the event. It was her first public function outside Tokyo for 20 months. She was escorted around the British pavilion, inspected a stuffed Siberian mammoth and 'the world's biggest kaleidoscope', and then jumped back on the train to return to the palace. 'She was smiling, but you could see the light had gone out of her eyes,' says royal-watcher Toshiya Matsuzaki. 'Look at her!' He tosses a copy of *Josei Jishin* magazine onto the table, which features a cover close-up of a smiling Masako at the Expo, wearing a smart grey jacket and white slacks, with a gold chain around her neck and pearl pendants dangling from her ears. 'They had to touch this up quite a lot – the make-up wasn't enough to cover up all the zits on her face, and you could see she had lost a lot of weight. She didn't look well at all.'

That *tekiou shogai* diagnosis had turned out to be another piece of deceitful double-talk designed, at least in part, to protect the royal family from any 'taint' of mental illness. But what exactly is it? 'Adjustment disorder', according to the World Health Organization's ICD-10, the international bible of mental illness, is not the most serious condition in the pantheon of what can go wrong with wiring of the mind. It is often caused by a stressful life event such as an illness, bereavement or separation. It is characterised by 'a depressed mood, anxiety, worry, a feeling of inability to cope, plan ahead or continue in the present situation'. It is, of course, a lot more complicated than this, but the key thing to remember is that the condition does not last longer than six months before clearing up by itself, or with the help of counselling and mild short-term medication. If it does last longer, it is not, by definition, adjustment disorder, but something much more serious.

For nearly two years now the *Kunaicho* has been insisting that Masako's condition is improving, that her illness is a temporary aberration, that she is gradually resuming her official duties. Unfortunately, that is not borne out by the observable facts. Nor is it a view shared by any of the eminent psychiatrists I consulted in Australia, Japan, or the United States. Although, of course, they have not been able to examine or assess the princess, they were unanimous in their diagnosis. Masako is suffering from depression, serious depression, and unless her environment is improved – read, unless she is given more freedom to pursue her personal interests and find a fulfilling public role – no amount of treatment is going to cure her.

Clinical depression is defined in Webster's Dictionary as 'an emotional condition, either neurotic or psychotic, characterised by feelings of hopelessness, inadequacy, etc.' Those who confuse its symptoms with merely feeling down in the dumps should read the scarifying descriptions in *Darkness Visible – a Memoir of Madness*, by the Pulitzer Prize-winning novelist William Styron, author of *Sophie's Choice* and another famous victim of depression. This is how Masako must be feeling:

Depression is a wimp of a word for a howling tempest in the brain . . . Like anyone else I have always had times when I felt deeply depressed, but this was something altogether new in my experience – a despairing, unchanging paralysis of the spirit beyond anything I had ever known or imagined could exist . . . All capacity for pleasure disappears, and despair maintains a merciless daily drumming.

It is also an ancient affliction, not some trendy modern therapist's concoction. There are recognisable pictures of 'manic' and 'melancholic' people from up to 3000 years ago, in the works of Hippocrates, Galen and Homer, as well as in the New Testament, in St Paul's Letter to the Corinthians. The list of famous people known to have suffered from it is as long as your arm, and includes such historical figures as George Washington, Napoleon Bonaparte and Ludwig van Beethoven. High-achievers like Masako, particularly creative people, are especially vulnerable. The Impressionist master Monet suffered from it after the death of his first wife, Camille, and attempted to commit suicide; Marilyn Monroe treated herself with hospitalisation and the drugs which finally killed her; a depressed and ageing Nobel laureate, Ernest Hemingway, blew his brains out with a shotgun; Princess Diana talked about her depression after the birth of Prince William, and later developed the eating disorder bulimia. She survived, only to die in a car crash, but it is an uncomfortable fact of life that some 15 per cent of people who suffer from severe depression kill themselves. In Australia it claims more lives than the road toll.

Although more than 100 million people worldwide suffer from it, it is only in relatively recent times that depression has begun to lose its stigma. Britain's wartime leader Winston Churchill suffered from manic depression, or bipolar disorder as it is now known, but he never discussed his illness publicly and it is only through the diaries of Lord (Charles) Moran of Manton, his physician and friend, that we know he coined the phrase 'my black dog' to describe his condition. Nowadays in the West, with the advent of modern psychoactive drugs, it is increasingly being seen as something that can be successfully treated, rather than a death sentence – which is just as well, considering that, by some estimates, one person in five will suffer from depression at some stage in their life. But in Asia, and particularly in Japan, any kind of mental illness is still seen as something shameful to be kept secret – especially if it occurs in a family as eminent as that of the emperor.

To learn a little of what Masako is going through, and to try and understand the causes of her depression and her prospects of recovery, I visited one of Australia's most distinguished psychiatrists. Professor Gordon Parker is executive director of the Black Dog Institute which is located behind the sprawl of brick and concrete buildings that make up Sydney's Prince of Wales Hospital. Named after Churchill's famous phrase, the institute bills itself as 'the premium mood disorder centre' in the southern hemisphere, and has treated more than 3000 patients, many suffering from depression. The place has an air of comfortable informality – no psychiatrist's couch, and photos on the walls of Christo's famous wrapping art, beginning with his first major effort when he trussed up two kilometres of Sydney's Little Bay in woven white erosion control fabric.

Parker is an amiable man in his mid-sixties wearing a tie decorated with camels who was for two decades Director of the School of Psychiatry at the University of NSW, and whose experience in Asia includes two years as research director of the Institute for Mental Health in Singapore. He is the author of *Dealing with Depression – A Commonsense Guide to Mood Disorders*. In his spare time he is also a scriptwriter – he once wrote for the TV comedy *The Mavis Brampton Show*, and is co-author with Neil Cole of the play *Personality Games*. Like his colleagues, Parker is in no doubt that Masako is not suffering from adjustment disorder. 'By clinical definition this class of disorders lasts less than six months,' says the professor. 'These events are very transitory [lasting] minutes or days at the most. The Wallabies lose, you feel depressed, you go off and have a beer and you feel better.'

From what he has read of Masako's condition, it sounds more like 'a chronic stress-induced mood disorder', triggered by the pressure she would be under in the 'gilded cage' of the palace. She would feel a sense of powerlessness and helplessness. 'An example in an Australian context might be where a woman is married to a pig of a bloke and he beats her up and demeans and humiliates her. She's got lots of young kids and no money and she feels that she just can't get away from that scenario. If you feel in life that nothing that you do will get you out of your present situation, then most of us would fall into some form of chronic depression.' Masako, says the professor, might at times feel so mentally down that she would be unable to even get out of bed or have a bath or a shower. She would feel a chronic lack of energy. Her sleep would be disrupted. Naruhito and others around her would find it impossible to cheer her up.

There is a famous and rather cruel experiment performed 40 years ago, which all psychiatrists study. In it, a researcher named Martin Seligman put dogs in 'shuttle-boxes' and harnessed them so that they could not escape. Then he ran an electric current through the floor. Initially the dogs howled and whimpered and tried to escape from the shocks, but eventually they gave up and lay on the floor without struggling. Even when, the following day, they were put back in the boxes and released from their restraints so that they could escape if they wanted to, most of them did not – they just lay there suffering. This is called 'learned helplessness' and it underpins our understanding of depression today. In Masako's case it is not electric shocks but the iron embrace of the Imperial Household Agency that has caused her illness.

As well, she must be feeling the burden of the stigma

mental illness carries in Japan – particularly since she has long been expected to bear the heir to the throne, and mental illness is regarded there as a hereditary condition, passed on in the genes. Japan has already had one emperor in modern times who was unable to reign in his own right – Hirohito's father, the Taisho Emperor Yoshihito – and has no desire to have another. In the West, our understanding of mental illness is rather more subtle. Scientists at the University of NSW have quite recently found a link with a variation in the gene governing the release of serotonin, the 'brain chemical' that regulates mood. But this 'bad gene' seems merely to make people more *susceptible* to adverse events such as a major illness, job loss, poverty, divorce or death of a loved one – it does not *guarantee* that depression will follow.

Professor Ian Hickie is another highly regarded psychiatrist, executive director of the Brain and Mind Research Institute, a neuroscience research institute, and a clinical advisor to Beyond Blue, the anti-depression initiative established by the former Victorian Premier, Jeff Kennett. This shrink-tank occupies a renovated underwear factory which still carries the image of Australia's iconic Chesty Bond on its chimney, overlooking a pleasant park in the inner-Sydney suburb of Camperdown. Hickie's views are important because he has made a particular study of attitudes towards mental illness in Asia. He cites, for instance, a recent World Health Organization study which shows that of seven Asian countries surveyed, Japan came equal last with China, behind Korea, Malaysia and Thailand, in its treatment of the mentally ill. Psychiatric epidemiology there is 'still in its neo-natal stage', says the report. This, rather than more robust mental health, helps to explain the apparently low incidence of mental illness. Officially,

Japan has fewer than half as many 'major depressive disorder' cases as Western countries with more enlightened attitudes – about three people in 100, compared with more than six in Australia.

But if you look instead at the figures for suicide you will see a very different picture. Japan appears to have a *more* serious problem than almost any other country in the world, particularly since the shocking advent of internet suicide pacts among troubled young strangers who meet on-line. Suicide there is more culturally acceptable than in the West as a 'solution' to situational crises and in cases of chronic loss of face. According to the WHO's latest figures, 36 Japanese males and 14 females in every 100,000 kill themselves every year – it is commonly said that women try more often, and men succeed more often. These are nearly double the figures for Australia (21 and 5) and more than treble the suicide rate of the United Kingdom (11 and 3). Only the traumatised countries of the former Soviet Union and Sri Lanka have higher suicide rates than Japan. So how to reconcile this with the fact that Japanese report less mental illness? The statistics are camouflaged by a refusal to seek help.

Most Japanese, certainly people as prominent as Masako, would rather go to their GP to get a potion for their 'sleeping difficulty' or 'upset stomach' than admit that there may be a deeper underlying psychological cause for their problems. It is also common among older people to try and deny that they have a medical problem at all, explaining their depression in terms of the philosophical concept of a disorder of the *ki* or 'vital energy'. In part this is because of a well-founded fear that they may be drugged to the eyeballs and clapped in an old-fashioned mental institution. Japan has a huge over-supply of hospital beds of all sorts, and as a result patients – who are called 'treasure' by greedy hospital owners – may find themselves trapped for weeks or months in a Kafkaesque medical nightmare. The average length of hospitalisation for mental illness in Japan is 390 days, more than a year, compared with the American average of 10 days.

In recent times, attitudes do appear to have been changing. To try and counter the unwillingness to trust medical intercession – and, of course, to increase their sales – the pharmaceutical industry has been running an extensive TV advertising campaign encouraging people to talk to their doctors about their problems. In one ad I saw, an attractive young woman smiles at the camera and coos, 'I went to a doctor and now I am happy.' There has been greatly increased media attention, particularly since Japan's first 'celebrity mental patient', the film star Nana Kinomi, talked publicly about her postmenopausal depression; and a flood of more than 100 books on the subject has hit the market. All this has helped demystify mental illness, with many more people now seeking psychiatric help, and sales of the few antidepressant drugs which are available in Japan trebling in the past three years. But in spite of this, mental illness there is still little understood compared with in the West, and people seeking treatment can still expect to be shunned.

'In Japan there is an emphasis on the family, or the social group, as being more important than the individual,' explains Hickie. 'If you declare that you have a mental health problem it is often a source of very great shame for yourself, your family, your company or your social group. People go out of their way not to disclose [mental illness] and there is active discrimination against them. In Hong Kong, until recent times you couldn't join the armed services if you had a relative with a mental disorder. There is a fearfulness around mental illness.'

Nor do the experts have much confidence in Japanese psychiatric treatment. Parker says therapy there is 'very unusual, very quaint, very idiosyncratic, often quite bizarre'. Doctors frequently dispense drugs themselves, leading to gross, but highly profitable, over-prescription. 'It's like dispensing sweets. The theory is that if one drug works, two will work even better, so they will dispense three or four of them,' says the professor. This is why Japanese have become the world's champion pill-poppers, taking twice as many drugs as even the Americans. They spend more than $100 billion a year on medications, more than the entire Japanese defence budget and double what they spend on their staple food of rice. The media has coined a phrase for this: *kusuri zuke shakai*, or 'drug pickled society'.

But unfortunately, says Dr Atsumi Fukui, they are not always the right drugs. Fukui, who has been in Australia since she was a child, was for many years the only practising Japanese-born psychiatrist in the country. She says that many modern medicines used to treat psychiatric disorders are not approved in Japan. The popular Prozac, for instance, never made it to Japanese dispensary shelves, because its US manufacturer, Eli Lilly, did not believe there was a market for it – depression was not generally acknowledged as a real illness, even as recently as the 1990s. Pfizer's Zoloft – currently the world's most popular front-line drug for treating depression – has only just been approved, more than a decade after it was first available in Australia. Partly this is because Japanese regulators, with more than 14,000 drugs listed for government-funded medical benefits (Australia has about 600), demand more stringent proof that a new drug is not only safe, but more effective than those already on the market. But there is more than a suspicion that this is just window-dressing for a government policy designed to protect Japan's fragmented and backward pharmaceutical industry from foreign competition.

In view of all this, it is hardly surprising that Masako and the people around her refused for months, possibly years, to confront the truth – that she is suffering from a serious mental illness – and attempt to deal with it. The precise details of her treatment have never been disclosed – in fact, at the time of writing there had only been one bulletin on her health. But as 2005 ground to a close, it became an open secret among Tokyo's chattering classes that her condition, far from improving as her minders would have the world believe, was getting worse. It was impossible to conceal the fact that her behaviour was becoming increasingly erratic, leading to more cancelled engagements and miffed officials. Captive to her Black Dog, she was spending much of the day shut in her quarters reading economic texts until two or three in the morning, and playing music to herself. She could not bring herself to talk to the staff and sometimes communicated with them by slipping notes through a crack in the door. Relations with the *Kunaicho* had deteriorated to such an extent that Shingo Haketa, the former chief of the Health and Welfare Ministry who had been appointed the new head of the agency, confirmed that she had refused even to meet him.

Masako was also quite unable to deal with her ladies-in-waiting, the people who controlled – or tried to control – her life on a day-to-day basis, from waking her up in the morning to choosing her clothes to drawing her bath at night. These attendants, half a dozen of them, are not professionals but middle-aged women – usually widows and spinsters – whose jobs are handed down from generation to generation by families of the old nobility. Many of them have been 'in service' at the palace for decades and, far from trying to accommodate Masako, insist on their own inflexible ways of doing things. It seems she could not abide their insufferable meddling. Three senior members of the household found various excuses to resign, but the rest of the household seemed determined to stay put, and trying to replace them, Masako discovered, was as futile as a prisoner trying to sack his warders. These bitchy biddies are the source of much of the malicious gossip about Masako that has been finding its way into the tabloids.

Of the 300 or so public events which Naruhito was obliged to attend during 2005, Masako had only been able to appear by his side on about a dozen occasions. She did not go to the big winter sports carnival in Hokkaido – even though, as gossips were quick to point out, she had been well enough to take her little daughter Aiko on her 'skiing debut' just a few weeks before. This 'up and down' behaviour has come to characterise Masako's life and is typical of someone with her condition. One day she will be gaily entertaining old school-friends at afternoon tea; the next she will be seen leaning against a wall with her eyes closed, barely able to support herself, as she tries to supervise Aiko at play.

She gave up going on the annual outings, popular with the Tokyo diplomatic corps, to the imperial duck-pond where Naruhito had first proposed all those years ago. She turned down another chance for an overseas trip, cancelling a planned visit to Mexico in the spring of 2006 to attend an international water conservation conference –

Naruhito would have to go alone. She even snubbed the emperor and empress on several occasions, reported the magazines. Once, she cancelled an invitation to them to attend her birthday party at short notice. Then, on Akihito's seventy-second birthday, the night before Christmas, Masako and Naruhito had gone to the imperial palace for a slap-up celebratory dinner. When the time came for Aiko to be sent home with a nursemaid the little girl threw a tantrum and Masako had to take her back to the East Palace herself. She did not return to the dinner party until almost three hours later, ruining the feast, complained the chef, and the whole night, carped her critics. No one thought to ask what had been going through her troubled mind during those missing hours.

These might sound like trivial tiffs, but in a culture where appearances are so important, any real or imagined slight is taken very seriously, particularly when it is magnified through the microscope of the media. Illness is no excuse. And even more significant than these social lapses, at least in the eyes of the palace's crusty courtiers, she was unable to attend to the sacred rituals that come with the job. Masako was missing for a solemn commemorative service on the anniversary of the death of the Taisho Emperor on Christmas Day. And she did not turn up in her ceremonial garb to join New Year's prayers for the peace and prosperity of the Japanese people at the imperial shrine, the most important religious ritual of the year on the royal calendar. 'She has no idea,' a *Kunaicho* official fumed anonymously to a magazine journalist. 'This is not supposed to be fun, [these ceremonies are] even more important than her public duties.' Much more important, it goes without saying, than the mental health of the suffering princess.

In December, more than two years after Masako's illness was first disclosed, the public was at last given a glimpse behind the sick-bay curtains. A new specialist had arrived on the scene, Dr Yukata Ono, a professor of psychiatry at Tokyo's highly regarded Keio University. Ono is a disciple of Dr Aaron Beck, Professor of Psychiatry at Pennsylvania University and the founder of a widely endorsed school of treatment for people with depression called cognitive behavioural therapy. He is a specialist with a string of professional publications to his name, including one on suicide prevention among elderly residents in the boondocks of rural Aomori Prefecture. Ono is also the author of a book called *Treating Depression*, and a recognised authority on the subject, at least in Japan. Finally someone was taking Masako seriously.

It is not known exactly how the professor came to be Masako's psychiatrist, but her frantically worried mother Yumiko must have played a part. During flying visits to Tokyo from The Hague, she had taken to calling on her daughter, over the protests of the palace officials, and demanding that they stop harassing her and help her get proper treatment. No doubt she also obliquely reminded Naruhito of his wedding promise to protect her daughter 'from any possible hardships'. When she learned that Masako did not trust the palace doctors, and had been refusing to see her official physician, Yumiko put the word out on her network that she was looking for a respected psychiatrist, one who embraced modern thinking on the treatment of mental illness, and one in whom, most importantly, her daughter could confide. Analysis in any language is a demanding enough task without having to negotiate the platitudinous circumlocutions of Japanese courtly language.

Professor Ono filled the bill. 'Talk therapy' sessions began, supplemented by what I am told is a regime of medication – probably paroxetine (marketed as Aropax in Australia) or fluvoxamine (Luvox). Both these drugs are older antidepressants approved in the US in the early 1990s, and now largely superseded in the West by a newer generation of drugs with fewer side-effects – but they are a great deal better than nothing. At year's end, after endless toing and froing by the *Kunaicho* about the text, a three-page report was released on Masako's condition. Unsurprisingly, the words *utsu byo* ('mood disorder', or 'depression') had been censored out somewhere along the way. Just as no one would acknowledge that an IVF specialist had been brought in to help Masako have an IVF baby, so no one was admitting that a depression specialist had been brought in to treat her depression.

It may seem obvious to the Western mind, but in Japan the proprieties must be observed, and even though most informed Japanese now understood what was wrong with the princess, the stigma of officially using the word had to be avoided. So, publicly at any rate, the palace stuck to the diagnosis of *tekiou shogai*, or adjustment disorder, even though Ono, of all people, must know that, by definition, this could not possibly be what Masako was suffering from. 'They say it is *tekiou shogai*,' sniffed Dr Shizuo Machizawa, a psychiatrist at Tokyo's Rikkyo University, 'But it is nothing other than depression. She [Masako] cannot bear to be sitting there like a doll on a *hinadan*.' (A *hinadan* is a tiered stand on which tiny decorative ceremonial dolls representing a prince, a princess and courtiers, all in Heian era costume, are displayed.)

That report, bland though it seems after the endless ex-purgations through which it must have gone, nevertheless points the finger squarely at *Kunaicho* officials as having caused Masako's mental illness. The condition, said Ono, was caused by 'chronic stress'. The stress was caused by her 'environment' (read the rigid regime of the palace) and triggered by something all working mothers will be familiar with – the demands of having to care for a small child while trying to perform a demanding job. Masako, said the report, found her official duties too onerous, and she needed to find a personal mission in life – a research project, presumably one a little more demanding than the care of injured beetles. If she was ever to recover, Masako must be allowed more time to 'exercise and enjoy herself in private', and must be given the freedom to go out more on her own. The psychiatrist appealed to the staff of the East Palace to support her so that she could recover and resume her official duties.

The only thing surprising about Ono's report was that there were no surprises. Nothing in it could not have been said 13 years before, on Masako's wedding day. Here is an ambitious, intelligent woman who cannot bear the stifling constraints of life as a royal puppet; a woman from a family with a tradition of public service denied a real role in life; a woman with a Harvard education, a master of languages, who is denied meaningful discourse, and urged to amuse herself with pursuits such as the dissection of catfish or the study of medieval barges. *Kunaicho*'s response to the report was that they would 'study' it – code for doing nothing. And, as any psychiatrist would tell you, that is not an option. No matter how effective Ono's treatment, if the underlying causes of Masako's depression are not removed – if her life in the palace does not improve – she will never get better, and may even be driven to take desperate measures.

In spite of the findings of her psychiatrist, many influential Japanese still refused to acknowledge that she was really ill, and were by now openly criticising Masako. Although Harumi Kobayashi and her Masako fan-club were still happily clicking away, the tide of public opinion was turning against her, at a time when she most needed support. In the absence of any informed debate in the media, the unregulated internet became the battleground, in much the same way as what became known as the 'War of the Wales' dominated the British media when Charles and Diana's marriage was on the rocks, with the public taking sides, and the media fed by partisan leaks from the two camps. On Channel Two, a new on-line chat-site, a character calling herself (himself?) No Name Kimi No Seisa commented cruelly: 'She is useless. I hope she dies soon so Naruhito can remarry. She has become neurotic because of the pressure on her to have boys.' Others were insulting: 'How come she hasn't fixed her teeth?' And an element of racism even crept in: 'She likes white faces.'

Leaks, pretty obviously from the household staff, pointed out that although Masako's illness might prevent her from fulfilling many of her public duties, it did not appear to interfere with her private pleasures. An understanding of the roller-coaster of her depression was obviously beyond them. She was spotted sight-seeing at the Tokyo Millenario, a colourful Christmas light-show near Tokyo's main railway station; she attended a concert by the world-renowned violinist Itzhak Perlman; she had been seen horse-riding, and enjoying herself at a party with some of Naruhito's old school-friends; she was looking forward to a holiday at the Hotel Grand Phoenix, a luxury ski-lodge with a palatial royal suite on a mountainside in the middle of the Japan Alps. Some prominent royal writers with close contacts in the bureaucracy began to suggest that, in spite of all the evidence, Masako's illness was not real and she was merely out to enjoy herself, while selfishly shirking her duty.

'She is *goman* [arrogant],' says Toshiaki Kawahara, one of those critics. He is a well-known writer who has been reporting on the imperial household since 1952 – in fact, he has written an extraordinary 21 books about the royals. His most famous scoop was a two-hour interview with Naruhito when the prince was at Oxford. He is a frail, white-haired man in his mid-eighties who walks with the aid of a pearl-handled walking stick. Like many men of the older school, he believes that the marriage was a mistake from the beginning:

> One of the main reasons things are going badly is that Masako is egotistical and selfish. She doesn't compromise. She is too intellectual, and she cannot get along with the people around her. She speaks too much, like English women . . . that is why the crown prince fell in love with her. [But] Japanese women have a responsibility to act modestly and to act somewhat obediently. She would not make a good empress – she is too strong [and] she tries to put her opinions forward on any issue.

But whether or not they believe Masako is sick, critics like Kawahara cannot ignore the central dilemma of the drama – unless something radical happens, in 40 or 50 years' time when Naruhito and his brother Akishino die, the Japanese imperial line will also come to an end. And Japanese, unlike the citizens of most other countries, which got rid of their monarchs long ago, seem reluctant to see that happen. Polls consistently show that more than 70 per cent are in favour of an emperor, though this figure may be quite unreliable owing to the biased way in which polling questions are loaded in Japan. 'Do you feel very close, a little close, or not close at all to the imperial family?' asked one recent newspaper poll.

Nevertheless, few Japanese would be happy to see their monarchy abolished – even the Communist Party has been quiet on the subject in recent years, and its big-selling newspaper *Akahata* covers the doings of the royals. I doubt whether the number of Japanese supporting a republic would even reach the 20 per cent of Britons who tell pollsters they want to get rid of their queen. And I suspect none would be as sanguine as Kenneth Ruoff, Akihito's American biographer. Although he doesn't believe the government would ever allow it to happen, Ruoff doesn't think the end of the monarchy would make a blind bit of difference to the way Japan is run, its economy, its institutions of state, or the prosperity of its people. 'You could run a subway under the palace,' he suggests irreverently – Tokyo's underground rail system is contorted around it to avoid the indignity of undermining the emperor's residence. 'You could make [the palace grounds] into a really nice park for all the people of Tokyo. You could save the cost of about one jet fighter [a year] from the national budget – after all, why should this one family be supported on the dole? But in the long run I don't think it [abolishing the monarchy] would make much difference.'

Japan's ageing band of right-wing extremists would be furious, says Ruoff. But they would soon come up with a new symbol of national pride, just as in republican France, which got rid of its last emperor 130 years ago, the ultra-nationalist Jean-Marie Le Pen has adopted Joan of Arc as his rallying cry, filling his house with devotional statues of the martyred saint. 'It's not like the far right would disappear,' he says, 'they would just come up with something different to prove that Japan is a little bit more unique with a capital "U" than any other country.'

Japan may not be ready for such a radical change, but how, with no male heir, can the imperial line be maintained? That was the question that preoccupied Japan's politicians, bureaucrats and journalists, through the long, hot summer of 2005. In the old days, of course, Naruhito would simply have dropped his handkerchief at the feet of one of the court concubines, who would dutifully follow him into the bedchamber and produce the required offspring nine months later. The Meiji Emperor, remember, produced 15 children in this way. But, as we have seen, the practice died out with Hirohito, and there is no provision for it in the current law of succession.

Remarkable to relate, even today bringing back concubinage to save the monarchy has its supporters. As the debate raged, Prince Tomohito of Mikasa, Akihito's eldest cousin, let it be known through a newsletter column he writes that this was his preferred option. 'Using concubines like we used to is one option,' he wrote. 'I'm all for it, but this might be a little difficult considering the social climate in and outside the country.' Few agreed with the ageing, cancer-stricken prince, who is closely aligned with the conservative Right. Most Japanese regard the idea of a royal harem as an embarrassing anachronism best left to the Swazis, as, most certainly, would Masako and Naruhito.

As far back as 2001, the *Kunaicho* had begun its own deliberations on the issue – after all, if the monarchy ceased to exist, so would their jobs. They came up with two alternatives – expand the gene-pool by allowing more distant (male) imperial relatives to succeed; or allow women to return to the Chrysanthemum Throne for the first time in more than two centuries. Of these, hardly surprisingly, the one which gained support among die-hard monarchists was the proposal to recruit a member of one of the families which had been kicked out of their palaces 50 years before in the wake of the MacArthur reforms. The new prince would have to be legitimised by adoption by one of the male heirs to the throne.

Under the most convoluted proposal to circumvent the succession law, the conscripted prince would be adopted by Prince Tomohito, and then marry one of his own half-sisters, Akiko or Yohko, Tomohito's two eligible daughters. Scholars delved back into history to find precedent to justify this 'adoption solution', and discovered that it had been used three times before, in the sixth, fifteenth and eighteenth centuries, when distant relatives took the throne after the family's main line ran out of heirs. No one thought to ask the two young princesses, both smart, university-educated graduates, what *they* thought of the idea, of course.

At the news that adoption was being considered, some discreet jostling began among the surviving ex-royals. According to research by Richard Lloyd Parry, seven of the families stripped of their royal rank in 1947 survived, and five of them had sons of marriageable age, a total of eight eligible bachelors carrying the imperial blood-line. Among these, three front-runners soon emerged, ordinary Tokyo *sararimen* who by an accident of birth were being considered as potential emperors: Tsuneyasu Takeda, then aged 29, is a writer who is an expert on imperial family history; Asatoshi Kuni, 33, who worked for the trading house Itochu Corporation; and Mutsuhiko Higashikuni, 24, a car salesman. Authenticating their claims to the throne would, however, require a genealogical spreadsheet the size of a table-top and a great deal of patience. My own research showed that Higashikuni is, in fact, the grandson of Hirohito's daughter, Shigeko, the former Princess Teru, and thus would be ineligible to carry on the male lineage. Takeda's and Kuni's ancestry disappears in the mists of the nineteenth-century aristocracy.

The obvious solution to the succession crisis was staring everyone in the face: change the law to allow a woman to succeed. There are plenty of eligible royal woman – eight princesses, in fact, including Masako and Naruhito's little daughter Aiko, who remain in their palaces on the public payroll until they marry, when they are required by law to surrender their titles and depart. Polls showed that the public overwhelmingly favoured this solution, with 75 per cent in favour of a female emperor, and only 16 per cent opposed, according to one survey by the Kyodo news agency.

Elsewhere this would be uncontroversial. Seven European monarchies now allow women to succeed to the throne (although Britain insists that males have priority), as does Asia's only other important surviving monarchy, Thailand. Sweden abolished its men-only law in 1980 when faced with exactly the same situation as Japan – the heir to the Swedish throne is now Crown Princess Victoria. Monaco, on the other hand, took a different route. The minute Mediterranean principality changed its constitution in 2000 to allow its monarch to be chosen from a wider field of royal relatives because the ruling Prince Albert has no legitimate heir. He does, his subjects were shocked to learn, have two illegitimate children, one a son by a Togolese flight attendant. But the snooty Monegasques apparently don't want any suggestion of illegitimacy, let alone duskiness, in their sovereign.

But Japan, as we have seen, is a rather sexist society, and those 16 per cent opposed to female succession come mainly from the influential conservative right wing of politics. Almost as soon as the issue of a female emperor was raised, hundreds of Shinto priests, representing the country's 80,000 shrines, gathered in Tokyo to express their opposition to what they referred to as 'the modern concept of gender equality [which gives] little considera-tion to the centuries-old tradition of the paternal bloodline of the imperial family'. As well as regarding itself as the custodian of ancient tradition, the priesthood forms an important support-base for the ruling LDP. Prominent politicians, led by an influential former prime minister, 88-year-old Yasuhiro Nakasone, and several senior members of Prime Minister Koizumi's own Cabinet, announced they would fight any attempt to change the legislation. The succession crisis was morphing into a political battle which would pit the traditionalists against those seeking to modernise the monarchy.

Keen to promote himself as a reformist politician at war with the autocratic old factional barons of the LDP, the populist Koizumi sniffed the breeze of public opinion and announced early in 2005 that he was personally in favour of a change in the law, and he was appointing a committee of worthies to investigate and make recommen-dations. As in the West, no prime minister of Japan would initiate such an inquiry without ensuring that it would come up with the 'right' answer. In this case, the commit-tee was stacked, not with imperial historians who would be expected to favour continuing the men-only tradition, but with judges, university professors and civil servants who might bring a more open mind to the issue. Heading it was Hiroyuki Yoshikawa, a distinguished former president of the University of Tokyo, but a man whose expertise is in, of all things, robot engineering.

With what is, by Japanese standards, almost indecent haste – only 17 meetings, a total of 30 hours of deliberation over 10 months – the committee reached consensus and recommended that the law be changed to allow a woman to become emperor. Koizumi welcomed the finding, and declared that – even though more than 100 members of his own party were now in open revolt, threatening to cross the floor and bring down the government – he would press ahead with the legislation in the parliamentary session which began in March 2006. The change would mean that the eight princesses, providing they did not marry first, would now join the ranks of the princes eligible to succeed to the throne, with Princess Aiko now second in line after her father, Naruhito. The report left unanswered a number of thorny constitutional issues, such as whether or not the daughter of a female emperor would be next in line to the throne. But one can imagine the sigh of relief that echoed around the East Palace at the decision. One of the greatest pressures on Masako – to have another round of IVF treatment in an attempt to have a boy – would now be lifted from her shoulders. There was light at the end of the long, dark tunnel of depression.

But as so often happens in Japan, things were never going to be that simple. In February of 2006, a few months after the committee reported its findings, came a bolt from the blue. Koizumi was presiding over a televised parliamentary budget committee meeting when an attendant passed him a note, and he looked up in surprise. NHK, the national broadcaster, was running a story that, 11 years after the birth of their last child, Naruhito's brother Akishino and his wife Kiko were expecting another, their third. An ultrasound scan had revealed that she was six weeks pregnant, and, all going well, the baby would be born in September.

The news broke just days before the prime minister was due to introduce the highly contentious legislation into the parliament. It has to be said that modernising the imperial family would not be top of his must-do list. Modernising his antiquated, corrupt, undemocratic and faction-ridden ruling party has long been a priority. Japan's economy, emerging from a decade and a half in the doldrums, needs further radical reform – particularly the privatisation of the postal savings bank on which Koizumi staked his leadership in the election of 2005. The crumbling health, pension and aged care systems all need drastic revitalisation if they are to cope with the demands of the world's most rapidly ageing society. The hawkish Koizumi was also keen to rewrite Japan's 'peace constitution' to recognise the reality that Japan is a regional military power, with a wider role to play in global security. Alongside these challenges, allowing a woman to inherit the throne would be seen as a third-order issue, popular with the public, a gesture to Japan's feminists, but hardly worth the civil war it would cause within the party.

Conspiracy theorists were quick to suggest that giving Koizumi a face-saving way of backing down on his commitment was the very reason why the *Kunaicho* had leaked the news so quickly. Normally, pending royal births are not announced until the third month of pregnancy, in case of a mishap. The prime minister mulled it over for a few days, then let it be known that, in view of the royal pregnancy, the need for urgency had evaporated and the legislation would not be introduced during the summer session of the *Diet*. If at all.

The news could not have come at a better time for the opponents of a female emperor as it threw the entire succession plan into turmoil. If the child was a boy the imperial dynasty could continue without the law having to be changed. Akishino's son could follow him or Naruhito onto the throne. However, if it was another girl the crisis would continue, but without the dynamic Koizumi to champion the cause for reform. The factional barons who rule the LDP had made it clear that, after four years as prime minister, it was time for someone else to have a turn. Unless there was another unexpected turn of events, in September 2006 Koizumi would have to stand down. Without him to lead the push for change, political observers fear the reform will wither on the vine. And the pressure on Masako to bear a boy would continue relentlessly.

10

No Happy Ending

T HE DIE-HARD FANS HAVE BEEN WAITING SINCE JUST AFTER
dawn, six o'clock on a muggy, overcast summer's
morning, sheltering under the overhang of a rural
railway station. As on Masako's wedding day all those
years ago it is raining – this time golden showers backlit
with flashes of sunshine, what Japanese call 'fox's wedding
rain'. 'This is nothing,' says one stocky middle-aged
woman, towing a suitcase on wheels containing a change
of clothing, lunch and several thousand dollars' worth of
state-of-the-art digital camera equipment. 'Once when
they were delayed we had to wait thirty hours!' Her
friends nod sympathetically.

Unfortunately, Harumi Kobayashi can't make it today.
She has rung us, distraught, from Tokyo's main station to
say that she has run out of money for the fare. 'No one
understands me,' she wails. 'Not my husband, not my
boss, not my children. I think I'll just forget about it
and burn all my photos.' Fortunately she later relents,

ambushing the royal couple as they are escorted through the station and adding yet more pictures to her mammoth collection.

But the rest of the Masako fan-club has turned up in good spirits, sipping green tea from their thermos flasks and nibbling rice-balls as they stake out the best spots for photographing their idol. They have travelled overnight for hundreds of kilometres, from Saitama, Kanagawa and Aichi prefectures, to seize this rare opportunity to snap her – Masako has not been seen in public for months. Five of them are veterans – they have been stalking Masako, in the nicest possible way, since her engagement was announced 13 years before. One followed the couple to Australia, while another trailed Naruhito all the way to Belgium to snap him at a royal wedding. They are led by the doyenne of the paparazzi, the formidable 'Mrs Sakai' who won't give her full name 'in case the *Kunaicho* punishes me'. Even Masako's most devoted fans are scared of the palace officials.

I have left early, too, just as the huge halls of the Tokyo station were beginning to rumble with the million and more commuters who stream through this transit hub every working day of the week. Armed police are on duty for the royal occasion, to back up the railway guards standing stiffly to attention on top of little wooden lookout boxes, placed at strategic intervals around the concourses. I am bound for Nasushiobara, a sparsely populated region of mountains, forests and hot springs north of Tokyo, which has been a favourite getaway for Japan's rulers since the time of the Tokugawa shoguns. After ploughing through the cuttings, talking to the princess's friends, colleagues and sundry expert commentators on four continents, and pleading in vain with the royal minders for an interview,

I am finally going to catch a glimpse of the couple for whom I have taken more than a year out of my life.

Although the palace officials might shudder at the idea of their royals riding around on bicycles, no one raises an eyebrow at them catching a train. In fact it's by far the easiest way to travel around the Japanese countryside. Nasushiobara station is 158 kilometres away, but the dolphin-nosed *shinkansen*, capable of 240 kilometres an hour, will make it in 75 minutes, half the time of a car on the congested roads. The royal couple won't exactly be strap-hanging in a crowded aisle with the hoi polloi either. The crown prince is entitled to his own special carriage; when he becomes emperor he will get a whole train to himself, much as Europe's royals used to. And forget tea-bags and sand-wiches with curled-back crusts – Japan's railway food, the famous *ekiben*, is worth the trip alone, tasty snacks dispensed by smiling young women from loaded trolleys which tinkle as they pass up and down the aisles. My trip passes in foam-cushioned comfort, while I catch up on the latest magazine gossip about Masako and Naruhito.

The previously taboo subject of divorce is now being openly discussed, no doubt a whispering campaign begun by the *Kunaicho*, who would love to see the back of Masako. Officials are said to have been 'studying' this 'solution' for more than a year. Not only is she not fit to become the empress, say their mouthpieces in the media, but divorce would allow Naruhito to remarry, produce a male heir, and avoid the need to change the law to allow female succession. Perhaps not so curiously, no one seems to have consulted the couple about the idea.

As the grey of the dreary city high-rises morphs to a yellow-green blur of ripening rice-paddies, I read that some commentators are stretching rather a long bow, comparing the couple's predicament with that of Britain's Edward VIII, the king who abdicated his throne for the love of the American divorcee Wallis Simpson. Others compare their plight with that of Charles and Diana, but this seems to rather miss the point. Although in both cases the royal family and the palace courtiers regarded the bride as unsuitable, Naruhito is still, from all outward appearances, deeply in love and committed to supporting his ailing princess. Yoko Tajima, a professor of women's studies at Tokyo's Hosei University, was closer to the mark when she wrote that the real problem was the restrictions on Masako's life, both public and private, which were denying her basic freedoms and human rights. 'Please let Masako free,' she pleaded. But how?

Although divorce has been increasing in Japan since the 1960s, it is still only a fraction of the rate seen in Western countries. Annually, there were 1.92 divorces per 1000 people in 1998, fewer than Australia (2.6), and less than half the number of the United States (4.1), where one marriage in two ends in tears. Partly this reflects social stigma, partly the economic reality of supporting two households in Tokyo, one of the world's most expensive cities, where women still face formidable barriers to re-entering the workforce. More common than formal divorce is what Japanese call 'in-house divorce', where the couple co-exists under the same roof, living lives of quiet misery until one or the other dies.

It is commonly said that divorce is forbidden to members of the imperial family who are on, or in line to, the throne. Says Kenichi Asano, the professor of journalism and imperial critic: 'There are two families in Japan that you can never leave – the *yakuza* [crime gangs] and the royal family.'

This is a colourful quote, but it is not quite true. It is correct that in the history of the Japanese monarchy, only one royal, a distant cousin of the Meiji emperor named Prince Kitashirakawa, divorced, and that was way back in 1889. A number of others are known to have lived emotionally if not physically apart from their wives, with one prince not so long ago scandalising Tokyo by maintaining a glamorous bar hostess as a mistress in an apartment he bought for her. But constitutionally, if not by custom, divorce is permitted. Article 14 of the Imperial Household Law specifically provides that in the event of divorce, the wife of a prince shall lose her status as a member of the imperial family.

But the commentators promoting divorce do seem to have overlooked two important things. The first is that Naruhito is still devoted to Masako. It would require an immense sacrifice for the crown prince to discard the love of his life, even for what his parents and his advisors may imagine to be the good of the country. The second is that, if the law allowing female succession is ever enacted, Aiko would be next in line to the throne after her father, and the officials would never allow a future emperor to be taken from the palace. What mother would willingly pay that price for her freedom – to allow her young, and only, child to be taken from her and turned into the *Kunaicho* ideal of an obedient royal robot?

So what of Aiko? Apart from a few stilted videotapes released by the agency, and some still photos of her cultivating mustard-spinach in the palace garden and finger-painting at kindergarten, we have not seen a lot of the tot who many hoped would one day become Japan's first female emperor since the eighteenth century. Approaching her fifth birthday, Aiko bears a striking resemblance to her father, a small, quiet, rather passive child. Both parents are obviously devoted to her, particularly Masako for whom the little girl appears to be a ray of hope in the darkness of her life in the palace. Masako devoted her 2006 New Year's *waka* poem to her daughter:

> *When one in the circle laughs*
> *so does another,*
> *and the children's laughter spreads more and more.*

Naruhito has stuck to his promise to play a more fulfilling role in his daughter's upbringing than traditional Japanese dads. When she was a baby he fed the child, bathed her and played with her – although it is not known whether he went as far as changing the nappies, as Kenneth Ruoff had hoped. When they are out in public, he will hold Aiko's hand, piggy-back her or cradle her in his arms. At his last birthday press conference, Naruhito spoke with obvious feeling of his 'love and affection' for the child, and of the importance of Aiko learning how to relate with 'normal' children outside the palace, acquiring, as well as formal skills such as calligraphy, the 'simple rules of [social interaction]'. He quoted with approval the famous folksy aphorism, *Children Learn What They Live*, by the American family counsellor and writer Dorothy Law Nolte, who has apparently become for this generation of royals what Dr Spock was for Naruhito's parents.

Inevitably, there have been clashes with the *Kunaicho* over Aiko's upbringing. The 'good old days' when Minoru Hamao, Naruhito's chamberlain, would be given permission to whack the boy and shut him in a dark cupboard are over. The chambermaids charged with looking after Aiko have complained that the child is becoming spoilt, throwing tantrums and offending people by telling them what she really thinks of the presents they give her, rather than smiling polite thank-yous. In a minor concession by the bureaucrats, they have permitted a genuine expert on child-care to be brought into the East Palace to look after Aiko's education, putting the noses of the amateur aunties of the *Kunaicho* seriously out of joint. Mikiko Fukusako, a highly qualified professional in early childhood education, has proved not only to be a good teacher, but has become a friend and ally of Masako in her war with the palace staff. She also attended Denenchofu Futaba school, three years ahead of Masako, and the two women obviously share both experiences and values.

From the age of three, twice a week, Aiko attended a kindergarten in Aoyama called the National Children's Castle, where she mixed with other kids in a playgroup, learning 'wordplay, basic etiquette and socialisation'. She has been taken on carefully choreographed outings, or 'debuts' as the media like to call them, to parks, the zoo, a farm, skiing, ice-skating. She watches the sumo wrestling on TV, and knows the names of all the champions. Her parents have done their best to bring her out into the real world, while protecting her from the mobs of mobile-phone-camera-wielding *okake* mums who crowd around whenever they are out in public, eager to snap her photo.

From the spring term of 2006, her formal education began at Gakushuin, where Naruhito and all the other royals began their education. As with her father, the teachers and fellow students were urged not to treat Aiko differently from the other kids when she turned up on the first day with her home-made *bento* lunch in her hand. But this will only work up to a point. From now on, she will be reminded daily that she is living a life apart from 'normal' folk – each day a chambermaid will bring her to school, and will then wait in the special 'royal waiting-room' provided until the child is ready to return to the palace.

I am thinking about the little girl who was once seen as the only hope for the survival of the monarchy when the bullet-train slides into Nasushiobara station, the doors open, and a crowd of holiday-makers emerges, trundling their bags along the platform. Although it is a large, modern building, the station retains a kind of country charm, and an obvious pride in its local produce. A shop sells packs of preserved *ayu*, a freshwater fish, sweet potato skins, puffed barley, ropes of *udon* noodles, and vicious-looking hornets pickled in honey. It also displays photos of the crown prince and princess, no doubt hoping to imply royal patronage, until a railway official notices me photographing them and sidles over to order the owner to take them down. So keen are they to avoid offending their royal guests, that officials have even instructed the popular 7-Eleven convenience store chain to tone down its garish green, red and orange sign. The shop at the bottom of the street where Masako and Naruhito will stay has been repainted a less obtrusive black and white.

I have half a day to kill because the *Kunaicho*, with its usual paranoia about the foreign media, has refused to reveal which train the royal couple will be taking. In fact, the only reason I know they will be coming at all is thanks to Mrs Kobayashi and her groupie grapevine. A local taxi-driver is happy enough to take me on a $200 tour of the royal sights, beginning with the *goyotei*, the imperial retreat where they will stay. It is a huge estate of forest and meadows in the shadow of twin mountain peaks which Naruhito likes to scale, a semi-wilderness with streams, and a hot spring, where snakes slither and wild bears roam. It was once a hunting lodge. On display at the station is an enormous iron pot, two metres across – the sort of thing in which cannibals boiled missionaries in childhood comic-books – which the hunters used to stew their game. Unfortunately, the police have blocked off the street in preparation for the royal arrival, so we cannot catch a glimpse of the rambling old timber homestead where Masako and Naruhito will holiday.

A few minutes' drive away is Gioia Mia, a local restaurant said to be a favourite of the couple. Maintaining the royal tradition of a public display of modesty, this is no temple of haute cuisine, but a rustic timber-floored Italian-style café with Japanese touches. People are already queuing at noon for $18 pizzas and pasta with a topping of salmon roe and shredded *shiso* leaf. We stop off at Yumi Midori, the bakery where little Aiko goes for her *choux crèmes*, the zoo they visit, and Épinard Nasu, a $500-a-night luxury country club resort where the couple sometimes plays tennis. They will have only a handful of servants to look after them, and it seems like an altogether more relaxed lifestyle than living under the thumb of the *Kunaicho* back at the East Palace. Masako plans to spend a fortnight recuperating here, though Naruhito will have to go back to Tokyo to attend to his interminable official duties.

After a lunch of barbecued *ayu*, I join the small crowd gathering outside the station. It has now swollen to about 100, with pompous bureaucrats from the local prefecture scurrying around trying to herd everyone into little enclosures, marked off by plastic planter-boxes full of pink begonias. Everyone now has a little paper Japanese flag which a bulky gentleman, presumably a foot soldier for one of the ultra-nationalist groups, has handed out. Media representatives jostle for position – as well as local and

Tokyo TV there is a crew here from Germany filming a series on royals of the world, complaining bitterly that in three months they have been unable to get even an appointment with the palace press office. Lined up like ducks in a shooting gallery on their little stools are the ladies of the royal fan-club, now wielding a formidable array of the latest digital camera gear.

Above us on the elevated track, a *shinkansen* glides to a halt. Twenty minutes go by, time for the royals to smarten up for the reception. And then they emerge from the VIP waiting-room, escorted by the station-master and a band of uniformed flunkies. Smiling those forced smiles and waving that funny little royal wave, they walk towards their silver people-mover van which is waiting in the fore-court. It is 13 years since I have seen them, but from outward appearances neither has changed as much as I would have expected. Naruhito leads the way, wearing his smart-casual gear, charcoal pants, an open-necked shirt, and a blazer. I look through my telephoto lens to check that his eyes are open. Masako follows a step or two behind and to one side, wearing a plain white dress with a navy blazer, her hair pulled back revealing shell-like earrings. She looks thinner than I remember, pale beneath her heavy make-up, walking slowly with an anxious eye on her daughter. Little Aiko, in a shell-blue milkmaid's smock with white booties, seems dazed after her trip, clutching her mother with one hand, and a bag full of children's toys with the other. They pause for a minute or two to allow the groupies to snap away and shriek 'Masako-*sama*' and 'Aiko-*sama*' over and over again. Then they climb into the van, draw the curtains, and are whisked away, flanked by a police motorcycle squadron.

'She looked fine,' says Mrs Sakai. The other ladies nod.

'Maybe she is getting better?' Or maybe Masako was just happy to be getting away from her minders, away from the suffocating formality of the palace.

Certainly in the months that followed, she showed no sign of returning to public life and sharing the taxing burden of royal engagements with Naruhito. Her public appearances remained few and far between – even turning down that chance for an overseas trip, to Mexico, which she would once have jumped at. Her isolation and loneliness continued to gnaw.

No fresh medical bulletin was issued, leading to the inevitable conclusion that nothing had changed, that Masako's depression remained as intractable as before. The gossip columnists report that she continues to have nightmares, and sometimes lacks the strength to get up, spending the entire day in bed. She cannot even find the energy to get dressed or apply her make-up. She is prone to sudden bouts of uncontrollable crying. When she faces a stressful day, she runs a fever and vomits – sometimes so severely she has to be given fluids with an intravenous drip.

As the psychiatrists had predicted, without a change in her environment, no amount of drugs or psychotherapy is going to cure what ails Masako – the crushing burden of ancient, inflexible tradition unable to adapt to the needs of a modern, independent woman; a husband unable to keep his promise to protect her; a society unwilling to modernise an archaic institution to create a more relevant role for its monarchy in the twenty-first century.

And so, as the New Year celebrations came around again, the royal couple were stuck with a debilitating dilemma. The magazines began to speculate that the only way out might be for Naruhito to renounce the throne and leave the palace, together with his wife and child, saving

Masako's sanity, but at the cost of forfeiting the job for which he had been preparing all his life – and, inevitably, being shunned by his family for his dereliction of duty. Abdication, he would be well aware, has occurred many times in the history of the Japanese imperial family, and the renunciation of the throne by a crown prince is specifically provided for in the 1946 Imperial Household Law, perhaps prompted by the sad case of the dotty Taisho Emperor:

> *Article 3. When the Imperial heir is suffering from an incurable disease of mind or body, or when any other weighty cause exists, the order of succession may be changed by decision of the Imperial Household Council . . .*

It is hard to imagine that Masako's depression would not constitute a 'weighty cause', nor that the Imperial Household Council would refuse. The problem with this 'solution' is that Naruhito's brother would then be in line to inherit the throne, and an Emperor Akishino would be an unpopular monarch with both the Establishment and ordinary Japanese, who regard him as lacking the moral authority and dedication to duty they expect in an emperor. He can protest as much as he likes that reports of his carousing down in Bangkok are 'smoke without fire'. And an added complication would be that if the law is ever changed to allow a female emperor, Aiko would no longer be eligible to succeed – a refugee from the palace, living as a commoner in the suburbs of Tokyo, Boston, Oxford, or wherever Masako and Naruhito decided to make their lives after they escaped.

There is no happy ending to this story. In fact, there is

no ending at all. As we went to press, there were reports once again that Masako was on the mend – she had just made her first 'solo outing' in two years, a visit to Tokyo's renowned St Luke's International Hospital. She and Naruhito had been spotted at the United Nations University, a postgraduate research institute where a study had been set aside for Masako, although plans for her to resume her long-abandoned studies apparently came to nothing. Relations with the in-laws had apparently thawed a little, and they had been invited back to the palace for dinner. At the press conference before he flew off to Mexico in March, alone again, Naruhito said that Masako had been 'making efforts towards recovery in accordance with the course of treatment prescribed by the doctors. She has been recovering steadily, with increased opportunities recently for private outings and physical activities which the doctors recommend, as well as gradually taking on official duties little by little'.

Oliver Oldman and his wife Barbara, Masako's minders from her Boston years, were the last 'outsiders' to visit Masako and Naruhito that I contacted. They spent a 'jovial time' with her at the East Palace over cake and cups of *hojicha*, roasted Japanese brown tea. They reported that Masako was getting on better with her minders – particularly her new chief lady-in-waiting, a bilingual US university graduate named Megumi Kusada – and was planning to increase her public appearances. Oldman said he was 'upbeat' about Masako's recovery, and was hoping that she would be able to pay a visit to Harvard – if the *Kunaicho* could be persuaded to approve it.

However, the fact remained that almost three years after her breakdown, Masako was still not well enough to resume her round of official ribbon-cutting. In August the *Kunaicho* did deem her fit enough for an overseas trip, the first the family had undertaken together. However, the arrangements merely underlined the ongoing seriousness of her condition. It was to be a strictly private summer holiday, with no official engagements – Masako, Naruhito and little Aiko would be sequestered in Het Oude Loo, a seventeenth century baroque royal palace in Holland, taking time out to visit Masako's parents in The Hague. Even more extraordinarily, for the two weeks she was away she would have to be accompanied by her psychiatrist, Professor Ono. Hardly surprisingly the Tokyo rumour-mill broke into a frenzy. *Newsweek* magazine even received a tip-off that Masako was planning to 'defect' and claim asylum on the grounds that her human rights had been violated.

Normally, with the sort of expert care she finally appears to be receiving, her illness should have been resolved long before this. But, as the psychiatrists had warned, unless the circumstances which triggered her depression – the rigid grip of the Men in Black on her life – change, then it is pointless to talk about a 'cure' because the depression will simply recur, over and over again. And it is obvious that the *Kunaicho* is not yet ready for its great leap forward into the modern world. The only token concession it has made is to appoint a new, and hopefully more sympathetic, bureaucrat as head of the East Palace household, a former diplomat known to Masako's father. As Kenneth Ruoff summed it up: 'The hopes expressed at the time of her engagement that this modern career woman would revolutionise the throne overnight now seem especially unfounded.'

Even the birth – at last – of the first royal male in more than 40 years seemed unlikely to relieve Masako's gloom.

On 6 September, after a difficult pregnancy which saw her confined in hospital for a month, there was celebration in the streets of Tokyo – literally – when Masako's sister-in-law, Princess Kiko, was delivered of a baby boy, Prince Hisahito, by caesarian section. Passers-by paused to yell *banzai*, and a troupe of women in red and white *yukata* swigged sake and performed a congratulatory folk dance near Gakushuin University, Akishino's and Kiko's *alma mater*. The media reflected the importance the public attached to the 'male delivery' as it was quickly dubbed – newspapers brought out four-page special editions for the boy, but had planned only two pages if it had been a girl. Overnight, Japan had a new sweetheart. The demure and unassuming Kiko had stepped in to save the monarchy, even though at the age of 39 – and 11 years after the birth of her last child – she must have known there would be no guarantee of success, and serious risks attached. Masako, once the darling of the online chat-rooms, was rejected and reviled. 'What use is she now?' growled one of her critics.

Hisahito will be third in line to the throne, after Naruhito and his father, Prince Akishino, and his arrival ensures the survival of the monarchy without the need for the government to grapple with the contentious alternatives involved in modernising the law of succession. But it will be only a temporary reprieve, because now the entire burden of keeping the sacred imperial Y chromosome alive rests on the shoulders – or rather the loins – of this scrawny, underweight, premature baby, lying in his crib with a ceremonial sword on the pillow beside him. What if he does not survive? If he turns out to be infertile? Or gay? What if no-one will marry him – which would hardly surprise considering the fate of his aunt and his grand-mother? Or if he is simply unwilling to accept his royal obligation to father a family? The crisis has merely been postponed for a generation.

As for Masako, she would have felt a mixture of emotions when Akishino telephoned the East Palace with the news, a few minutes after the baby's birth: happiness, relief . . . and grief. Happiness, of course, that Kiko and the child had survived a risky birth; relief that there would be less pressure on her now to bear a baby boy; and grief that the royal line of Naruhito would be extinguished and that the crown pass to the house of Akishino, the jealous younger brother who had dwelled in his shadow all his life. Aiko will never be emperor, though Masako must surely be secretly happy that her daughter will now one day be allowed to leave the palace, marry and lead a normal life, free from the training and the travails, the proscriptions and restrictions at the hands of the *Kunaicho* that have driven her mother to the brink of mental and physical collapse.

Thinking things over as the *shinkansen* rockets back to Tokyo in the gathering gloom, it seems to me that the alternatives for Masako are stark. Barring the unthinkable – suicide, which claims the lives of so many depressed people who see no other escape from their torment – they can be summed up as follows: divorce, flight from the palace, or a revolution in the palace guard. The first is implausible, if for no other reason than that Masako and Naruhito appear to be still in love, with each other and with little Aiko. The second, that Naruhito should renounce the throne, is equally unlikely – this is the job for which the dutiful prince has been groomed for his entire life. As for anything more than minor concessions from the *Kunaicho*, the experience of the past 13 years shows that this is the least likely scenario of all. Modernising the monarchy to allow Masako to use her talents for her country has met with their implacable opposition from day one. As a critic quoted by Lesley Downer sniped, after Masako found herself seated at a banquet between Bill Clinton and Mikhael Gorbachev, chatting alternately to them in English and Russian: 'The royal family are not ambassadors. She doesn't need to be able to speak English, she has interpreters for that. Her job is to smile.' And, she might have added, bear a baby boy.

And so it seemed, as the fourteenth anniversary of their wedding loomed, that there was nowhere to go, no alternative to Masako continuing to sacrifice herself for the sake of her country's outdated imperial institutions – and her father's family honour. When she is invested as the empress in a few years' time, she will find it to be an even more painful crown of thorns. Far from giving her new power and authority, the restrictions on her life will redouble. She seems condemned to suffer the fate of her mother-in-law, stoically bearing the burden of her illness as the years go by, the light fades from her eyes, and all we hear from her are some whispered platitudes every few years when she is wheeled out to meet the media. She may discover her life's real mission is to share her husband's new enthusiasm for drawings of medieval ox-carts, or use her Harvard education to further the propagation of Michiko's silkworm collection. She will watch Aiko grow into womanhood, moulded by her *Kunaicho* mentors into an obedient royal puppet. One by one her friends and her family will drift away.

She will live to regret the rainy summer's day that she surrendered to well-meant notions of duty and honour and gave up her life for her country.

Glossary

Japanese words and phrases can have many meanings, or no exact equivalent at all in English. The following interpretations have been chosen because they best suit the context in which they are used in this book.

Amakudari	'Descent from the gods' – the practice of bureaucrats being appointed to well-paid sinecures after retirement.
Ayu	Sweetfish, similar to a small trout.
Babaa	An insulting term for an older woman like 'old bag'.
Bakufu	'Tent' or military government – another word for the shogunate which ruled Japan from 1603–1868.
Banzai	'Ten thousand years' – a celebratory cheer similar to 'Hurrah!'
Bento	Single-portion 'takeaway' meal.
Besso	Holiday house.

Bunraku	Traditional Japanese puppet theatre.
Buraku	Relating to *burakumin*.
Burakumin	'Village people' – a socially discriminated-against underclass, descended from people who performed 'unclean' jobs such as leather-work.
Bushido	'The way of the warrior' – the code of honour espoused by the samurai class.
Chikan	Gropers.
Daigenshu	Supreme commander.
Daiginjoshu	Highest grade of *sake*.
Daikon	Giant white radish.
Daimyo	Regional warlords during the shogunate.
Denka	Highness.
Denki	To do with electricity; a light fitting.
Diet	Japan's parliament.
Ekiben	Railway lunch-boxes.
Gagaku	Type of classical music played with antique instruments at the imperial court.
Gaimusho	Japanese Ministry for Foreign Affairs.
Geisha	Traditional female entertainers.
Genro	Coterie of elder statesmen who advised the emperors.
Genshu	Head of state.
Go	Or *Igo*, a Japanese board-game.
Goman	Arrogant or obnoxious.
Goyotei	Villas in the country where the imperial family holidays.
Hakama	Long, divided skirt-like pants sometimes worn on formal occasions.
Hara kiri	Ritual suicide by self-embowelment.
Heian	Era (794–1192 AD) when the imperial court was at Kyoto.

Hinadan	Tiered wooden 'stairway' on which ceremonial dolls in Heian court attire are arranged.
Hojicha	Roasted Japanese 'brown tea'.
Honke	The male line of a family.
Honne	Inner truth or reality.
Honseki-chi	Council office where one's family registry is kept.
Ikebana	Japanese art of flower arrangement.
Inari	The rice deity, whose shrines are guarded by white foxes.
Jimujikan	'Administrative vice-minister' or head of a government department.
Ji-san	'Old man', one of Naruhito's nicknames.
Juni Hitoe	The 12-layered ceremonial robe worn by royal brides.
Junshi	The samurai custom of following one's lord into death by committing suicide.
Kabuki	Traditional Japanese theatre.
Kaiseki ryori	Seasonal Japanese haute cuisine served as a progression of small dishes.
Kamikaze	The 'divine wind' that destroyed the invading fleet of Kublai Khan in 1281; fighter pilots who flew suicide missions in World War II.
Kampo	Traditional herbal medicine.
Kanji	Chinese characters incorporated into written Japanese.
Karei raisu	Rice and curry.
Kashikodokoro	The Shinto shrine in the imperial palace grounds where royal weddings are solemnised.
Kazoku	The 'floral families' of Japan's modern aristocracy, 1869–1947.
Kendo	Martial art of fencing with wooden or bamboo 'swords'.

Ki	Used in traditional medicine to mean something like 'vital life force'.
Kikokushijo	'Returnee children' re-entering the Japanese education system after studying abroad.
Kisha kurabu	'Clubs' of journalists attached to the organisations on which they report.
Kobun	In the often life-long hierarchical relationships formed at school and in the workplace the *kobun* or *kohai* is the 'underling' owing allegiance to the senior *oyabun,* or *sempai.*
Kohai	See *kobun.*
Koi	Colourful and expensive pet carp.
Koishimaru	Species of silkworm.
Kojiki	The 'record of ancient things', Japan's oldest book, said to be based on oral history dating to AD 712.
Kojukei	Bamboo partridge.
Koseki	Family register.
Koto	Stringed musical instrument like a small horizontal harp.
Kuge	Ancient Japanese aristocratic classes, dating back to Heian times.
Kunaicho	Imperial Household Agency, the public servants who administer the royal family's affairs.
Manyoshu	'Collection of 10,000 leaves', a compendium of ancient Japanese poetry.
Ma po dofu	Spicy Szechuan bean curd dish.
Matsuri	Seasonal festival, usually in late summer.
Matsutake	Pine mushrooms, the most prized and expensive in Japan.
Mazakon	Contraction of *mazaa konpurekkusu*, 'mother complex'.

Miso	Bean-paste used for soup and stuffing sweet-meats.
Mitsuba	The herb trefoil or 'Japanese parsley'.
Mochi	Buns made of pounded glutinous rice.
Nasake	Word with no English equivalent which conveys feelings of compassion, empathy and kindliness.
Nenashi gusa	'Grass without roots', or as we might say in English 'a fish out of water'.
Nihonshoki	Japan's second oldest historical work, said to have been completed in AD 720.
Nori	Dried seaweed used for wrapping sushi.
Obi	Ornamental sash worn around the waist of a woman in a kimono. The special *obi* presented to Masako during her pregnancy was an *iwata-obi*, worn next to the skin, to provide support and ensure a safe birth.
Obon	A Buddhist holiday to honour the spirits of one's ancestors.
Oh eru	'OL' or 'office lady'.
Okake	Fans; people who chase pop 'idols'.
Omiai	Introduction arranged by an intermediary with a view to matrimony.
Onii-chama	Big brother.
Oninoho	Billowing orange pantaloons, part of the traditional costume worn by Japanese crown princes when they marry.
Onsen	Hot spring, typically at a spa resort where Japanese go to bathe.
Origami	Art of folding paper into shapes resembling flowers, birds, etc.
Oyabun	See *kobun*.
Pachinko	Popular gambling game played on a vertical pinball machine.

Pekopeko	A fawning or grovelling way of bowing.
Pinchi hitta	Pinch hitter, a baseball term for a specialist batter brought in as a substitute when a run is badly needed.
Ronin	Samurai who has lost his master.
Ryotei	High-class Japanese guest-house serving traditional cuisine.
Saikeirei	Low, worshipful bow.
Sakaki	Sacred tree related to the camellia.
Sake	Has two meanings, depending on the *kanji* characters used – 'salmon', and 'rice wine'.
Samurai	'One who serves', a member of the feudal warrior class.
San san kudo	Wedding toast in which the couple exchange sips of *sake*.
Sarariman	Salaried employee.
Sempai	See *kobun*.
Sensei	Respectful title accorded teachers, doctors, politicians, etc.
Shaku	Many meanings, here a royal sceptre.
Shinkansen	High-speed 'bullet trains'.
Shitsuke	No English equivalent, combines the virtues of discipline, good upbringing and behaviour.
Sho	Antique 17-pipe bamboo flute.
Shogun	'Barbarian-subduing generalissimo' – Japan's temporal rulers 1603–1868.
Shoji	Translucent screen made of wood and rice-paper.
Soba	Buckwheat noodles.
Sokaiya	Niche gangsters who extort money from corporations by disrupting, or threatening to disrupt, their shareholders' meetings.
Taiko	Huge traditional drums, usually played at festivals.

Tanka	17-syllable Japanese verse form.
Tarento	'Talent' or popular culture stars.
Tatami	Mats of woven rice-straw used in traditional Japanese homes.
Tatemae	Façade or outward pretence concealing the *honne* or inner reality.
Tekiou shogai	Adjustment disorder.
Tenno	'Heavenly ruler above the clouds'; Japan's emperor.
Togu Gosho	Crown prince's palace, the East Palace.
Tonkatsu	Crumbed, fried pork loin.
Torii	Vermillion-painted timber archways which guard Shinto shrines.
Tsuji giri	Word from samurai days meaning 'to try out a new sword on a passer-by'.
Tsuyu	'Plum rains' which fall in June and July.
Udon	Thick wheat-flour noodle, usually served in soup.
Utsu byo	'Mood disorder' or depression.
Wagyu	Breed of Japanese beef cattle famous for its fatty meat.
Waka	Historic form of 31-syllable verse traditionally composed by Japan's royals.
Wakatta	'I understand.'
Yakiniku	Cooking meat and vegetables, usually at the table, over a burner on a griddle.
Yakuza	Members of Japanese organised crime gangs.
Yukata	Light, casual dressing-gown-style robe often worn at summer festivals or after bathing.
Yuzu	Type of Japanese citrus fruit.

References

The main written sources used for background for this book are:

Books

Bix, Herbert P., *Hirohito and the Making of Modern Japan*, HarperCollins US, 2000.

Hamao, Minoru, *Message to the Crown Prince and Masako**, Shincho-sha, Tokyo, 1993.

Harvard Student Agencies Inc., *The Unofficial Guide to Life at Harvard 2004–2005*, USA, 2005.

Hills, Ben, *Japan – Behind the Lines*, Sceptre, Australia and New Zealand, 1996.

Jounouchi, Yuzuru, *Kunaicho – Behind the Chrysanthemum Curtain**, People-sha, Tokyo, 1993.

Kawahara, Toshiaki, *Michiko to Masako – the Making of a Princess**, Bungei Shunju, Tokyo, 1993.

Kawahara, Toshiaki, *Masako's Love and Joy**, Kodan-sha, Tokyo, 2001.

Kinoshita, June and Palevsky, Nicholas, *Gateway to Japan*, Kodan-sha, Tokyo and New York, 1998.

Matsuzaki, Toshiya, *Michiko, Masako and Aiko**, Tachibana Shuppan, Tokyo, 2003.

Empress Michiko, *The Naruhito Constitution**.

Crown Prince Naruhito, *The Thames and I – a Memoir of Two Years at Oxford*, Global Oriental, UK, 2005.

Ruoff, Kenneth J., *The People's Emperor – Democracy and the Japanese Monarchy 1945–1995*, Harvard University Asia Centre, New York and London, 2001.

Vogel, Ezra F., *Japan As Number One: Lessons for America*, Harvard University Press, USA, 1979.

Watanabe, Makoto, *If You Were Invited to an Imperial Dinner Party**, Kadokawa, Tokyo, 2001.

Watanabe, Midori, *Michiko and Masako – Days of Tears and Strengthening Bonds**, Kodan-sha, Tokyo, 2001.

* In Japanese.

Magazines

The Economist, Forbes, Japan Close-Up, Josei Jishin, Josei Seven, Newsweek, The New Yorker, Shukan Asahi, Shukan Gendai, Shukan Josei, Shukan Post, Shukan Shincho, Vanity Fair, Vogue.

Newspapers

Asahi Shimbun, Boston Herald, Chicago Sun-Times, The Harvard Crimson, The Irish Times, Los Angeles Times, Mainichi Shimbun, The New York Times, Nihon Keizai Shimbun, The Scotsman, The Sydney Morning Herald, The Times (London), The Washington Post, Yomiuri Shimbun.

On-line

The Chrysanthemum Throne, by Lesley Downer (www.etoile.co.uk/Columns/PandorasBox/041012.html), *Genealogy of the Japanese Imperial Dynasty* by Jeffrey W. Taliaferro (www.geocities.com/jtaliaferro.geo/genealogy2.html), the Imperial Household Agency (www.kunaicho.go.jp), *The MacArthur Archives* (www.nancho.net/nancho/ghqemps2.html), Wikipedia (www.wikipedia.org).

Index

Ben Hills is one of Australia's best-known investigative reporters and most experienced foreign correspondents, having reported wars, elections, scandals, celebrities and social issues for the Fairfax newspapers from more than 50 countries over three decades (see benhills.com). He was based in London in the 1970s, mainly covering Africa and the Middle East, in Hong Kong in the 1980s, and in Tokyo in the 1990s, where he first reported on Masako and Naruhito. Ben is a winner of the Walkley Award, Australia's premier award for journalism, and the Graham Perkin Award for Australian Journalist of the Year. He is the author of two previous books: *Blue Murder* (Sun Books), about the Wittenoom asbestos disaster, and *Japan – Behind the Lines* (Sceptre) about his three years reporting from Japan. Ben lives in Sydney with his wife, the photographer Mayu Kanamori. He can be contacted at benhills@benhills.com.